Fallenness, Sustainment, and Judgment

Fallenness, Sustainment, and Judgment

Analyzing Coherency in the Thematic Trajectory of Qohelet

ALBERT R. PORTILLO JR.

Foreword by Ashley E. Davis

WIPF & STOCK · Eugene, Oregon

FALLENNESS, SUSTAINMENT, AND JUDGMENT
Analyzing Coherency in the Thematic Trajectory of Qohelet

Copyright © 2025 Albert R. Portillo Jr. All rights reserved. Except for brief quotations in critical publications or reviews, no part of this book may be reproduced in any manner without prior written permission from the publisher. Write: Permissions, Wipf and Stock Publishers, 199 W. 8th Ave., Suite 3, Eugene, OR 97401.

Wipf & Stock
An Imprint of Wipf and Stock Publishers
199 W. 8th Ave., Suite 3
Eugene, OR 97401

www.wipfandstock.com

PAPERBACK ISBN: 979-8-3852-3512-4
HARDCOVER ISBN: 979-8-3852-3513-1
EBOOK ISBN: 979-8-3852-3514-8

01/17/25

Unless otherwise noted, Scripture quotes are from the ESV® Bible (The Holy Bible, English Standard Version®). ESV® Text Edition: 2016. Copyright © 2001 by Crossway, a publishing ministry of Good News Publishers. The ESV® text has been reproduced in cooperation with and by permission of Good News Publishers.

Scripture marked NASB20 is from the New American Standard Bible®, Copyright © 1960, 1971, 1977, 1995, 2020 by The Lockman Foundation. All rights reserved.

Scripture marked NIV is from THE HOLY BIBLE, NEW INTERNATIONAL VERSION®, NIV® Copyright © 1973, 1978, 1984, 2011 by Biblica, Inc.® Used by permission. All rights reserved worldwide.

Scripture marked NRSV is from the New Revised Standard Version Bible, copyright 1989, Division of Christian Education of the National Council of the Churches of Christ in the United States of America. Used by permission. All rights reserved.

For my father, Albert Roque Portillo Sr.
(March 5, 1961–September 26, 2024)

My greatest inspiration for pursuing God's call on my life

Contents

Foreword by Ashley E. Davis | ix
Acknowledgments | xi
List of Abbreviations | xiii
Introduction | 1

PART I. BACKGROUND ANALYSIS

Chapter 1: Wisdom Tradition in the Ancient Near East and Israelite Culture | 23

Chapter 2: Canonicity of Qohelet in the Wisdom Corpus and the Bible | 40

Chapter 3: The Universality of Qohelet's Message | 58

PART II. ANALYSIS FOR COHERENCE

Chapter 4: Modern Scholarly Attempts to Find Coherency in Qohelet | 77

Chapter 5: Coherency in the Theological Trajectory of Qohelet's Projectile Themes | 95

PART III. QOHELET'S THEOLOGICAL AFFINITY TO THE METANARRATIVE OF THE BIBLE

Chapter 6: The New Testament and the Trajectory of Qohelet's Theology | 115

Chapter 7: Qohelet as a Guide for Life in the Trajectory of Fallenness, Sustainment, and Judgment | 132

Conclusion | 147

Appendix: Chart of Correlating Themes and Passages in Qohelet | 163

Bibliography | 171

Index | 177

Foreword

CONTEMPORARY BIBLICAL SCHOLARSHIP IS full of opinions, some good and some bad. The goal of biblical academic scholarship is to *advance* the study of texts that have been seemingly lost to the mists of antiquity. The texts of the Hebrew Bible so often go unnoticed, or are often swept under the rug, in favor of New Testament texts that espouse the name of Jesus. However, Christ is present in the themes of the Hebrew Bible as his presence is foreshadowed in the verses of books like Qohelet. The knowledge drawn from connecting biblical themes in the books of the Hebrew Bible is regarded as paramount in current studies, and this work is no exception to that rule. Tracing the thematic themes, or projectiles, as Dr. Portillo notes, shows a coherency in a cyclic theme of fallenness, sustainment, and judgment. This theme is akin to the sin cycle—the cycle that is characteristic of our very lives. The content, then, is of utmost importance for understanding how we find Christ in the midst of seeming inconsistencies.

Questioning canonicity and textual emendations can be a dangerous path to travel down. Throughout Jewish antiquity, the theology of Qohelet and its placement in the canon of Scripture had caused many to raise their eyebrows due to seeming inconsistencies in voice and statements. However, its placement in the canon cannot be ignored. If one believes in the divine inspiration of the biblical text, and markedly meticulous work of the ancient scribes to preserve the text, one will find that Qohelet upholds the character of the Divine and instills a strong eschatological hope for the believer. God's character in the book of Qohelet is not compromised by the inconsistencies; it is arguably strengthened through the lingering messages and themes inherent in the sin cycle. Qohelet demonstrates not only that man's life is lived in the midst of a fallen nature, but that it is subsequently sustained in the goodness of Christ while everything in his creation is held together, in one way or another, as he serves as Divine Adjudicator.

FOREWORD

Sound orthodoxy thus rests in the thematic themes, or threads, that one finds throughout the Hebrew Bible, notably here in the book of Qohelet. It is all connected. It is all about the One to whom we so dearly owe our lives. And Qohelet so vividly demonstrates that in a life full of vanity and shame, Christ stands in the midst of it all as the great Redeemer and Purveyor of our faith.

Ashley E. Davis, PhD
Professor of Hebrew Bible and Doctoral Mentor
Liberty University School of Divinity

Acknowledgments

I thank Dr. Ashley E. Davis for being the most elaborate person in this project. Her patient and compassionate mentorship has been exceedingly helpful in making me a better writer and scholar overall. With her balanced approach to critique and free reign, I was empowered and encouraged to maintain my own style of writing while at the same time being challenged to think about areas of research essential to this project that might have otherwise been missed. Dr. Davis will forever be a mentor to me, for which I am incredibly honored and privileged. I am forever indebted to Dr. Davis for all her graceful support and affirmation in producing a publish-worthy manuscript.

I would also like to thank my father, Pastor Albert R. Portillo Sr., for the countless hours of discussion around this topic. These discussions allowed me to evaluate my thought process throughout the progress of this project. For this, I am forever grateful.

List of Abbreviations

ABD	David Noel Freedman, ed. *Anchor Yale Bible Dictionary*. 6 vols. New Haven, CT: Yale University Press, 2008.
AD	*anno Domini* (in the year of our Lord)
BC	before Christ
BDAG	Walter Bauer, Frederick W. Danker, W. F. Arndt, and F. W. Gingrich. *Greek-English Lexicon of the New Testament and Other Early Christian Literature.* 3rd ed. Chicago: University of Chicago Press, 2000.
BDB	Francis Brown, S. R. Driver, and Charles A. Briggs. *Hebrew and English Lexicon of the Old Testament.* Oxford: Clarendon, 1906.
BTB	*Biblical Theology Bulletin*
CBL	The Complete Biblical Library
cf.	*confer*, compare
DOT	Tremper Longman III and Peter Enns, eds. *Dictionary of the Old Testament: Wisdom, Poetry and Writings.* Downers Grove, IL: IVP, 2008.
Eccl (or Qoh)	Ecclesiastes (or Qohelet)
e.g.	for example
ESV	English Standard Version
HALOT	Ludwig Koehler, Walter Baumgartner, and M. E. J. Richardson, eds. *The Hebrew and Aramaic Lexicon of the Old Testament.* 5 vols. Leiden, Netherlands: Brill, 2000.
Heb.	Hebrew
ICCS	Institute for Classical Christian Studies
i.e.	that is
ISBE	Geoffery W. Bromiley, ed. *International Standard Bible Encyclopedia.* Rev. ed. Grand Rapids, MI: Eerdmans, 1979.
IVP	InterVarsity Press

LIST OF ABBREVIATIONS

JPS	The Jewish Publication Society
KJV	King James Version
LEH	Johan Lust, Erik Eynikel, and Katrin Hauspie, eds. *Greek-English Lexicon of the Septuagint*. 3rd corrected ed. Stuttgart: Deutsche Bibelgesellschaft, 2015.
LXX	Septuagint (the Greek Old Testament)
NASB	New American Standard Bible
NIDNTTE	Silva, Moisés, ed. *New International Dictionary of New Testament Theology and Exegesis*. 2nd ed. 5 vols. Grand Rapids, MI: Zondervan, 2014.
NIDOTTE	Willem A. VanGemeren, ed. *New International Dictionary of Old Testament Theology and Exegesis*. 4 vols. Grand Rapids, MI: Zondervan, 1997.
NIV	New International Version
NLT	New Living Translation
NRSV	New Revised Standard Version
OT	Old Testament
RSV	Revised Standard Version
s.v.	*sub verbo,* under the word
TDOT	G. Johannes Botterweck and Helmer Ringgren, eds. *Theological Dictionary of the Old Testament*. Rev. ed. 15 vols. Grand Rapids, MI: Eerdmans, 2006.
Tg. Onq.	Targum Onqelos
v(v).	verse(s)
ZAW	*Zeitschrift für die alttestamentliche Wissenschaft*
ZEB	Moisés Silva and Merrill C. Tenney, eds. *The Zondervan Encyclopedia of the Bible*. Rev. ed. 5 vols. Grand Rapids, MI: Zondervan, 2009.

Introduction

ONE OF THE PRIMARY components essential to the study of any biblical book is its need for coherence with the testimony and progression of the grand narrative of the Bible. Although written at different times, by different authors, to different audiences, and for different purposes, coinciding themes run seamlessly throughout the biblical record of salvation history and its anticipated eschatological future.[1] Each book of the canon contributes in its own way to the Bible's one story, which is undoubtedly true for the book of Qohelet (the Hebrew name for Ecclesiastes).[2] This introduction begins by explaining the need for coherence in Qohelet and how this can be accomplished with a proper approach to charting the trajectory of Qohelet's message through its most prominent theological themes. Like any trajectory followed by a projectile with a target aim, so is the canonical and theological message depicted in the thematic framework of Qohelet. Hence, following the discussion on the need for coherence, hermeneutical boundaries are set through a suggestive approach for charting a thematic course of trajectory in Qohelet's theology, along with a synopsis of how this

---

1. The concept of coinciding themes running seamlessly throughout the biblical record of salvation history, and its anticipated eschatological future takes the "Progressive Covenantal" position of an extensive debate between Covenantal and Dispensational theologies. The full spectrum of this debate consists of four positions, with Covenantalism and Progressive Covenantalism on one end and Progressive Dispensationalism and Dispensationalism on the other. On the one hand, Covenantalism and Progressive Covenantalism see the progression of covenants as the outworking of one unifying plan of God. On the other hand, Dispensationalism and Progressive Dispensationalism see the plan of God worked out through a succession of dispensations distinct and separate from each other. For more exploration on these topics and debate, see Gentry and Wellum, *Kingdom Through Covenant*; Meade, "Circumcision of Flesh"; Horton, "Covenant Theology"; Williamson, *Sealed with an Oath*; Saucy, *Case for Progressive Dispensationalism*; Horton, *Introducing Covenant Theology*; Merkle, *Discontinuity to Continuity*.

2. Qohelet is the Hebrew name for Ecclesiastes and will be used predominately in this study.

INTRODUCTION

study plans to demonstrate that the target aim of Qohelet's message is an appeal to righteous living and eschatological hope.

THE SEARCH FOR COHERENCE IN QOHELET

Over centuries of church history, a broad interpretative spectrum of Qohelet has been developed with some satisfying and unsatisfying characterizations.³ The book of Qohelet has, thus, become one of the most diversely approached books in the canon, leading to a quest for coherence that has yet to establish a unifying agreement among scholars. According to Barry G. Webb, "There are virtually no assured results of scholarly study to provide a foothold for us. Ecclesiastes has effectively scattered the academic field rather than drawing it together around any widely held conclusions."⁴ The fact that there are vast differences in the approach taken to the study of Qohelet shows that there is still a significant need for coherence. Most of the leading arguments thus far in the quest for coherence in Qohelet have been focused on dealing with its supposed contradictions and inconsistencies. Michael V. Fox states, "One of the first reported discussions of Qohelet centers on the book's contradictions. . . . I take Qohelet's contradictions as the starting point of interpretation. . . . The contradictions in the book of Qohelet are real and intended. We must interpret them, not eliminate them."⁵ Fox's statement is correct, but the question remains, "How does one approach the interpretation of these contradictions?" The answer to this question is where the diversity in the study and interpretation of Qohelet has derived, leading to the unresolved quest for coherence. Although not every argument developed in the study of Qohelet can be examined in this study, three convincing and leading arguments for coherence that will be discussed as a segue to the central thesis are the arguments by J. A. Loader, who argues for an "adequate literary explanation" of Qohelet in

---

3. The term "unsatisfying" here does not necessarily mean that an interpretation should be rejected but rather acknowledges that the interpretation either deliberately or unintentionally misrepresents Qohelet's theology in a manner that fails to provide a balanced interpretation or to satisfy coherence with the integrity of God's character and affinity to the Bible. For a few sources providing unsatisfying characterizations of Qohelet, see Neusner, *Mishnah*; "Vayikra Rabbah 28:1"; Walsh, "Despair as a Theological Virtue"; Levine, "Humor in Qoheleth."

4. Webb, *Five Festal Garments*, 83.

5. Fox, *Time to Tear Down*, 1–3.

the tensions he calls "polar structures,"[6] Michael V. Fox, who argues that "harmonization is a proper and necessary part of the reading process of Qohelet,"[7] and Eunny P. Lee, who argues that the contradictions in Qohelet have "their place in the author's overall rhetorical strategy."[8] It is not that these particular arguments dominate the study in the quest for coherence in Qohelet, but, on the one hand, they are each placed on widely separate areas of the interpretive spectrum of Qohelet, making them good examples of how diverse the approach to Qohelet has been. Jimyung Kim states, "The contradictions in Ecclesiastes have motivated many scholars to deal with the problem of the contradictions, and they have generated diverse interpretations or controversies."[9] On the other hand, however diverse these arguments of interpretation may be, their different approaches share the common goal of making sense of the supposed contradictions.

The contradictions of Qohelet are often found in the passages and theological motifs dealing with vanity, joy, and judgment. According to Edward M. Curtis, "There are discernible themes, but no clear linear structure, and Qoheleth likely makes a point through this lack of coherence."[10] Additionally, Katharine J. Dell states, "The book of Qoheleth considers a range of theological themes that are profound and existential. Indeed, some have seen it more as a philosophical treatise than a theological work."[11] While there is agreement with these statements, for the sake of this study's argument, it is essential to distinguish between the terms "themes" and "motifs." In the broader view, the term "themes" will refer to the theological themes used in charting the trajectory of Qohelet's theology, whereby its framework can be outlined and traced. In the narrower view, the term "motifs" will refer to the repetitive catchwords inherent to the broader themes. Hence, this distinction will set the basis for the approach of this study's quest for coherency in Qohelet.

It is important to clarify that the search for coherency in the contradictions of Qohelet is not just for making sense of contradictions. Instead, a more significant theological danger of misrepresentation lingers when a

---

6. Loader, *Polar Structures in Qohelet*, 1.
7. Fox, *Qohelet and His Contradictions*, 22–23.
8. Lee, "Vitality of Enjoyment," 1.
9. Kim, "Reanimating Qohelet's Contradictory Voices," 2.
10. Curtis, *Interpreting the Wisdom Books*, 70.
11. Katharine J. Dell, "Reading Ecclesiastes with the Scholars," in Firth and Wilson, *Exploring Old Testament Wisdom*, 88.

INTRODUCTION

proper approach is not taken to interpret Qohelet, such as the misrepresentations of certain rabbinic sages or Tannaim, whose views are recorded in the Mishnah. According to Fox, "Certain Tannaim are reported to have expressed concern that the words of Qohelet might 'cause an inclination to heresy' (*Qoh. Rob.* 1.4). Significantly, the verses they quote as examples of this danger, Qoh 11:9aβ and 1:3, are not the ones modern commentators consider most radical."[12] In other words, some of the statements of Qohelet have been misconstrued as sounding lustful and shameless, opening the potential for risk of being misrepresented as unorthodox, such as the statement, "Rejoice, O young man, in your youth, and let your heart cheer you in the days of your youth. Walk in the ways of your heart and the sight of your eyes" (Qoh 11:9). This has raised questions about Qohelet's theological worldview, leading to doubts about Qohelet's theology which have inevitably impacted views on its canonicity and placement within the Bible. Throughout Jewish antiquity, for instance, the content of Qohelet has sparked controversy, whereby P. R. Williamson states, "Polarized positions were adopted by the rival schools of Shammai and Hillel in the first century AD. Even though positive, Hillelite assessment of the book's canonicity prevailed, objections continued to be raised until at least the fourth century AD."[13] Although the acceptance of Qohelet's canonicity has come a long way since the fourth century AD, making it more widely accepted in modern scholarship, the debate surrounding Qohelet's supposed inconsistencies lingers, begging the question of how Qohelet functions within the one story of the Bible. According to Daniel J. Estes, "It is undeniable that Ecclesiastes contains numerous inconsistencies both in its voices and its statements. This fact has led to many theories of multiple sources, unmarked quotations, and interpolations, in which 'the radical and pessimistic message of the 'original Qohelet' has been countered later by more orthodox glossators' (Seow 1997c: 39)."[14] While it is true that the supposed inconsistencies are what have attracted the attention of extensive scholarly analysis, the modern scholarly approaches to Qohelet, thus far, have not allowed for a single conclusion but have only created a myriad of diverse interpretations.

Also surrounding the search for coherence in the inconsistencies of Qohelet have been the arguments of authorship, language, date of

---

12. Fox, *Qohelet and His Contradictions*, 149.
13. Williamson, "Canon," 39–40.
14. Estes, *Handbook on the Wisdom Books and Psalms*, 277.

composition, and its message as wisdom literature compared to the other wisdom books of the canon, such as Proverbs. With a primarily unified consensus that Solomon authored the wisdom books of Proverbs and Song of Songs, where the message and theology have been said to contrast that of Qohelet, arguments for authorship have fallen within three theories. Either the author of Qohelet was Solomon (who at times referred to himself in the third person), one of King David's other descendants, or an Israelite from a later period using a Solomonic personality. According to Dell, "Whether we see the book in terms of a dialogue or simply as an inner struggle to comprehend, citing traditional opinions in order to contradict them, there is an overarching thematic unity and the sense of a voice—the repetitive 'I' that contrasts with the epilogue's third-person description."[15] This study takes the position that a redactor (also referred to as the frame narrator) completed the final form of Qohelet but that this redactor maintained the integrity of the original composition of the text, which points to Solomon, the son of King David, as the composer and teacher. Although there may never be a unified consensus on a single conclusion for the interpretation of Qohelet, it is, nonetheless, vital that an approach be made to Qohelet that upholds an affinity to its canonicity within the wisdom corpus and the entire Bible, as well as a fidelity that upholds the integrity of God's character, revealed through salvation history and the future eschatological hope of the Bible. While fidelity to the Bible and the character of God is fundamental in the approach to the search for coherence, this still does not mean there will ever be unity in the interpretation of Qohelet. Although it may not solve the problem of inconsistencies caused by the contradictions of Qohelet's teaching, it, nonetheless, creates boundaries for an appropriate start in the quest for coherence. According to Fox, "For Qohelet, the absoluteness of God's control means that each individual case is an ethical microcosm, so that the local absurdities—and there are many—are irreducible. Qohelet generalizes from them no less than from acts of divine justice. As a result, no matter how much right order we see, the absurdities undermine the coherence of the entire system."[16] Hence, without a coherently sound approach and interpretation of Qohelet, the door is left open to many misrepresentations and caricatures of God's character. The search for coherence in this study seeks to keep the interpretation of Qohelet within the boundaries of biblical

---

15. Katharine J. Dell, "Reading Ecclesiastes with the Scholars," in Firth and Wilson, *Exploring Old Testament Wisdom*, 85.

16. Fox, *Qohelet and His Contradictions*, 143.

and theological affinity, whereby harmony in what we learn about God's character through his work in salvation history and what we learn about God's character in his plan for the eschatological future is not compromised by contradicting the entire canon.

The study will, therefore, argue for coherence in Qohelet from a thematic approach, where the entirety of Qohelet's teaching is understood in light of the one story of the Bible. Charting the trajectory of Qohelet's theology from a thematic approach provides consistency with the theological course of the entire Bible. According to Curtis, "Qoheleth sees God as both creator of all things and as the one who, through his providence, oversees all of life. The sage connects the work of God in the world with both the blessings that allow people to find enjoyment and delight, and with God's judgment on evil (3:17; 11:9; and 12:13)."[17] As mentioned earlier, while the view of authorship might bear some weight on the acceptance of Qohelet as a theologically sound teaching of orthodoxy, its inclusion in the canon bears witness to several other factors regarding Scripture. Williamson states, "Some have suggested that the inclusion of Ecclesiastes within the canon is due in no small part to the implicit associations of Qohelet with Solomon, but the fact that other such books (e.g., the apocryphal *Odes of Solomon* and Wisdom of Solomon) remained excluded suggests that other factors played a much more significant role in recognizing its status as Scripture."[18] These significant factors are more prevalent in the themes guiding the tensions, harmonization, and rhetoric of Qohelet's framework, whereby its entire message functions as a witness to God's character and plan of redemption testified in the rest of the canon of Scripture. The character of God and his redemptive plan in the coherency of Qohelet becomes evident in its witness to reality in the ontological and metaphysical realities of life. Although presented as paradoxical rhetoric, Qohelet is not merely fixated on a horizontal view of all things "under the sun" but primarily a vertical view that points to a *hopeful future*. In this case, there is no need for a pessimistic approach to making sense of Qohelet's content. Instead, the methodology is crucial when approaching Qohelet in the quest for coherence. In speaking of methodological approaches to biblical interpretation that maintain an affinity to the character of God through time and eternity, Henri Blocher states, "Qohelet, whom we have already mentioned, develops in his own style parallel thoughts on the divine arrangements, with their baffling and

---

17. Curtis, *Interpreting the Wisdom Books*, 77.
18. Williamson, "Canon," 40.

humbling diversity, the failure of our attempts at complete systems, and yet the privileged relationship of the human heart to ʿôlām (3:11). The function of memory and commemoration looms large in both Testaments."[19] In part, Blocher's view of methodology that does not surrender to pessimism will be at the forefront of this study's approach to coherence in Qohelet. While tension, harmonization, and rhetorical patterns are acknowledged as inherent attributes of Qohelet's frame of thought,[20] an argument for a more satisfying coherence in Qohelet will be presented in a contextual-theological approach to Qohelet's thematic trajectory.

Hence, in the following two sections of this introduction, a discussion will be presented explaining the concept of projectile themes that will serve as a basis for charting Qohelet's theological trajectory, and a synopsis will be given explaining how the course of Qohelet's theological trajectory will be charted with a canonical and theological aim that coincides with the message of the entire Bible. Each chapter of this study is meant to contribute systematically to the search for coherence in Qohelet by analyzing its three most prominent themes. Fundamentally, this study argues that *while meaningful advances have been made in the search for coherence in the literary approach to Qohelet's contradicting motifs, there is still an unsettled incoherency in the overlay of Qohelet's theology. In taking a thematic approach, however, the inconsistencies of Qohelet take on a function of thematic underpinning, whereby coherence in the course followed by the projectile themes of fallenness, sustainment, and judgment forms a framework guiding a theological trajectory aiming at an appeal to righteous living and eschatological hope.*

THE CONCEPT OF PROJECTILE THEMES

Themes are an essential component of any text, whereby the author sets a basis for the problems or issues addressed within the text. Themes give the reader a broad perspective crucial for understanding the immediate context of a text and interpreting its meaning. According to Grant R. Osborne, "By noting the broader perspective of a book, we can more easily

---

19. Blocher, "Yesterday, Today, Forever Time," 188–89.

20. Chapter 4 will discuss previous attempts to find coherency in Qohelet from modern scholars, such as J. A. Loader, who argues for an "adequate literary explanation" of Qohelet in the tensions he calls "polar structures"; Michael V. Fox, who argues that "harmonization is a proper and necessary part of the reading process of Qohelet"; and Eunny P. Lee, who argues that the contradictions in Qohelet have "their place in the author's overall rhetorical strategy."

interpret correctly the details of particular statements."[21] For Qohelet, this is especially true, yet the focus on themes in the search for coherence has been secondary to the statements that have been misrepresented as contradictions and have become the center of the debate. For this reason, this study will take a thematic approach by focusing primarily on the three most prominent themes of fallenness, sustainment, and judgment as the basis for charting Qohelet's theological trajectory.[22] This approach, however, shall not negate the linguistic aspects of the text, whereby the arguments from contradictions and inconsistencies have been derived. Instead, the intent is to demonstrate how the themes of fallenness, sustainment, and judgment bring clarity to Qohelet's statements expressed from his frame of thought.[23] Although space does not permit for an all-extensive exposition of Qohelet's thematic and literary parts, the process of this study does take on some aspects of Osborne's hermeneutical spiral whereby "each unit of the surface structure will be analyzed in detail, tracing themes through all the extant parallel passages and noting the deep structure underlying it with its effect on the total message of the surface structure. The result will be a continuous spiral upward toward the intended meaning of the text in terms of both the parts and the whole."[24] Hence, the three themes of fallenness, sustainment, and judgment, as derived from the surface structure of Qohelet, set the basis for tracing the lines of trajectory that function as a guide to Qohelet's theological framework in the premise that humanity enters a fallen world, God sustains humanity amid the fallenness, and God preserves the lives of those who fear him on the day of judgment. Like any other trajectory a projectile follows, so is the theological trajectory of Qohelet, followed by themes functioning as projectiles guiding the frame of thought in Qohelet's teaching.

This study, therefore, introduces the concept of *projectile themes*. While the general concept of themes and their function within the biblical text remains the same, the term "projectile" only describes, as an adjective, how those themes function. In other words, *projectile themes* function as the basis for charting the trajectory of Qohelet's frame of thought in

21. Osborne, *Hermeneutical Spiral*, 38.

22. The terms "thematic trajectory" and "theological trajectory" will be used interchangeably only when the terms "thematic" and "theological" are combined with the term "trajectory."

23. The terms "frame of thought" and "framework" will be used throughout this study as synonymous terms as it relates to the purview of Qohelet throughout his teaching.

24. Osborne, *Hermeneutical Spiral*, 139.

themes such as fallenness, sustainment, and judgment. As a trajectory will generally consist of a path charted by a projectile often aimed at a specific point, *projectile themes* imply that these themes (i.e., fallenness, sustainment, and judgment) function as projectiles aiming to convey particular points and emphasis in the trajectory of Qohelet's message. According to Osborne, "The reader must study carefully the plot and miniplots within narrative books in order to determine the developing themes and characterizations of the author."[25] That is, themes may only sometimes be explicit but are derived from the text with clues such as catchwords and motifs. In cataloging features that support a unified composition in Qohelet, Eunny P. Lee provides three features, two of which support features of developing themes, such as "(1) hints of organization on a macro level that point to a broadly coherent design; (2) the use of numerous catchwords and linking devices that effectively connect various aspects of the author's thoughts into a meaningful whole."[26] In a sense, the concept of *projectile themes* follows the mode of analysis to make contradictory statements coherent, as described by Jimyung Kim. This mode consists of three strategies, with some form of the second strategy adopted in the concept of *projectile themes*. This mode and strategy, according to Kim, "enables the reader to take the text as a whole . . . insists on the unity and coherence of Qohelet by minimizing certain aspects of the text in favor of a dominant view is one that we can call 'the progression of thoughts' perspective. . . . With this strategy, the reader is to take the most developed ideas as the book's final message."[27] Hence, in taking the themes of fallenness, sustainment, and judgment as a progression of Qohelet's thoughts, the function of these themes as the most prominent and unifying of Qohelet's teaching take on the function of *projectiles* aiming at conveying a message that can be traced along a path of trajectory. These projectile themes give the reader insight into the mind and theology of Qohelet. What lies beneath the surface of these themes are the literary and often literal catchword expressions of how Qohelet has observed sin in the world, God's grace in the sustainment of his creation, and the hope of redemption. Hence, *projectile themes* form the framework for Qohelet both literarily and theologically, whereby coherence can be traced across every aspect of Qohelet's teaching.

25. Osborne, *Hermeneutical Spiral*, 208.
26. Lee, "Vitality of Enjoyment," 13.
27. Kim, "Reanimating Qohelet's Contradictory Voices," 9–11.

INTRODUCTION

The essence of forming a framework that can be traced through a projectile (i.e., projectile themes) allows for the charting of a trajectory. According to the *Merriam-Webster's Collegiate Dictionary*, the noun definition of a projectile is "a body projected by external force and continuing in motion by its own inertia."[28] The adjective definition is "projecting or impelling forward."[29] In general, these definitions describe the function of themes in the narrative of a text. In other words, themes are developed from a frame of thought projected from the mindset of the author. *Projectile themes* are carried along by the literary motifs that convey either implicitly or explicitly the message or story of a text. According to Richard Alan Fuhr Jr. and Andreas J. Köstenberger, "Thematic context involves the consideration of theological motif as a form of context. The theological message of the Bible is communicated through repeated themes; when a theme repeats itself and carries prominence, it is labeled a 'motif.' Motifs can be seen in each book of the Bible, and certain motifs transcend individual books."[30] Biblically speaking, when themes transcend an individual book, there is an implication that external factors and sources are likely influencing the author's frame of thought. When a motif is repeated in the content of a book, this typically functions as a clue toward the subject matter. Motifs help guide the reader to a coherent reading and keep the reader in tune with the author's flow of thought, whether implicitly or explicitly expressed. Hence, in charting the trajectory of a text, themes function as projectiles that move the narrative forward with a particular aim. Conceptually, *projectile themes* are projected forward, guiding the reader through the narrative's literary context, whereby coherence and meaning can be achieved in the reader's understanding. Some themes may be carried along by more complex devices and motifs, making it more challenging to interpret the narrative. Nonetheless, the projectile function of a theme remains the same.

In addition to the concept of projectiles, there are related aspect trajectories. According to *Merriam-Webster's Collegiate Dictionary*, the noun definition of trajectory is "a path, progression, or line of development resembling a physical trajectory."[31] Just as a trajectory is followed by a projectile and generally aimed at a specific target in the scientific study of ballistics, so are the functions of themes. For example, speaking of William

---

28. *Merriam-Webster's Collegiate Dictionary*, s.v. projectile.
29. *Merriam-Webster's Collegiate Dictionary*, s.v. projectile.
30. Fuhr and Köstenberger, *Inductive Bible Study*, 205.
31. *Merriam-Webster's Collegiate Dictionary*, s.v. trajectory.

INTRODUCTION

J. Webb's view of the redemptive trajectory of the entire biblical text, Walter C. Kaiser Jr. states, "He viewed biblical texts on a redemptive trajectory, which was assisted, of course, by the Holy Spirit and which encouraged the interpreter to go beyond the culture-bound letter of the text. It was one that aimed at love, justice, and equality."[32] As the trajectory of each biblical book of the Bible has a theological aim that contributes to the overall story of the Bible, it is within the course of the trajectory that themes establish the boundaries for interpretation. A proper interpretation will always result from the thematic projection of the text, whereby thematic boundaries maintain affinity in a coherent understanding, meaning, and application. According to Osborne, "Biblical narratives contain theology, and there are principles or themes that are intended for the reader."[33] Speaking on Wolfgang Iser's view of themes from a reader-response criticism approach, which may be an accurate response to Qohelet, Osborne also states,

> For Iser the themes of the text bridge to the readers and guide as well as correct their interpretation. Iser speaks of the "indeterminacies" or gaps in the text that force the reader to become involved in its textual "world." Thus it is in the dialectic between the indeterminate signs of the text and the perspective supplied by the reader that "understanding" occurs. However, for Iser the text provides the impetus, engaging readers and drawing them into its narrative world. It does this via a textual "repertoire" or configuration that provides an internal sequence (plot, dialogue and so forth) perceived by the reader. The actantial units or developing sentence structure sets up a series of anticipations that involve the readers in the plot line and force them to complete its textual meaning.[34]

In other words, themes are the basis for making sense and finding meaningful coherence in the literary development of a text, which involves its infrastructure, such as plots and dialogue. Essentially, the literary infrastructure gives clues to its themes, and at the same time, themes give coherence to the literary infrastructure—an interdependent relationship between the literary and thematic context that characterizes the text.

While the concept of *projectile themes* is not new, the use of the term "projectile" in conjunction with the term "themes" may be. This conjunction,

---

32. Kaiser and Silva, *Introduction to Biblical Hermeneutics*, 88–89.
33. Osborne, *Hermeneutical Spiral*, 220.
34. Osborne, *Hermeneutical Spiral*, 478–79.

however, describes particular themes that summarize the main ideas and topics underlying the message being conveyed. According to Millard J. Erickson, "Bearing in mind that the biblical teachings were written to specific situations and that our current cultural setting may be in some respects considerably different from that of the biblical writers, we must make sure that we not simply reexpress the biblical message in the same form. We must discover the underlying message behind all its specific forms of expression."[35] Erickson's reasoning for discovering the underlying message is that there is less risk of re-expressing a biblical message irrelevant to the current time. The example Erickson uses is the danger of preserving the transient expression of the sacrificial system. When the underlying message is discovered, the timeless expression of a message is identified, which can then be coherently understood and applied. Hence, *projectile themes* are the sum of all expressions deriving from a text's underlying message.

While commentaries have traditionally focused on the literary infrastructure of a text, such as words, phrases, and textual units, modern scholarship has now turned the focus toward theological themes as an interpretive thread tying all other textual elements together. According to Fuhr and Köstenberger, "With the resurgence of biblical theology, many commentaries are now devoted to the analysis of relevant themes, no longer relegating these to treatments outside of the scope of verse-by-verse exposition. When commentaries give adequate attention to theological motifs within the text, this analysis helps readers see the theological threads that impact interpretation."[36] In tracing theological trajectories, *projectile themes* set the course for theological interpretation, meaningful coherence, and contextual application, all of which are projected from the theological worldview of the author. *Projectile themes* allow the reader and listener to follow the transitions of an author's and teacher's mindset as they move from one point to the next or back and forth between points. *Projectile themes* guide the author, teacher, and student through the navigation of the message, whereby the literary infrastructure is the space that is traveled. Hence, *projectile themes* are the progression of thematic trajectories whereby the biblical text is theologized. According to R. J. Lubeck, "The task of the theologian is therefore to identify the thematic trajectories in the OT and trace them through the successive historical contexts with a view toward finding the high points (= the context in which the motif is

---

35. Erickson, *Introducing Christian Doctrine*, 20–21.
36. Fuhr and Köstenberger, *Inductive Bible Study*, 275.

seen in its greatest clarity)."³⁷ Hence, *projectile themes* are the textual themes that are most clear in their literary, theological, and canonical contexts. In biblical studies, contextual clarity maintains and preserves the integrity of God's character and the authority of the text as it is expressed and testified in the progression of salvation history and the eschatological future. This concept is especially true of the wisdom texts, as Curtis states, "Wisdom texts must be interpreted in the light of the major themes that permeate the wisdom books."³⁸ Hence, in taking the major themes in Qohelet, this study seeks to provide a contextual-theological analysis of Qohelet's framework by focusing on three lines of trajectory that are referred to from here on out as *projectile themes*. The projectile themes of fallenness, sustainment, and judgment chart these lines of trajectory.

CHARTING THE COURSE OF TRAJECTORY IN QOHELET THEOLOGY

Charting the course of Qohelet's thematic trajectory requires more than just literary and theological analysis. Each chapter in this study is meant to build upon one another systematically, whereby the argument of coherence in Qohelet's projectile themes is supported by the background and canonicity of Qohelet's composition. Before any approach can be made to charting the trajectory in Qohelet, a few essentials must be understood. Hence, this study is split into three parts, with part 1 consisting of chapters 1–3 seeking to establish a basis for approaching Qohelet as a canonical and theological composition. In part 1, it is essential to establish recognition of Qohelet's composition in the wisdom tradition of both the ancient Near East and Israelite cultures. Similarities and dissimilarities in the wisdom genre lay between the ancient Near East and Israel, whereby a shared form of wisdom literature is designated in prose, learned sayings, aphorisms, and teachings. According to R. S. Hess, "Much of the biblical wisdom literature has contemporary and earlier parallels in the major civilizations of the ancient Near East.... Much of this wisdom is shared between nations."³⁹ Additionally, G. T. Sheppard states, "Ancient Israelites often borrowed forms of wisdom from non-Israelite sources, through oral and literary interactions

---

37. Lubeck, Review of *Theological Diversity*, 487.
38. Curtis, *Interpreting the Wisdom Books*, 118.
39. Hess, "Wisdom Sources," 895–96.

with Edom, Egypt, Mesopotamia, and other nations."[40] Understanding the contemporary world of Qohelet affects how readers receive and respond to its content and context. Hence, the aim of chapter 1 is to begin with a general analysis of wisdom as an attribute and genre, then transition to a more specific analysis of wisdom in the ancient Near East and Israelite culture. While this chapter will discuss the similarities of wisdom between the ancient Near East and Israel, the primary purpose is to mark the distinction between the ancient Near East and Israelite's perception of wisdom as an attribute expressed in their wisdom literature. According to Sheppard, "A specialized 'wisdom' knowledge in Scripture is more than just a naturalistic or humanistic appraisal, for it presumes an awareness of the limits to wisdom in relation to what is revealed elsewhere and the freedom of God to intervene in ordinary affairs (e.g., Prov. 21:30f.)."[41] Wisdom as a genre can only truly be understood through understanding wisdom as an attribute. The attribute of wisdom seeks to perceive reality from an ethical and moral basis, whereby different cultural expressions of worldview derive among nations. Hence, chapter 1 establishes a foundational layer fundamental to reading Qohelet canonically and theologically.

Another essential to charting the trajectory of Qohelet is its canonicity in the wisdom corpus and the Bible. Tremper Longman III says, "The book was accused of contradictions, secularity, and even outright heresy. Indeed, all three accusations were interrelated in that Ecclesiastes was said not only to contradict itself, but also to contradict other Scriptures, which meant that its author was a heretic."[42] These accusations grossly misrepresent Qohelet and fail to recognize its thematic framework guiding Qohelet's theology on sin, grace, and judgment. These accusations also fail to recognize the art of rhetoric playing out in some forms of the wisdom genre, thus interpreting its message at face value rather than the motives often playing out in the sage's mind. In taking the thematic approach to chart Qohelet's theological trajectory, a discussion on Qohelet as a stand-alone book, as a book part of the wisdom corpus of the Old Testament, and as part of the one story of the Bible is presented to settle these misconceptions and show its affinity to the canon. In other words, if Qohelet can be theologically coherent in its canonical placement, then it can be shown to be theologically coherent in the infrastructure of its literary context. According to Kathleen A. Farmer,

40. Sheppard, "Wisdom," 4:1074.
41. Sheppard, "Wisdom," 4:1076.
42. Longman, *Book of Ecclesiastes*, 26.

"On the one hand, Qohelet reminds his audiences of the limited nature of proverbial truths by appealing to his own contrary experiences 'under the sun.' On the other hand, his continual references to what can be said to be true 'under the sun' function as subtle suggestions that 'under the sun' may not be all there is."[43] Hence, by embracing Qohelet as a message for all nations and all times, its boundaries stretch beyond the confines of its literary infrastructure to which most scholars have given the most attention. However, when recognizing Qohelet as a book whose message was not meant to be confined to time, place, and audience, its theological trajectory can be charted over the span of the canonical spectrum, whereby its function within the wisdom corpus of the Old Testament and the Bible as a whole eliminates much of its misconceived contradictions. Michael V. Fox makes a good point: "The belief that Solomon was the author of Ecclesiastes made its acceptance as Scripture possible. Once it was included among the sacred scriptures, exegesis found ways to make it theologically palatable."[44] Therefore, after establishing the canonicity of Qohelet in chapter 2 by discussing its function as a book that stands alone, a book within the wisdom corpus, and a book within the one story of the Bible, it is subsequently essential to establish the universality of Qohelet's message by arguing that Solomon was the author.

Despite the frame narrator of Qohelet, there is good reason to believe that Qohelet was a redaction of King Solomon's work as a teacher, and if Solomon is received as the author of Qohelet, the authority of wisdom in the teaching of Qohelet is better established. In accepting Solomon as the author and teacher of Qohelet, the premise of chapter 3 is that Solomon, being the wisest man who ever lived and a teacher of nations, not only was the most qualified person to teach with such artistic rhetorical strategy but that his message was presented with the element of universality, whereby those who came from the ends of the earth to hear his teaching were able to receive it in as much as the wisdom tradition that was shared between nations. To speak of the universality of Qohelet is to speak of its message as an admonition and call to all people in all times and spaces. In arguing for a social reading of Qohelet, Yat-Shing Edwin Mung states, "Qoheleth's composition is intended to be read rhetorically, as affirmed by its epilogue, while the theme of social justice is a universal and global concern that is

---

43. Farmer, *Who Knows What Is Good?*, 198.
44. Fox, *Ecclesiastes*, xv.

responsive to a social reading."[45] Mung's argument for a social reading of Qohelet is worth considering, with Solomon having been positioned to speak on such matters of global affairs to global leaders. Additionally, David George Moore and Daniel L. Akin state, "There are also some good arguments for favoring Solomonic authorship. . . . the requirements of being 'son of David, king in Jerusalem' (1:1) points to Solomon. . . . parallels between 1 Kings and Ecclesiastes fit the life of Solomon. For example, there are similarities in what both say about Solomon's wisdom (Eccl. 1:16; cf. 1 Kgs. 3:12) (Kaiser, 26)."[46] With internal evidence pointing to Solomon as the most qualified king in Jerusalem to be the author, the authority of Qohelet's wisdom and rhetorical strategy become more coherent than in the theory of an anonymous author. Hence, the aim of chapter 3 is to establish the Solomonic authorship view and the universality of Qohelet's teaching, whereby the theological trajectory of Qohelet can be charted thematically from a canonical spectrum spanning the time and space of the Bible.

Part 2 consists of chapters 4–5, focusing on the analysis for coherence. As an offering of contribution to the search for coherency in Qohelet's theology, it is only necessary to review some of the leading contributions made thus far in the study of Qohelet. Hence, the focus of chapter 4 will be given to three different approaches to coherence in Qohelet proposed in modern scholarship. To reiterate from earlier in this introduction, chapter 4 explores coherence in Qohelet from the approach of J. A. Loader, who argues for an "adequate literary explanation" of Qohelet in the tensions he calls "polar structures,"[47] Michael V. Fox, who argues that "harmonization is a proper and necessary part of the reading process of Qohelet,"[48] and Eunny P. Lee, who argues that the contradictions in Qohelet have "their place in the author's overall rhetorical strategy."[49] In essence, this chapter functions as a segue to the following chapter not only by providing insight into what has already been contributed to the search for coherency in Qohelet but also to help distinguish what will be contributed through the argument of this study. One common thread in these approaches to coherence is that they all strongly focus on the literary infrastructure of Qohelet, such as literary structure and devices, which are necessary elements inherent to

---

45. Mung, "Qoheleth and Social Justice," 233.
46. Moore and Akin, *Ecclesiastes, Song of Solomon*, 5.
47. Loader, *Polar Structures in the Book of Qohelet*, 1.
48. Fox, *Qohelet and His Contradictions*, 22–23.
49. Lee, "Vitality of Enjoyment," 1.

its themes. By understanding these views, the main argument of this study presented in chapter 5 will contribute by taking these views and bridging their gaps with an analysis of their function within the thematic trajectory of Qohelet. The primary purpose of chapter 4 is to show that there is still a need for balance in the coherency of Qohelet.

Hence, chapter 5 seeks to argue the central thesis for the study by focusing on three overlaying themes, which are referred to as projectile themes. Since it is the purpose of this study to find coherence in the thematic trajectory of Qohelet, the concept of projectiles will be used as adjectives for describing how the themes of fallenness, sustainment, and judgment guide the framework of Qohelet's teaching charted by his theological worldview on sin, grace, and judgment. According to Frances Tsai-Fen Chang, "The theological themes frame what a book of the Bible is saying because they affirm the ultimate source and reason of the recorded events of history and the ultimate basis of the teaching expressed."[50] Additionally, inherent to the projectile themes of fallenness, sustainment, and judgment, projectile momentum is given by the motifs of vanity, striving after wind, and vexation in the theme of fallenness; joy, gift, and eternity in the theme of sustainment; and the deeds of the wicked and the righteous, death, and the hope of the God-fearer in the theme of judgment. As Richard Alan Fuhr began his analysis on the inter-dependencies of prominent motifs in Qohelet with the "presupposition that the prominent motifs observable within the text should in fact complement one another, . . . from the assumption that if compositional unity can be established, then one ought to assume thematic unity,"[51] this study also begins with a similar presupposition that focuses on the unified themes that take the same aim in the culmination of Qohelet's "end of the matter" point stated in Qoh 12:13 of the epilogue. Hence, a contextual-theological analysis that leads to balanced coherence and meaning in the overall message of Qohelet, from both the literary infrastructure and trajectory of its projectile themes, will be presented in contribution to the study of Qohelet in modern scholarship, whereby coherence in the projectile themes of fallenness, sustainment, and judgment forms a framework guiding a theological trajectory aiming at an appeal to righteous living and eschatological hope.[52]

---

50. Chang, "Suffering and Enjoyment/Hope," 156.

51. Fuhr, "Analysis of the Interdependency," n38.

52. As charting the course of trajectory in Qohelet's theology is discussed, the assertion is that the thematic trajectory of fallenness, sustainment, and judgment follows

Part 3 consists of chapters 6–7 and focuses on showing how Qohelet is a theologically coherent message that contributes to the metanarrative of the Bible. According to Williamson,

> Biblical theology is arguably best thought of as a holistic enterprise tracing unfolding theological trajectories throughout Scripture and exploring no biblical concept, theme or book in isolation from the whole. Rather, each concept, theme or book is considered ultimately in terms of how it contributes to and advances the Bible's meta-narrative, typically understood in terms of a salvation history that progresses towards and culminates in Jesus Christ.[53]

Chapter 6, therefore, examines what the New Testament reveals about Qohelet's theology and how Qohelet's trajectory takes aim at an anticipated future messianic revelation. That is, the projectile themes of fallenness, sustainment, and judgment in Qohelet show to be rooted in salvation history with an aim at an unfolding revelation of messianic and eschatological hope advanced in the New Testament. Hence, three points of aim regarding Qohelet's trajectory and what the New Testament reveals about Qohelet's theology will be discussed. These points of aim are the New Testament on the fallen state of creation and humanity, the New Testament on the sustaining grace of God, and the New Testament on the eschatological judgment and hope of glory. These three points of aim are not only correlated with the fallenness, sustainment, and judgment projectile themes of Qohelet but are also inherent to the unfolding revelation of the Bible as a whole. According to Iain Provan, "Ecclesiastes, as part of the Scripture that is given us for shaping faith and life, offers us such advice, correlating as it does so with extensive sections of the New Testament that also touch on such themes."[54] Hence, chapter 6 seeks to strengthen the coherency argument of this study by analyzing correlating themes between Qohelet and the New Testament, whereby salvation history culminates in Christ's call to repentance, grace, and redemption.

When approaching Qohelet with the metanarrative of the Bible in view, the trajectory of fallenness, sustainment, and judgment in Qohelet's

---

a premise that humanity enters a fallen world, God sustains humanity amid the fallenness, and God preserves the lives of those who fear him in the day of judgment. If this premise is inherent to these themes, it may be asserted that Qohelet is teaching from the all familiar theology of sin, grace, and judgment, thus affirming his intentions of the supposed contradictions.

53. Williamson, *Sealed with an Oath*, 17.
54. Provan, *Ecclesiastes, Song of Songs*, 42.

INTRODUCTION

teaching functions as a guide for life for every believer. At the forefront of the Bible's message throughout salvation history and the New Testament have been the warnings against sin, the promise of sustainment in God's grace to persevere in righteousness, and the eschatological hope of withstanding in the final judgment for those who fear God. Inherent to this message is the teaching of Qohelet, whereby the appeal is a call to righteous living and eschatological hope. According to Peter Enns, "Ecclesiastes has applicatory implications beyond how we can view despair, suffering, God, and so on. Wrestling with Ecclesiastes will also affect how we today as Christians understand the nature of Scripture and what, as a result, we are to do with it—that is, how do we read Scripture?"[55] Sensitivity and patience are crucial elements in the approach to Qohelet, and if articulations are too narrow, then conflict will inevitably arise between the interpretation and application of the text. Hence, only after analyzing all that has been discussed in the previous chapters can the applicatory implications in the function of Qohelet as a guide for life now be addressed. The question in focus for chapter 7 will be: How do the concepts and themes of fallenness, sustainment, and judgment guide the believer in righteousness and hope? By focusing on three points of discussion relating to the theological trajectory of Qohelet's projectile themes, the realities of life in the fallen state of humanity, life in the sustaining grace of God, and life in the imminent judgment inform our understanding of how humanity ought to live in the world while under the sun. Hence, chapter 7 seeks to understand the applicability of Qohelet's theology to Christian living, whereby the universal appeal to live righteously in fear of God is correlated with the themes of fallenness, sustainment, and judgment.

Finally, the conclusion will be quite simple in its presentation by providing a summary and reflection on what has already been discussed in the previous chapters. Hence, concluding comments on the theological appeal in the trajectory of Qohelet will be offered, along with comments on the overall theological message of Qohelet as a coherent call to righteous living and eschatological hope. Last but not least, a final proposal for reading and teaching Qohelet will be given in hopes that the reader, teacher, and student of Qohelet can find a more satisfying coherence in the thematic approach to its literary infrastructure. Hence, the conclusion will combine everything discussed in the previous chapters for one unified conclusion in the thesis argument. As stated earlier in this introduction, the thesis of

55. Enns, *Ecclesiastes*, 197–98.

this study is to argue that *while meaningful advances have been made in the search for coherence in the literary approach to Qohelet's contradicting motifs, there is still an unsettled incoherency in the overlay of Qohelet's theology. In taking a thematic approach, however, the inconsistencies of Qohelet take on a function of thematic underpinning, whereby coherence in the course followed by the projectile themes of fallenness, sustainment, and judgment forms a framework guiding a theological trajectory aiming at an appeal to righteous living and eschatological hope.*

PART I.

Background Analysis

Chapter 1

Wisdom Tradition in the Ancient Near East and Israelite Culture

RECOGNIZING GENRE IS A fundamental starting point for approaching any piece of literature. By classifying literature into genres, rules are set for the author-reader relationship. In other words, genre provides boundaries determined by its author for how its audience should respond to, and receive, its message. Justin Marc Smith states, "Genre serves as the literary bond that holds subjects and audiences in relationship. We would add that genre is the literary bond that holds authors, subjects and audiences together in relationship, as the author chooses the genre that will best communicate the subject to the audience."[1] If overlooked, these literary bonds of genre become disconnected. Especially due to the complexity of wisdom literature, sensitivity to these bonds is critical as the genre of wisdom is often conveyed in overlapping forms of subgenres, such as prose, learned sayings, aphorisms, instruction, and teachings. Additionally, the genre of wisdom is significant in that its very name is an attribute of ethical and moral perception expressed in the worldviews of culture. For Qohelet, wisdom takes its form from the ancient Near East and Israelite cultures, whereby participation in cultic religion and social justice is often the influence. In examining the genre and attribute of wisdom and how these functioned in the ancient Near East and Israelite cultures, the characterization of Qohelet's literary and theological expression is better understood.

---

1. Smith, *Why Βίος?*, 3.

PART I. BACKGROUND ANALYSIS

WISDOM AS AN ATTRIBUTE AND GENRE

Scholars have challenged the genre of wisdom as not being a genre that existed in the time and setting of the ancient Near East and Israel.[2] According to Roland E. Murphy, "'Wisdom' is a term that can be used to indicate certain books which deal particularly with (biblical) wisdom, or it can refer to a movement in the ancient world associated with 'teachers' or sages, and it can also suggest a particular understanding of reality which presents some contrasts with other biblical books."[3] Although wisdom literature existed, it was not a genre nor a specialized faction or school, as was the philosophical schools of the Greeks. On the one hand, scholars such as Mark Sneed and Will Kynes have challenged the authenticity of wisdom literature. Sneed does not believe there was a genre classification called "wisdom literature" but would prefer a literary classification defined by its "mode" of function. In other words, when the classification of literature is defined by its mode, how that piece of literature functions in its presentation to its contemporary audience is the primary consideration. Regarding wisdom literature, the mode of function can take on the forms of teaching, preaching, admonishing, or a call to knowledge and understanding. More extreme is Kynes's complete rejection of the term "wisdom literature." Kynes believes that the term "wisdom literature" has been used in many ways that have not been adequately defined for the classification of a genre and would prefer the term not be used at all. In other words, according to Kynes's view, although the wisdom tradition had a place in its ideological setting, it was not classified as a literary genre, nor can it be classified by a term that cannot be adequately defined.[4] On the other hand, scholars like Fox advocate for acknowledging the terms "wisdom literature" and "genre" as a reference for classifying comparable texts. Speaking of Kynes and Sneed's view on the wisdom genre, Fox states, "These observations do not justify abandoning the concept of wisdom literature or the recognition of wisdom literature as a genre. . . . Wisdom literature is a heuristic genre, which is valid insofar as it helps bring together texts that can be fruitfully compared, both for similarities and differences."[5] But if texts are to be compared for genre

2. For background on the different views of wisdom as a genre, see Kynes, "'Wisdom Literature' Category"; Lambert, *Babylonian Wisdom Literature*; Sneed, "Is the 'Wisdom Tradition' a Tradition?"; Perdue, *Wisdom and Cult*.

3. Murphy, "Wisdom in the OT," 920.

4. Sneed, *Was There a Wisdom Tradition?*, 75.

5. Sneed, *Was There a Wisdom Tradition?*, 75.

classification, what should be that criterion? Dell critiques Hermann Gunkel's broad view on genre, whereby Gunkel believes literature was uniquely derived from the context of its social and life settings. Although Gunkel stressed form and content in his genre classifications, he did not see an authorial or compositional intent on arrangement.[6] For this reason, Gunkel was primarily interested in a genre's social context beginning with the origins of its oral tradition. Dell, however, argues against Gunkel's broad view and believes there is a criterion for classifying wisdom literature into a genre characterized by its narrower view of literary form.[7] In other words, where Gunkel saw the life setting of literature as the primary factor for genre classification, Dell saw the literature's form and content as primary. If Gunkel's view is correct, then the narrow literary view of genre classification becomes an issue because wisdom literature has many overlapping subgenres and thus overlapping social and life settings. Dell and Sneed would agree that the classification of wisdom literature from a narrow literary analysis shows that not all literary works, such as Job, classified in the wisdom genre are strictly wisdom.[8] Unlike Proverbs, which is unarguably wisdom literature in its form, content, and context, works like Qohelet, Job, and Song of Songs strongly overlap with other genre forms. Dell, however, acknowledges that among the overlapping genres of a literary work classified as wisdom, there is an overarching genre that makes up its larger category, whereby the overarching layer that makes up the category of the wisdom genre consists of contextual themes and modes. According to Dell,

> Sneed (2011, 57) also argues that genre classification has to be at the smaller level and that "Hebrew wisdom literature should be described as a mode of literature and not strictly a genre." Mode of literature is a broader category, but surely genre categorization can operate on a number of different levels so that small sections and whole works or groups of works can be described using this terminology.[9]

The term "mode" is best thought of as the method of presentation, such as teaching and instructing, whereby genre is best thought of as a classification of all elements of a piece of literature, including its mode. Although

---

6. For more background on Hermann Gunkel's formulation on form-critical categories, see Lyon, *Reassessing Selah*, ch. 2.

7. Sneed, *Was There a Wisdom Tradition?*, 148.

8. Sneed, *Was There a Wisdom Tradition?*, 148–49.

9. Sneed, *Was There a Wisdom Tradition?*, 149.

PART I. BACKGROUND ANALYSIS

Sneed prefers the categorical term of "modes" over "genres," modes do not consider the inherent aspect of literary expression but only delivery. Nevertheless, when mode and context are considered part of a whole, the mode is simply a genre presentation. In terms of wisdom, the mode can be teaching, instructing, or reflective (Proverbs and Qohelet), poetic or prose (Job and Song of Songs), or a combination thereof. Hence, when discussing the genre of wisdom, it is essential to acknowledge the varying forms of presentation (e.g., teaching and instructing) and the varying forms of subgenres (e.g., sayings, riddles, admonishing, rhetorical questions, didactic narratives). Qohelet is wisdom literature that is presented in the form of instructing and teaching, whereby Kynes states, "Instruction directly addresses a party in need of teaching, who is either called upon using the imperative to adopt a way of behaving and acting that is beneficial for life or is led through persuasion and self-reflection to the knowledge of what should or should not be done."[10] This is not, however, a characteristic unique to Qohelet but to wisdom literature in general. For instance, Solomon begins Proverbs by beckoning his son to heed his instructions. Proverbs are presented in the mode of instruction for living wisely, such as with Qohelet. If the sages could be classified in a social setting all of their own, then the broad category of wisdom is the oral tradition of teaching and instructing. Hence, understanding wisdom literature in a genre classification that is holistic to all elements of a text helps in not only the identification of its mode of presentation but also its form and content (narrow view) and context (broad view). However, recognizing wisdom as a genre is only one side of the coin necessary for defining wisdom literature as the starting point of interpretation. The wisdom genre is a classification of literature that Fox describes as literature that "teaches the profitability of wisdom, promises wealth and happiness, and professes the certainty of justice."[11] These characteristics of wisdom literature can only be understood through the attribute of wisdom inherent to its appeal to the world and humanity. Hence, the attribute of wisdom is the other side of the coin defining wisdom literature. On one side of the coin are its broad and narrow literary elements and on the other, its attributes.

The Hebrew word for wisdom, used primarily in the wisdom corpus, is חכם (*rhkhm*) This word appears 149 times in the Hebrew Bible and 89 times in the wisdom books of Job, Proverbs, and Qohelet. According to

---

10. Kynes, *Oxford Handbook of Wisdom*, 361.
11. Fox, *Time to Tear Down*, 76.

the Complete Biblical Library *Hebrew Dictionary*, "This noun may refer to 'skill,' 'good sense,' 'general wisdom,' or 'godly wisdom.'"[12] These definitions deal with the principles of doing justice, such as justice in skillful discipline, justice in making sound decisions, justice in common sense, justice in living civilly, and justice in living piously. Hence, the attribute of חכם carries the concept of being trained to deal with and act ethically and morally wisely. Becoming trained in wisdom also spans other ancient Near East civilizations, whereby Gerald H. Wilson states,

> Outside the Bible, the root חָכַם is known in the Akkadian verb *ḥakāmu(m)*, G and D stems, know, understand; Š stem, inform, explain; N stem, be understood or be recognizable. Ugaritic knows the verb root *hkm* with a sense more closely related to that of the biblical verb, be wise. The nominal root חָכָם, wisdom, is known from Phoenician. In the Imperial Aramaic of the *Aḥiqar* text, the pael verb is found with the meaning instruct and give answer (to a test of wisdom) and the adjective חכים, wise, is also employed.[13]

Significantly, wisdom literature is characterized by these attributes, whereby the sage's teaching and instruction appeal to ethics and social justice. Inherently, the attributes of ethics and social justice are associated with theology, whereby God and the human response are the two focuses of social justice. That is to say, God is sovereign and righteous and sets an absolute standard for morality, and humanity is responsible for doing what is right according to God's standard. Additionally, wisdom is rooted in the doctrine of justification and righteousness, whereby humanity is to live in the sustainment of God's grace. In recognizing wisdom as a genre of literature with various modes and classifications influencing ethical and social justice behaviors, the framework for reading and studying wisdom literature becomes more apparent. This starting point becomes the essence of the approach to reading and studying wisdom literature thematically, literarily, and socially, whereby a balanced interpretation can be achieved. Hence, the study of wisdom literature must respect the inherent attributes rooted in cultic religion and social justice, whether Jewish, Christian, or ancient Near Eastern. On the one hand, L. G. Perdue states, "One necessarily concludes, on the basis of the sapiential traditions in Israel and the ancient Near East, that the sages not only engaged in teaching their

---

12. Gilbrant and Lint, *Old Testament Hebrew-English Dictionary*, s.v. "חָכְמָה," para. 85769.

13. Wilson, "חָכַם," 2:128.

students about various topics and practices of cultic religion but also instructed them to participate in its various dimensions of expression."[14] On the other hand, Curtis states, "While ancient Near Eastern parallels rarely transform our understanding of a biblical text, there are times when an understanding of the broader background can give us a richer understanding of certain features in the text."[15] Hence, in the following sections, the concepts of wisdom in the ancient Near Eastern and Israelite cultures will be discussed to deepen our appreciation for biblical wisdom literature with a shared relationship with the ancient Near East. Appreciation for the biblical wisdom literature is fully apprehended in the significance of its historical context of the geographical setting and social environment of its origins. When a comparative analysis is made between the wisdom literature of Israel and the ancient Near East, our understanding of wisdom's purpose and function becomes clear. However, it is essential to emphasize that the significance of the relationship between biblical and ancient Near Eastern literature is not so much in the similarities but the dissimilarities that make them distinct. Hence, when comparing the wisdom literature of the ancient Near Eastern and Israelite cultures, although containing elements that share in the classification of wisdom genre, it is essential to recognize the divergence between the two worldviews, whereby we find illumination in the uniqueness and significance of Yahweh, as his character is revealed through Israelite wisdom literature and the Bible as a whole. The biblical wisdom literature's divergence and illumination can only be emphasized when viewed externally and internally within the scope of its cultural setting. From interaction with the surrounding cultures and their immediate culture, the wisdom literature of the Bible, according to P. Pitkänen, "fits into the picture."[16] Hence, the external and internal analysis of biblical wisdom literature in its cultural and social settings is necessary to understand the wisdom traditions in both the ancient Near East and Israel. In this cultural interaction, similarities and divergence in worldviews are discovered, whereby wisdom literature in the ancient Near Eastern and Israelite cultures reveals the significant expression of the biblical worldview and evidences the authority of the wisdom corpus of the Bible. Emphasizing the distinctions between the differing worldviews of the ancient Near East and Israel helps define the content of biblical wisdom, such as in our

14. Perdue, "Cult, Worship: Wisdom," 83.
15. Curtis, *Interpreting the Wisdom Books*, 121.
16. Pitkänen, "Historical Criticism," 285.

study of Qohelet. Hence, understanding wisdom as an attribute and genre in the ancient Near East and Israel marks the starting point for approaching Qohelet theologically and literarily. It marks the starting point in the search for coherency, whereby Qohelet's theological and thematic trajectory can be traced. Wisdom as an attribute and genre defines the very essence of its content, making it a literature of theology. That is literature whereby Yahweh can be sought out and his character learned to live righteously in social justice and cultic religion (i.e., cultic devotion to Yahweh).

WISDOM IN THE ANCIENT NEAR EAST

Background studies in the ancient Near East have shown its value in biblical studies. Comparative analysis between Israelite and ancient Near Eastern cultures allows us to see the significance of Yahweh and his character amplified amid a world of paganism. The nation of Israel was embedded within the backdrop of the ancient Near East, thus inevitably influenced in some form, including its literature. Cultural boundaries overlap in close proximity, which means there are elements of culture that are shared and unified and elements of culture that are shared and distinct. Taking the modern world of the United States, for example, there is a geographically unified body of land that is inhabited by a vastly diverse group of cultures, which in some ways share in familiarity with common traits, and in other ways share in traits that are familiar yet distinct to a particular cultural group. For example, the inhabitants of America widely celebrate the holidays of Thanksgiving and Christmas, but elements of a family's immediate culture will determine how these are observed. In my home, in particular, aside from the traditional turkey (the commonly shared holiday dish), we eat Mexican cuisine called tamales every year, distinct to people within my immediate culture.

Similarly, overlap in cultural boundaries such as politics, religion, and education influenced the authors of ancient Near Eastern texts, whereby similarities and dissimilarities in shared and distinct cultural elements are evident in a diverse world. In particular, similarities and dissimilarities between the ancient Near Eastern and Israelite wisdom literature help us understand the cultural worldviews of societies within a world of diverse cultures, which are all familiar with a wisdom tradition. According to Matthews and Chavalas, "Wisdom includes understanding the natural world and the human world; society and civilization; the commoner and the king; the world of the gods and the world of nations."[17] For example, we see similarities and dissimilarities in the Egyptian wisdom literature called the "Teachings of Ptah-Hotep." In Column 5:8–10, there are three parallels with the biblical wisdom book of Proverbs, two of which are similar and one of which is dissimilar. The first stanza states, "My students, in all things, be intelligent, not arrogant, Be wise, not over-confident."[18] This stanza parallels in similarity with Prov 13:1, which states, "A wise son hears his father's instruction, but a scoffer does not listen to rebuke." Additionally, the second stanza states, "Seek advice from the powerless,"[19] which is paralleled in similarity with Prov 18:15 and 19:20, which state, "An intelligent heart acquires knowledge, and the ear of the wise seeks knowledge. . . . Listen to advice and accept instruction, that you may gain wisdom in the future." In contrast, the fourth stanza states, "Wisdom hides like precious green stones, But it can be found even in a young woman grinding grain."[20] In dissimilarity, this is in parallel with Prov 2:1–5, which states, "My son, if you receive my words and treasure up my commandments with you, making your ear attentive to wisdom and inclining your heart to understanding; yes, if you call out for insight and raise your voice for understanding, if you seek it like silver and search for it as for hidden treasures, then you will understand the fear of the Lord and find the knowledge of God."

There are further examples of parallels of similarity and dissimilarity in the wisdom literature of Mesopotamia, such as the literature titled "A Sufferer and a Friend in Babylon," which has parallels with both Job and Ecclesiastes. Regarding Job, parallels can be seen in the dialogue between Job and his friends discussing his suffering. According to Matthews and Benjamin, "All assume that the world is filled with suffering and that the existence of evil proves that the divine assembly cannot be just."[21] In the dialogue of lines 1–20 in "A Sufferer and a Friend in Babylon," the sufferer states, "When I was a child, fate took my father from me. The mother who bore me went to the land of no return. My parents left me an orphan without a guardian."[22] The friend responds, "You have blinded yourself to

---

17. Matthews et al., *IVP Bible Background Commentary*, "Poetic & Wisdom Literature: Introduction."

18. Matthews and Benjamin, *Old Testament Parallels*, 316.

19. Matthews and Benjamin, *Old Testament Parallels*, 316.

20. Matthews and Benjamin, *Old Testament Parallels*, 316.

21. Matthews and Benjamin, *Old Testament Parallels*, 255.

22. Matthews and Benjamin, *Old Testament Parallels*, 255.

common sense. Frowns have scarred your face."[23] In this dialogue are two parallels. First, in the broader sense, a parallel in the friend's response is similar to the book of Job, when Job's friends are trying to convince him that he is suffering for doing evil (Job 4–23). Second, in the narrow sense, a parallel in the sufferer's reflection of abandonment is dissimilar to Job 29:12, which states, "because I delivered the poor who cried for help, and the fatherless who had none to help him." The contrast is that in Job 29:12, the poor and orphan are helped and cared for, rather than abandoned, as in the dialogue of "A Sufferer and a Friend in Babylon." In emphasis, the dissimilarities between the two texts express two contrasting worldviews, whereby the wisdom of Yahweh and his people (the Israelites) are amplified amid the pagan cultures of the ancient Near East. In other words, where the wisdom of the ancient Near Eastern cultures sought to find order amid chaos through human activity and shared expectations of behaviors (i.e., cultural norms), wisdom in the Israelite culture seeks to find order amid chaos through the character of Yahweh expressed in his laws and ordinances (more on this in the next section).

The context of ancient Near Eastern wisdom literature spans a range of dimensions far beyond the textual parallels. Wisdom tradition was deeply rooted in the culture of the ancient Near East and has had its value in biblical studies since the nineteenth century. Over the past 150 years, archeological discoveries have added a new dimension to comparative literary studies in the ancient Near East, especially in the context of wisdom. The significance of the textual artifacts discovered in archeology is that many predate the wisdom literature of the Bible. Hence, artifacts found in ancient Near Eastern cultures such as Egypt, Sumer, Akkad, and Mesopotamia have provided a way for form critics to evaluate and reconstruct contextual settings of the biblical wisdom books.[24] Additionally, the discovery of textual artifacts has broadened the spectrum of influence from the cultures of the ancient Near East that expand a vast dimension of human activity and lifestyle. According to William W. Hallo and K. Lawson Younger Jr.,

> The "context" of a given text may be regarded as its horizontal dimension—the geographical, historical, religious, political and literary setting in which it was created and disseminated. The contextual approach tries to reconstruct and evaluate this setting, whether for a biblical text or one from the rest of the ancient Near

---

23. Matthews and Benjamin, *Old Testament Parallels*, 255.
24. Wells, "Hebrew Wisdom as the Sitz Im Leben," 61.

East. Given the frequently very different settings of biblical and ancient Near Eastern texts, however, it is useful to recognize such contrasts as well as comparisons or, if one prefers, to operate with negative as well as positive comparison.[25]

It may be said that ancient Near Eastern and biblical wisdom literature derive their parallels from this horizontal dimension mentioned by Hallo and Younger. Geographically, Israel is embedded within the backdrop of the ancient Near East. Historically, Israel and the ancient Near East are contemporary cultures. Religiously, Israel and the ancient Near East participated in cultic rituals, worship, and devotion. Politically, Israel and the ancient Near East had foreign relations. And literarily, Israel and the ancient Near East are both positively and negatively comparative. James Bennett Pritchard states, "The Egyptians delighted in compilations of wise sayings, which were directive for a successful life. To them, this was 'wisdom.'"[26] Some of these Egyptian texts, reflective of wise sayings in the mode of instruction, are *The Instruction of the Vizier Ptah-Hotep*, *The Instruction for King Meri-Ka-Re*, *The Instruction of King Amen-Em-Het*, *The Instruction of Prince Hor-Dedef*, and *The Instruction of Ani*. Other ancient Near Eastern wisdom literature focused on observation of life and world order are Akkadian texts such as *I Will Praise the Lord of Wisdom*, *A Pessimistic Dialogue Between Master and Servant*, and *A Dialogue About Human Misery*.[27] Hence, the vast majority of ancient Near Eastern texts predate the biblical wisdom books of Proverbs and Qohelet by a few centuries, thus giving the implication that the form and mode of delivery (e.g., instruction, teaching, and observation) of Proverbs and Qohelet were most likely influenced by the already existing wisdom tradition of the ancient Near East. However, it is essential to clarify that form, mode, and content do not mean context. Some of the most prominent comparisons are in the contextual similarities and dissimilarities of the ancient Near East and Israelite wisdom literature. However, if the contextual distinctions are not carefully considered between the wisdom traditions of Israel and the ancient Near East, then there runs the risk of parallelomania. According to Samuel Sandmel, "We might for our purposes define parallelomania as that extravagance among scholars which first overdoes the supposed similarity in

---

25. Hallo and Younger, *Canonical Compositions from the Biblical World*, xxv.

26. Pritchard, *Ancient Near Eastern Texts*, 412.

27. For an in-depth exploration into these ancient Near Eastern texts, see Pritchard, *Ancient Near Eastern Texts*; Hallo and Younger, *Context of Scripture*.

passages and then proceeds to describe source and derivation as if implying literary connection flowing in an inevitable or predetermined direction."[28] In other words, although content and form are essential components in comparative studies, if literary connections are to be made, comparisons in context should always precede the comparisons in content and form. Through the contextual comparisons of wisdom literature from the ancient Near East and Israel, the tradition of wisdom finds its most significant value in the task of biblical comparative studies. Distinctions are most significant in contextual comparisons, as there is no way to identify, let alone understand, the overlap between cultures without any comparison. In analyzing contextual settings and artifacts, however, cultural threads become visible as they overlap throughout the content and form of the overall spectrum of the wisdom tradition.

The fact that the ancient Near Eastern wisdom tradition runs deep in the backdrop of Israel is not a negative connotation of the biblical wisdom corpus. Instead, familiarity with the ancient Near Eastern wisdom tradition opens a whole other dimension to the interpretation of the wisdom books of the Bible. There is significance in how God chose to communicate and establish his covenant within the context of the ancient Near East, giving Israel a format that they were familiar with; as Matthews and Chavalas state, "It is evident in all of the above that as God included poetic and wisdom genres in his revelation to Israel, he did not design new literary styles to use or new issues to address."[29] As an interpreter of the biblical text in general and especially in the biblical wisdom literature, it is essential to invest time into the world of the ancient Near East. For instance, in the ancient Near Eastern wisdom literature dealing with ethics, a mythological and natural worldview can be perceived in the context of ancient Near Eastern culture. That is not to say wisdom attributes do not exist in the ancient Near East, but that the wisdom attributes derive from a naturalistic worldview of human thought, guided by the cultic religion of mythological pagan gods. Regarding the ancient Near Eastern ethical perspective dealing with the offense against humans, for instance, John N. Oswalt states, "Typically, the codes are said to have been authorized by a god. In Hammurapi of Babylon's case, it is Shamash, the sun god, who is said to give Hammurapi the right to dispense beneficence and order. But the laws themselves are understood

---

28. Sandmel, "Parallelomania," 1.
29. Matthews et al., *IVP Bible Background Commentary*, "Wisdom Literature."

to be human creations."³⁰ In this case, Mesopotamia's ancient Near Eastern culture believes their laws are authorized by divine authority. However, their judgments are based on cultural norms and customs shared among their society, which govern their expected behaviors. In contrast, the ethics and judgments of Israelite culture are derived from the theocracy constituted by the covenantal relationship of Yahweh and Israel. In other words, the culture does not set the standard whereby wisdom and ethics derive from human and natural mythological tradition but from a purely divine covenant lived out in the practical expression of God's people.

Hence, understanding wisdom in the ancient Near East is a valuable endeavor for understanding wisdom in the Bible. It is an essential task and responsibility of the biblical studies student to understand the context of the ancient Near Eastern pagan cultures, not for the sake of validating the truth of the Bible, but for the sake of validating our understanding of the Bible's truth.³¹ It is in spending the proper time and approach to comparative analysis between the ancient Near East and the Bible that the student of God's word becomes enlightened to the vast dimensions of similarities and dissimilarities marking the significance of God and his intervening throughout human history through a nation whose very culture is framed by divine covenant. Although wisdom traditions of the ancient Near East and Israel have shared forms, a distinguishing line is drawn between the reality of the biblical worldview derived from Yahweh's true and pure character and the ancient Near Eastern worldview derived from cultural norms and human expectations. Hence, wisdom in the ancient Near East is a valuable asset to biblical scholarship and is to be appreciated for its historicity and shared attributes with biblical texts.

WISDOM IN ISRAELITE CULTURE

Although wisdom in the Israelite culture shares similarities in form with the ancient Near East, the most significant difference is in the perceived realities of cultic religion and social justice. As mentioned in the previous section, ancient Near Eastern wisdom and ethics are derived from cultural norms forming their naturalistic worldviews. In the Israelite culture,

---

30. Oswalt, *Bible Among the Myths*, 86.

31. For more extensive background on the development of languages, literature, and wisdom traditions of the ancient Near East and Israel, see Kitchen, *Bible in Its World*; Kitchen, *On the Reliability of the Old Testament*.

WISDOM TRADITION IN THE ANCIENT NEAR EAST

however, wisdom derives from a worldview of their divine covenant with Yahweh. In other words, Israel's covenant relationship with Yahweh forms their worldview, not from cultural norms, but from divine justice in God's righteousness. For the Israelites, wisdom always starts with the fear of God. The fear of God concept is expressed in different phrases, such as "fear God" or "fear of God" (ירא אל), "fear before God" (ירא פנה אל), and "fear of the Lord" (ירא יה).[32] It is essential for a moment to focus the discussion on the concept of wisdom in the "fear God" phrases since it is in the concept of the "fear God" phrases that wisdom derives in Israelite culture.

The "fear God" phrases are significant in that they connote a yielding to God motivated not by a dreadful fear but a reverential fear, whereby wisdom, knowledge, and understanding are derived. According to Kelly M. Kapic, "The 'fear of the Lord,' spoken of throughout Scripture, is not normally meant to convey the idea of being frightened. Rather, it carries the idea of awe and wonder, of joy and hope."[33] In biblical wisdom, awe and wonder are the reverential aspects of fear, and joy and hope are the results of wisdom that come from covenantal knowledge, understanding, and expression of God's character. It is in the fear of God that Yahweh imparts his wisdom through the instruction of his law and ordinances. In this impartation, Prov 1:7a states, "The fear of the Lord is the beginning of knowledge." Suppose Israelite wisdom literature begins with the fear of the Lord. In that case, the student of biblical wisdom must have a reverential fear of the Lord in their approach to the Israelite corpus of wisdom literature. Although the fear of the Lord concept is explicitly emphasized in the wisdom literature of Proverbs, it is certainly a theme running through Qohelet and the entire canon of Scripture, whereby the instructional knowledge taught is expected to be put into practice.

The significance of the term "fear," in the context of the "fear God" phrases, is the connotation of a thing (i.e., noun) rather than an action (i.e., verb). To have the fear of the Lord is to have something in the nominal sense, whereby there is something to grasp. Another significance is the terms "God" (אל) and "Lord" (יה), whereby these are always a reference to Yahweh. To be precise, Yahweh (יה) denotes the proper name of God, as Terence Fretheim states, "The 'translation' LORD . . . is something of a problem, from various perspectives. LORD obscures the fact that Yahweh is a name and not a title

---

32. These phrases will be used synonymously as they carry the same concept in the context of wisdom.

33. Kapic, *Little Book for New Theologians*, 27.

or an epithet. The use of LORD is based on the post-OT Jewish practice of reading אֲדֹנָי (Lord) for Yahweh, because of an increased sense of holiness associated with Yahweh."[34] Hence, a more accurate way of translating the fear of God phrase is "fear of Yahweh" (cf. New Jerusalem Bible).

The "fear of God" phrases is an acknowledgment of Yahweh as the one true God and a yielding not only of the mind but the entire being of a person to Yahweh as Lord. In yielding to Yahweh as Lord comes the knowledge and understanding of truth, whereby wisdom and instruction become practical. Proverbs 2:3–7 states, "Yes, if you call out for insight and raise your voice for understanding, if you seek it like silver and search for it as for hidden treasures, then you will understand the fear of the Lord and find the knowledge of God. For the Lord gives wisdom; from his mouth come knowledge and understanding; he stores up sound wisdom for the upright; he is a shield to those who walk in integrity." M. G. Easton states, "Fear of the Lord—is in the Old Testament used as a designation of true piety (Prov. 1:7; Job 28:28; Ps. 19:9). It is a fear conjoined with love and hope, and is therefore not a slavish dread, but rather filial reverence."[35] Reverence for Yahweh in the fear of the Lord is, therefore, the root of knowledge and wisdom. Without reverence for Yahweh, the knowledge and wisdom of God cannot be understood or made practical in a person's life. Instead, as Prov 1:7b says, "fools despise wisdom and instruction," so is the person who does not revere the Lord Yahweh. The wise in Israelite culture are compared with those who hold the attribute of integrity. Proverbs 8:13 states, "The fear of the Lord is hatred of evil." Furthermore, Prov 14:27 says, "The fear of the Lord is a fountain of life, that one may turn away from the snares of death." Together, knowledge, understanding, wisdom, and instruction from the fear of the Lord give life and hope in this life.

Wisdom in the fear of God and its contextual settings throughout the Old Testament is influenced by righteousness. According to Michael J. Boda, "Fear of the Lord is the attitude of awe and of filial reverence, which befits the child of God over against his Maker and Redeemer. . . . To 'serve' Yahweh is to act as his loyal agent."[36] Additionally, Joseph Coleson states, "The fear of the Lord is, thus, the human covenantal response to Yahweh's gracious initiative and will be considered as foundational to a life

---

34. Fretheim, s.v. "Yahweh," 4:1, 293.
35. Easton, *Illustrated Bible Dictionary*, 254.
36. Boda, *1–2 Chronicles*, 368.

of wisdom (Prov 1:7)."[37] To have the "fear of the Lord" is to know and live in the righteousness that comes from understanding the knowledge and wisdom of Yahweh. In other words, the person who has the "fear of the Lord" lives according to the knowledge and wisdom of God, which results in righteousness.

As mentioned earlier, in the context of all references to the "fear of God" phrases, the underlying concept is knowledge and wisdom that lead in the way of righteous living (i.e., godly decisions). Righteous living is a life that is in submission to the lordship of Yahweh in both word and deed. For a person to submit to the lordship of Yahweh, they must first give reverence to God, whereby knowledge and wisdom can be imparted by the Spirit of God (cf. Isa 11:2). The significance is that the concept of fearing God in the wisdom of Israelite culture is perceived from a worldview motivated by righteousness. Wisdom rooted in righteousness is, therefore, wisdom that makes the purest sense of reality, bringing order to the cosmos and justice to social concerns. Speaking of biblical wisdom literature, particularly Proverbs, Roland E. Murphy states, "The verses underscore the purpose of the instructions and sayings that have been collected in the book. The saying about 'fear of the Lord' in 1:7 is programmatic for the wisdom enterprise (cf. 9:10; 15:33; Ps 111:10; Job 28:28)."[38] That is, the fear of the Lord concept is the foundation of the wisdom tradition of Israel and is the starting point to obtaining proper knowledge and understanding of God. This wisdom is divine and evidenced in the practical application in the life of the God-fearer. Wisdom in the "fear of the Lord" is, thus, something to be grasped and desired.

Wisdom literature in Israelite culture is expressed in various modes. The canonical wisdom books of the Bible consist of Job, Proverbs, Qohelet (Ecclesiastes), Song of Songs, and various Psalms. Other non-canonical (deuterocanonical or apocryphal) wisdom books originated in Israelite culture are the Wisdom of Ben Sira (Sirach) and the Wisdom of Solomon. In form, all of these books have overlapping genres, such as the saying, which are experiential and didactic, and instruction, which are commands and prohibitions. Job, Song of Songs, and the wisdom Psalms, however, are expressed in a more poetic mode, whereby J. A. Grant states, "As the name suggests, a wisdom poem is a poem (or hymn) that is rooted in the

---

37. Coleson, "Joshua," 171.
38. Murphy, *Wisdom Literature*, 54.

theology, form and content of Israel's wisdom tradition."[39] Despite their different and often overlapping forms, wisdom literature is classified as those books concerned with wisdom. This classification is convenient for designating literature of common modes and themes. The term "wisdom genre" may not have existed in the context of the ancient Near East and Israel, but the modes and themes certainly did and are evident in their very presentation, content, and form. The term "wisdom literature" has also, according to Murphy, "been adopted also by Egyptologists and cuneiform specialists to designate a variety of extrabiblical literature that is similar to the biblical works."[40] Especially for textual criticism, whether for the task of source, form, redaction, or literary criticism, the classification of literature aids in analyzing and grouping common literary works, such as the biblical wisdom corpus. Wisdom in Israelite culture, however, is not merely an influence of culture, literature, or the teachings of the sages, but rather has a deeper root perceived in the reality of their covenant with Yahweh. The covenantal framework is the defining component of the Israelite wisdom tradition. In other words, the Israelite worldview established in wisdom was a worldview derived from their covenantal fear and reverence for Yahweh and his character that is expressed through his law and ordinances. According to Murphy, "'Fear of God' is not lacking in the literature of the ANE (Barré 1981); reverence before the numinous is practically a given in the ancient world."[41] However, the difference between the ancient Near East and Israel is that reverence is more than deep respect for someone or something. Reverence to Yahweh is the source and origin of wisdom, knowledge, and understanding. Furthermore, as much has been said about the wisdom of Proverbs, Grant provides two observations significant to Job and Qohelet in the context of covenant and wisdom. On the one hand, Job's wisdom is expressed in the heart of his suffering, whereby his endurance reflects his reverence for God. At the heart of the covenantal relationship that Job has with God is his expectation of God's justice. Although full of lament, Job teaches us that there is a way to suffer in wisdom through continuous reverence toward God.[42] On the other hand, Qohelet's expectation of God's justice has led him into a quandary. For Qohelet, absurdity and meaningless in life "under the sun" derive from his covenantal expectation of God's justice.

39. Grant, "Wisdom Poem," 891.
40. Murphy, *Wisdom Literature*, 3.
41. Murphy, "Wisdom in the OT," 925.
42. Grant, "Wisdom and Covenant," 862.

And it is from the history of the covenant that Qohelet's wisdom derives, whereby he exhorts his audience to fear God.[43] Hence, it is significant that the wisdom books of Job and Qohelet give us wisdom from the experience of life's realities and a life lived in a divine covenant with Yahweh. However, the experiences between the two texts teach us two different aspects of how a person ought to face the experiences of life's realities. For Job, the lesson provides insight into how to suffer wisely in a world of uncertainty. While retribution was a shared worldview of the ancient Near East, Job teaches us that sometimes humans suffer without any cause for retribution. However, when that suffering comes, there is an enduring way that is wise: to suffer in fear of God, trusting in his justice. For Qohelet, there is uncertainty in life under the sun, whereby the same fate falls upon the righteous and wicked alike, but hope sustains those who fear God. While Job teaches us wisdom for suffering, Qohelet teaches us wisdom for living in a fallen world. In these two profound books of wisdom, the sapiential approach to bringing order out of chaos is expressed in its purest form.

Despite having roots in the ancient Near Eastern backdrop, wisdom in Israelite culture is very distinct in thought. Although wisdom literature generally shares similarities in form and content, the underlying influence draws the distinctions between cultural worldviews. According to R. S. Hess, "The wisdom literature of the Bible participates in forms and in some specific content with the wisdom literature of the West Semitic world and of the greater ancient Near East. However, the canonical text of the OT provides a distinctive source for important theological distinctives that do not occur elsewhere."[44] These theological distinctives give canonical placement to the biblical wisdom corpus of Scripture and significance to Israel's wisdom tradition in the ancient Near East. What is essential to recognize is that wisdom in Israelite culture forms the framework for a proper approach to life in godliness. That is a life of wisdom derived from the reverential fear of God.

---

43. Grant, "Wisdom and Covenant," 862.
44. Hess, "Wisdom Sources," 900.

Chapter 2

Canonicity of Qohelet in the Wisdom Corpus and the Bible

The canonicity of Qohelet has been questioned far too often throughout church history, causing its credibility as a book of the wisdom tradition, a book within the wisdom corpus of the Bible, and a book within the one story of the Bible to be mischaracterized. Arguments against Qohelet's canonicity have been primarily due to its anonymity (lack of reference to a direct author), its supposed unorthodox view of wisdom (in comparison to the book of Proverbs), its literary structure (supposed contradictions), and its theological worldview (its view on life and judgment). Considering Qohelet was accepted as authoritative by the Jewish community, Longman states, "It appears that, while Ecclesiastes was questioned, its canonicity was never rejected by the mainstream Jewish community. The question, in other words, was not, 'Is Ecclesiastes canonical?' but, since the book was considered authoritative, 'Why is this book canonical?'"[1] If the authority of Qohelet can be established by understanding its canonical attributes, its theological trajectory can be traced through the canonical framework from which it was composed. The following sections of this chapter will discuss Qohelet's canonical attributes highlighting its contribution to the wisdom tradition of Israel, its contribution to the wisdom corpus of the Bible, and its contribution to the Bible as a whole, all of which are fundamental to its study.

---

1. Longman, *Book of Ecclesiastes*, 28.

QOHELET AS IT STANDS ALONE

Qohelet (קהלת) is a Hebrew title that means "leader of the assembly, speaker of the assembly."[2] Its lexeme form used in the book of Qohelet appears seven times in the Bible and only in Qohelet. Its root, however, appears only four times as a place name and 173 times throughout the Old Testament. Qohelet (קהלת) has a semantic range denoting the act of assembling and the object of an assembly and congregation. The idea of the title Qohelet in the seven times it appears in the book of Qohelet coveys "the convener or leader of the congregation or community."[3] The Greek term for Qohelet is Ἐκκλησιαστής, from which the English title Ecclesiastes derives. In Greek and English translations, Ecclesiastes is translated with the titles "preacher" and "teacher." Qohelet, therefore, is to be understood not as a personal name but as the title of one who gathers an assembly for "preaching" and "teaching." Qohelet 12:9 states, "Besides being wise, the Preacher also taught the people knowledge, weighing and studying and arranging many proverbs with great care." With this descriptive statement in mind, it may be safe and reasonable to suppose that the context of Qohelet, whether a composition of one record or a redaction of many records, was not a composition as one might think of an author who is writing in isolation. Instead, Qohelet is most likely a composition derived from sermons and lectures preached and taught in a congregational setting or school of assembly.

Wisdom is attributed to Qohelet as a book that stands alone. In other words, as Qohelet is examined apart from the wisdom corpus of the Bible, it undoubtedly still presents characteristics inherent to the wisdom genre and tradition of Israel. The title alone (Qohelet) is indicative of the very type of literature and genre it has been classified and labeled as (i.e., wisdom). Although the content of Qohelet admittedly presents difficulties that some scholars have said are opposed to traditional wisdom,[4] neither literary nor thematic elements making up its theological framework should be negated. According to Peter Enns, "How one understands the overarching message of Ecclesiastes as a whole will affect how one handles the details of the book

---

2. *HALOT*, s.v. "קֹהֶלֶת," 3:1080.

3. Carpenter, s.v. "קֹהֶלֶת," 3:887.

4. Scholars such as James L. Crenshaw, Roland E. Murphy, and J. T. Walsh see the tensions and contradictions of Qohelet as a pessimistic form of wisdom literature as opposed to the traditional wisdom of Proverbs that is more optimistic about life. On the contrary, K. Schifferdecker sees Qohelet's view of a God-ordained order of the world as an echo of Proverbs' traditional wisdom.

itself, yet the book's overall message cannot be determined apart from the book's details."⁵ In other words, there is a cycle of reciprocity within the text of Qohelet, whereby its narrow and broad elements complement each other to bring about a coherently sound message of wisdom. Suppose the details of Qohelet are isolated without consideration of the overarching message. In that case, ambiguities linger, leading to a mischaracterization of Qohelet as a person, Qohelet as wisdom literature, and Qohelet as authoritative. Suppose the interpretive approach to Qohelet is taken from a literary approach to the neglect of its theological themes (or vice versa). In that case, its overall message will be misconstrued as it has been in the past. Enns asserts that there needs to be meaningful coherence in the overall message of Qohelet to make sense of Qohelet's literary contents. A meaningful coherence in Qohelet begins with accepting its compositional background as a unifying record of either one lesson or a compilation of multiple lessons. Some interpreters have even taken an autobiographical reflection view of Qohelet with good reason. According to Dell, "The book has the atmosphere of an older man looking back in philosophical mode and with the benefit of hindsight, but with the express purpose of instructing others in what he has learned"⁶ Although it is very plausible and most likely that Qohelet's wisdom has partly derived from life's experience and that his teachings may have been a product of his reflections, this does not constitute the composition of Qohelet as an autobiographical memoir of inner struggles. Instead, the fact that there is a frame narrator in the prologue (Qoh 1:1–11) and epilogue (Qoh 12:8–14) indicates that its composition and final form were a compilation of either a contemporary or later redactor. The function of the narrator, however, is to clarify the meaning of Qohelet's teaching (Qoh 1:12–12:7) by stating its thesis in the prologue and its main point in the epilogue. With the frame narrative of Qohelet in mind, Enns proposes three possibilities for the compositional character of Qohelet. According to Enns, "Qohelet may be (1) a fictional character created out of whole cloth, (2) the frame narrator's own alter ago (the vehicle by which he recounts his own struggles), or (3) a literary product that in some sense had an 'independent' existence before its adaptation by the frame narrator (which is not to imply it would have existed in the precise form in which we see it

---

5. Enns, *Ecclesiastes*, 1.

6. Katharine J. Dell, "Reading Ecclesiastes with the Scholars," in Firth and Wilson, *Exploring Old Testament Wisdom*, 84.

in 1:12–12:7)."[7] In addition, as stated in the introductory chapter, there are the views that Qohelet was a compositional character of either Solomon (who at times referred to himself in the third person), one of King David's other descendants, or an Israelite from a later period using a Solomonic personality. The view of this study takes the third compositional position presented by Enns that Qohelet had a prehistory of literary existence that was later redacted by the frame narrator, who put the works of Qohelet in their final form. In other words, the position adopted here is that the content of Qohelet 1:12–12:7 is the original work of Qohelet (the preacher and teacher). This supposition leads to the speculation that the original composition of Qohelet predates what has become widely accepted among scholars as a composition of the Second Temple period and further speculations that Solomon was the original author (more on this in chapter 3). Contrary to a later date (pre-exilic, Second Temple period), there is good textual reason to assert that Qohelet's roots run more profound within the historicity of Israel's culture, which is attested to in Qoh 1:1, stating, "The words of the Preacher, *the son of David, king in Jerusalem*." Although arguments for which one of David's descendants was or was not Qohelet linger, the question of Qohelet's compositional date hinges on this statement with implications that Qohelet is rooted deep in Israelite history and composed[8] (not redacted) during a time when Israel still had a king.

This brings us to the discussion of Qohelet's date of composition. Traditionally those who hold to Solomonic authorship date Qohelet early in Israelite history. However, up until the eighteenth and nineteenth centuries, critical scholars began rejecting an early date for Qohelet on the basis of language, and they began arguing for post-exilic dating. According to C. F. Keil and F. Delitzsch, "Not only the language, however, but also the style and the artistic form of the book, show that it is the most recent product of the Bible."[9] In other words, Keil and Delitzsch believe Qohelet's composition is one of the more recent of the Old Testament. In their argument for a later date, Keil and Delitzsch provide a list of the hapaxlegomena they say belong to a more recent period of the language. Most critical scholars have followed the criticism of Keil and Delitzsch, leading to most modern

---

7. Enns, *Ecclesiastes*, 6.

8. The terms "composed" and "composition" are to be used in distinction from the term "redaction." "Composed" and "composition" refer to the original autograph and development of the literary composition of Qohelet's text, and "redaction" refers to the development of its final form.

9. Keil and Delitzsch, *Commentary on the Old Testament*, para. 24444.

scholars advocating for a post-exilic date. For instance, Fox believes that there are hints of Persian elements within the text of Qoh 5:8 (7), which mentions the word *medinah* (מדינה), rendered as "province" in English, and hints of Hellenistic elements in the text of Qoh 9:11, which mentions the word *merotz* (מרוץ), rendered as "race." Fox supposes that "province" points to the post-exilic era when Jews lived in the Persian empire and that "race" points to the Greek athletic tradition of footraces, which puts his dating for the book of Qohelet between the second and third centuries BC.[10]

While the dating of Qohelet among critical scholars has often been propelled by the textual comparison of language and the use of Persian and Aramaic loanwords, Angel Sáenz-Badillos, referring to the comparison of languages in biblical studies, states,

> Comparative study raises many difficult issues mainly because of the vast differences in time among the various languages, almost 6,000 years in some instances, and because many African languages were not properly documented until the last or even the present century. In addition, comparative methods themselves, based primarily on morphology, phonetics, and vocabulary, are under constant review. Interference arising from contact between different groups, like Cushitic and Semitic in Ethiopia, makes this kind of study even more complicated.[11]

Yet another approach has been through the comparison of thought between Qohelet and Hellenists.[12] However, Longman argues, "This method, too, is dubious since connections can be made between Qohelet and earlier thought and literary forms and also with much later foreign thought."[13] As convincing as the arguments are for a later date, some scholars, such as Daniel Fredericks and Duane A. Garrett, make compelling arguments for the pre-exilic date of Qohelet. On the basis of Fredericks's devoted study of all of the arguments for the late dating of Qohelet, Longman states, "So little is known about the transmission of the biblical text during its earliest stages that we cannot rule out linguistic updating. The so-called late forms may not in fact have been original to the book but may reflect the updating

---

10. Fox, *Ecclesiastes*, xiv.

11. Sáenz-Badillos, *History of the Hebrew Language*, 26.

12. For more background on the arguments for a post-exilic dating of Qohelet, see Keil and Delitzsch, *Commentary on the Old Testament*; Fox, *Ecclesiastes*; Longman, *Book of Ecclesiastes*.

13. Longman, *Book of Ecclesiastes*, 10.

of vocabulary and grammar by later scribes so their contemporaries could understand the book better."[14] In addition, Garrett's comparative study of the ancient Near Eastern and Israelite literature showed that Qohelet was knowledgeable about the pre-exilic text that would not have been known to the communities of the post-exilic era. In counterargument to the post-exilic dating of Qohelet, Garrett states, "By contrast, strong evidence supports linking Ecclesiastes to the literary and intellectual world of the ancient Near East. Ecclesiastes is in many ways conceptually and structurally similar to examples from ancient Egyptian literature."[15] This Egyptian comparative literature includes the *Instruction of Ptahhotep*, the *Instruction of Duauf*, the *Instruction of King Amenemhet*, and the *Instruction for King Merikare*. Hence, all this that has been said regarding the dating of Qohelet is not to suggest the dismissal of one view over the other (a suggestion will be argued in chapter 3) but to consider how each view inevitably affects one's perception of Qohelet's authority and canonicity within the wisdom corpus of the Bible and Israelite wisdom tradition. If Qohelet is truly post-exilic literature, then only by hypothetical appeal can scholars justify its claim that Qohelet is a son of David and king of Jerusalem. Hence, the view suggested here, which will become more evident in the next chapter, is that Qohelet is a composition of pre-exilic dating, whereby the setting and authorship are in the era of a united kingdom. In maintaining this view, fidelity to Scripture and the entire canon is maintained, whereby a coherent reading and interpretation of Qohelet are more feasible.

Qohelet, as it stands alone within the backdrop from which it proclaims, is part of establishing its canonicity. Although of the minority view, the extent of Fredericks and Robert Gordis's research in counterargument to the critical scholars, holding to the pre-exilic language and dating of Qohelet, is quite feasible and testifies to the most obvious expression of Qohelet. In attributing a pre-exilic dating of Qohelet, its inherent elements of canonicity solidify the church's canonical recognition and authenticity. Regarding the arguments for post-exilic language and dating, Daniel J. Estes states, "As persuasive as this evidence appears, it may not necessarily be decisive in establishing a post-exilic date for the book."[16] Estes makes this suggestion on the basis of Fredericks, who argues "that its language 'should not be dated any later than the exilic period, and no accumulation

---

14. Longman, *Book of Ecclesiastes*, 10.
15. Garrett, *Proverbs, Ecclesiastes, Song of Songs*, 265.
16. Estes, *Handbook on the Wisdom Books*, 274.

of linguistic evidence speaks against a pre-exilic date.'"[17] Moreover, Gordis argues "that the Aramaic influences in the extant text could have originated in the common Northwest Semitic vocabulary stock, or they may have entered into Hebrew during times in Israel's history, such as during the reign of Solomon, when Israel and Phoenicia had extensive commercial and political connections."[18] In either case, for the dating and language of Qohelet, the evidence is inconclusive for a later date and should be considered with a grain of salt. The issues and concerns addressed in Qohelet are only relevant to part of the pre-exilic era. Instead, there are patterns of issues that can be traced throughout Israelite history and the ancient Near East. Furthermore, with the traditional view of Solomonic authorship, Solomon, who was a teacher of nations, would have had access to the literature of the ancient Near East and may have been well acquainted with various languages throughout such a diverse world. Hence, in the spirit of tradition held not only in strictly Jewish tradition but also the tradition of the church by early church fathers such as Didymus, Origen, and Gregory of Nyssa,[19] a significant canonical aspect of Qohelet is its date and setting. This setting and date testify to Qohelet's life setting (context) in which its language shares a similar stream with the ancient Near Eastern cultures, such as Egypt, Sumer, Edom, Akkad, Canon, and Phoenicia. This tradition establishes the recognition of Qohelet's canonicity among the wisdom corpus of the Bible.

QOHELET AS PART OF THE WISDOM CORPUS

The five books of the Bible's wisdom corpus (i.e., Job, Psalms, Proverbs, Ecclesiastes, and Song of Songs) are grouped differently depending on whether one holds to a Jewish or Christian tradition. In the Jewish tradition, for instance, these five books are grouped along with Ruth, Esther, Lamentations, 1 and 2 Chronicles, Ezra, Nehemiah, and Daniel in a corpus of Scripture called the *Writings* (*Ketuvim*). This collection was then divided into three subdivisions known as *poetic books* (Psalms, Job, and Proverbs), the *scrolls—Megilloth* (Ruth, Esther, Qohelet, Lamentations, and Song of Songs), and the other writings (1 and 2 Chronicles, Ezra, Nehemiah, and Daniel). According to Williamson, "Besides having additional material,

---

17. Estes, *Handbook on the Wisdom Books*, 274.
18. Estes, *Handbook on the Wisdom Books*, 274.
19. J. Robert Wright, *Proverbs, Ecclesiastes, Song of Solomon*, 190.

the LXX arranges the canonical books quite differently, appending Ruth to Judges, Lamentations to Jeremiah, including Chronicles, Ezra-Nehemiah and Esther with the Former Prophets, and grouping the poetical and wisdom books (Job, Psalms, Proverbs, Ecclesiastes, Song of Songs) together, along with Wisdom of Solomon and Sirach."[20] In the Christian tradition, Qohelet is grouped within the five poetic and wisdom books: Job, Psalms, Proverbs, Ecclesiastes (Qohelet), and Song of Songs, also called the *wisdom corpus*.[21] The wisdom corpus of the Bible consists of books that express every human experience of life relevant to every generation. In Job, the experience of human suffering is expressed in light of faith and faithful covenant with God, whereby the message is conveyed in poetic dialogue. Although many interpretations of Job have sought to answer the question of why the innocent suffer, Job teaches us that there is a way in which God expects humans (particularly the righteous) to respond to suffering, trusting in his justice in the "fear of God" expression (Job 1:9). Likewise, the expression of the Psalms portrays many elements of human experience from lament to consolation in God's redemptive history.[22] However, it is essential to note that not all Psalms are grouped within the *wisdom corpus*. When reference to the Psalms as wisdom is made, the connection is mainly to Pss 1, 19, 37, 49, 50, 73, 78, 112, and 119. In Proverbs, wisdom is a skill to be grasped in the "fear of the Lord," whereby living righteously before God results in the happiness and the skill needed to deal with all matters of life (Prov 1:1–7). Song of Songs is a poetic masterpiece, a love song expressing wisdom in the context of romance and marriage. And last but certainly not least, Qohelet (Ecclesiastes) teaches practical wisdom for living life in righteousness and hope that brings joy amid the fallenness of creation. Hence, according to Curtis,

> The wisdom literature, of course, is filled with practical, though often somewhat secular-seeming principles that have to do with everyday matters of life—things like civil speech, honesty, integrity, self-control, diligence, and other useful values. While some are deterred by the secular character of many of these principles, it seems likely that these practical guidelines for living are as integral

20. Williamson, "Canon," 36.

21. Although Qohelet falls within different literature groupings within the Hebrew and Protestant Bibles, wisdom corpus refers to the Christian grouping of Job, Psalms, Proverbs, Ecclesiastes, and Song of Songs.

22. The Psalms have been approached from differing views regarding compilation, use, and meaning throughout the history of biblical studies.

to God's purposes for his people as is the explicitly theological material that dominates many other parts of Scripture.[23]

Curtis makes a good point in that some get deterred by the secular aspects of life's issues expressed in the wisdom corpus of the Bible. This may be why many critical scholars have struggled to make sense of Qohelet's content and its placement within the canon of Scripture. Nevertheless, with the appeal to righteous living in the "fear of God," wisdom's paradoxical correlation between human and divine experiences contradicts a mere human secularist observation and interpretation. On the contrary, the human experience resides in the realities of the ontological (i.e., the objective reality of what is materially existent) and metaphysical (i.e., the subjective reality of what is existent outside the material world) realms, whereby life in the objectivity of all things "under the sun" and hope in the subjectivity of "the faith and assurance of redemption" meet. Hence, the wisdom corpus of the Bible is a collection of recognized canonical literature that gives the God-fearer divine wisdom for living in honest devotion to God. In the wisdom corpus, Qohelet finds its canonical placement and contribution to the Bible's appeal to live in righteousness before a righteous and holy God.

Although rabbinic authorities have questioned the canonicity of Qohelet due to its seemingly unorthodox and contradicting views compared to other parts of Scripture, it was never rejected by the mainstream Jewish community.[24] Longman states, "The predominant opinion was that Ecclesiastes indeed was canonical, and it is found in all the major early lists of authoritative books. The fact that it was found at Qumran implies that it had achieved that status before the time of Christ."[25] Although the Aramaic Targum translation of Qohelet is a paraphrase presented in more of an exegetical preaching form, the Latin Vulgate and Greek Septuagint agree with the Hebrew tradition of the Masoretic Text. These translations are so close together that the minor variants should maintain the confidence of their readers. Regarding the Greek translation's proximity to the Hebrew,

---

23. Curtis, *Interpreting the Wisdom Books*, 18.

24. For more background on the acceptance of Qohelet by the mainstream Jewish community, see Longman, *Book of Ecclesiastes*, 26–28. In this section, Longman discusses the canonicity of Qohelet and points out that evidence for mainstream Jewish acceptance of Qohelet can be found in its preservation with other texts discovered at Qumran and its recounts in rabbinic literature that reflect early Jewish opinions, such as in the "Talmudic" tractate *Berakot, Baba Batra (4a)*, which comes from the period of Herod the Great, and the tractate *Shabbat*.

25. Longman, *Ecclesiastes*, 255–56.

Fox states, "The mimetic (or formal-mapping) nature of the translation allows us to account for the resulting variants, unless obviously erroneous, as potentially valid alternative readings."[26] However, textual proximity was not the primary basis for accepting Qohelet as canon. The debates between rabbinic authorities argued whether Qohelet defiled the hands with its statements, such as Qoh 11:9, which seemed to contradict the teachings of Torah as in Num 15:39, stating, "And it shall be a tassel for you to look at and remember all the commandments of the Lord, to do them, not to follow after your own heart and your own eyes, which you are inclined to whore after." The idea was that if a text defiled the hands, it should be rejected as canonical. Still, a holy and divinely inspired book would "make the hands unclean" as it exposes the unworthiness of human hands, requiring holy rituals to handle the text with sacred reverence and care.[27] Although disputed by the rabbis, Qohelet has stood up to the recognized standard of divinely inspired authority. Hence, fourth-century church father Gregory of Nyssa (ca. 335–394) stated, "The teaching of Ecclesiastes pertains only to suitable behavior in the church, that is, how to direct a person in virtue. This book aims to elevate our minds above the senses, to abandon great, brilliant and noble appearances, to transcend the senses and to attain what transcends them."[28] That is to say that although Qohelet is explicitly observing the absurdities of all things, "under the sun," its message implicitly appeals to the divinely inspiring character of God, which transcends the senses of an ontological world. The implicitness of the message unites the text of Qohelet with the other wisdom corpus books, such as Proverbs, whereby Greg Goswell states, "Proverbs insists that no degree of mastery of the rules of wisdom can confer absolute certainty (e.g. Prov 16:1, 2, 9; 19:14, 21; 20:24; 21:30, 31). . . . Proverbs, as much as the other two books, stresses the *limitations* of wisdom."[29] These are unifying aspects of the wisdom corpus that scholars have failed to emphasize in their analysis, thus amplifying the supposed tensions between Proverbs, which has become the standard of wisdom literature, and Qohelet and Job, which have long been criticized against Proverbs. It is proposed here, however, that the canonicity of Qohelet is evident to the person with an open heart. David George Moore and Daniel L. Akin quote Michael Eaton's view on canonicity that

26. Fox, *Time to Tear Down*, 156.
27. Moore and Akin, *Ecclesiastes, Song of Solomon*, 7.
28. J. Robert Wright, *Proverbs, Ecclesiastes, Song of Solomon*, 192–93.
29. Goswell, "Order of the Books," 459.

involves faith, stating, "The person who is hostile to claims for authority in any religious document will bring his presuppositions to Ecclesiastes and find his doubts confirmed. Another person who comes to the Bible, perhaps to Ecclesiastes, with openness is ready to hear and find that the Preacher speaks to him as never before."[30] As valid as this statement is, this does not mean that the tensions should be dismissed but that they should be interpreted with integrity and sacred care. That is to say that there must be a fidelity to Scripture as a whole, whereby the interpretation of Qohelet maintains its testimony to the entirety of the wisdom corpus and the Bible. Although little is known about how the Old Testament books were determined to be canonical, what is explicitly known is that the canonical books of the Hebrew Bible explicitly include the book of Qohelet.

Nevertheless, if there are to be criteria by which a valid recognition of a text's canonicity can be measured, what should that be? Michael A. Eaton adds to the subjective criteria of canonicity, which involves faith, a satisfying set of objective criteria when he states, "Six factors may contribute to the recognition of inspiration in any document of Scripture: (i) its place in the history of redemption; (ii) its authorship or authorship associations; (iii) its content; (iv) its preservation; (v) the testimony of the church; (vi) the witness of the Spirit."[31] First, Qohelet's association with the history of salvation is evident in its overarching themes of fallenness (sin), sustainment (grace), and judgment (redemption). These themes follow a trajectory of salvation history that progresses throughout time and space and is witnessed in the metanarrative of Torah and the Prophets and the entirety of the Bible (more on these themes in chapter 5). Second, the traditional view of Qohelet's association with Solomonic authorship has also played a significant role in its canonical acceptance. Although scholars, such as Peter Enns, argue that the character of Qohelet was created to maintain a Solomonic connection, Enns also observes, although superficially, that,

> One could adduce, however, 1 Chr 29:25, in support of 1:16 being compatible with Solomonic authorship: "The LORD highly exalted Solomon in the sight of all Israel and bestowed on him royal splendor *such as no king over Israel ever had before*." This phrase is similar to what we see in Eccl 1:16. (The designation "in Jerusalem" is missing, which would now allow the inclusion of Saul along with David.) Since the reference here in Chronicles is

---

30 Moore and Akin, *Ecclesiastes, Song of Solomon*, 7.

31. Eaton, *Ecclesiastes*, 32.

clearly to Solomon, it lends a certain weight to reading Eccl 1:16 as likewise referring to Solomon.[32]

Third, Qohelet's content, which will be explored in more depth later, is an appeal to righteous living through the exhortation of ethical behavior and participation in social justice in the fear of God concept. Fourth, Qohelet's preservation has shown significance in that fragments of its manuscript were discovered among the many fragments of the sacred writings of the Old Testament at Qumran. Ernst Würthwein states, "The significance of the Dead Sea biblical manuscripts lies obviously, although not exclusively, in their great age. Many of them are more than a thousand years older than our long-familiar medieval manuscripts, reaching back to a period when some of the OT books were still being written and the biblical canon was not yet closed."[33] Fifth, although rabbinic scholars have wrestled with the acceptance of Qohelet as a book that "makes hands unclean," throughout the mainstream Jewish community and the testimony of our early church fathers, Qohelet has been regarded and embraced as sacred Scripture.[34] Sixth, the witness of the Spirit inherently rests in the divine inspiration of the text, whereby "the words of the wise are like goads, and like nails firmly fixed are the collected sayings; *they are given by one Shepherd*" (Qoh 12:11). Hence, in the words of fourth-century church father Evagrius of Pontus, "Ecclesiastes is Christ, the author of that knowledge. Or, Ecclesiastes is one who, having purified the soul by moral contemplation, leads his or her soul to the contemplation of the physical [world]."[35]

The canonicity of Qohelet in the wisdom corpus and the Bible is essential in charting the trajectory of Qohelet's theology with coherency. The mischaracterizations of Qohelet are gross misconceptions that fail to recognize the overlaying framework guiding Qohelet's theology on sin, grace, and judgment. The mischaracterizations need to acknowledge the art of rhetoric playing out in Qohelet's divinely inspired form of the wisdom genre. Suppose Qohelet is genuinely a divinely inspired work that the church has long embraced as authoritative for guiding and instructing in theologically sound doctrine for living righteously. In that case, its canonical associations and criteria give testimony to the one story of the Bible's metanarrative.

32. Enns, *Ecclesiastes*, 17–18.

33. Würthwein, *Text of the Old Testament*, 60.

34. For testimonials of the early church fathers on Qohelet as part of the canon of Scripture, see Bray and Oden, *We Believe in One God*.

35. J. Robert Wright, *Proverbs, Ecclesiastes, Song of Solomon*, 193.

PART I. BACKGROUND ANALYSIS

Hence, to truly understand the significance of Qohelet as authoritative, we must understand how it fits within the progression of God's redemptive program. As each individual book of the Bible contributes to the salvation history played out in God's covenants with Adam, Noah, Abraham, Israel, and David, so does the book of Qohelet contribute to the progression of this program.

Contrary to the short, pithy statements of Proverbs, however, the discourses of Qohelet have a strict inter-dependency that cannot be interpreted alone. The same is true on a broader scale, whereby the trajectory of Qohelet's frame of thought is best interpreted from the context of his theological worldview. If Qohelet were a king of a monotheistic nation with a strict upbringing and devotion to Yahweh, his theology would have weighed heavy on the motifs of his rhetoric, such as vanity, strife, evil, toil, and vexation in the context of a fallen world, and the fear of God, joy, and judgment in the contexts of grace, hope, righteousness, and redemption.[36] The correlation of these motifs shows the inter-dependencies within the book of Qohelet and inter-dependencies from the broader scope of the Old Testament in which Qohelet lived and most likely weighed his observations throughout his quest for meaning. Hence, the best interpretative approach to Qohelet is to consider its theological backdrop, which likely set the basis for Qohelet's frame of thought and rhetorical strategy. In doing so, Qohelet proves its place in the biblical canon from its connectivity to the wisdom corpus and the entire Bible.

QOHELET AS PART OF THE ONE STORY OF THE BIBLE

Scholars often find it difficult to conclude that the worldview of Qohelet is optimistic, hopeful, and vertical (in view of God), mainly because of the motif of *"hevel"* under the sun that sets off a pessimistic tone. Longman negatively states, "In brief, Qohelet's frequent use of the phrase *under the sun* highlights the restricted scope of his inquiry. His worldview does not allow him to take a transcendent yet immanent God into consideration

---

36. Chapter 5 will discuss these theological themes and motifs in depth and where they are demonstrated throughout the context of Qohelet. However, some of the most prominent verses that demonstrate these themes are Qoh 1:2, 14; 2:11, 23; 4:3, 16; 5:16–17; 6:1; 9:3; 12:8 in the context of a fallen world, and Qoh 3:13; 5:19; 8:12–14; 11:9; 12:14 in the context of grace, hope, righteousness, and redemption.

in his quest for meaning."[37] The problem with this statement is that it fails to recognize the rhetorical strategy of Qohelet, thereby overlooking the artistry of Qohelet to a worldview that is less than biblical. If we suppose rhetoric is an art as implied in the term "art of persuasion," then an artistic work of rhetoric, such as Qohelet, needs to be approached with artistry, as one might use in interpreting poetry. In poetry, there is often a hidden meaning from what is explicitly stated. Hence, just as Lee advocates for a strategy of rhetoric in Qohelet's placement of the joy passages,[38] it can also be advocated for a rhetorical strategy in Qohelet's use of the "fear God" motif, which forces the audience to consider a vertical view of life deriving from a righteous God, rather than a horizontal view emanating from fallen humanity. Hence, Qohelet's worldview can be depicted by his redirecting of the minds and perspectives of the audience to the hope and joy for those who fear God, not just in the sustainment of humanity in a world of *hevel* but in an eschatological hope that will allow the one who fears God to stand in the day of judgment. This is the same eschatological hope prophesied throughout the Old Testament and preached in the New Testament, thus setting a biblically correlated precedent in Qohelet's worldview.

Qohelet uses an artistic rhetorical strategy that the frame narrator interprets as leading to the conclusion, "The end of the matter; all has been heard. Fear God and keep his commandments, for this is the whole duty of man" (Qoh 12:13). This conclusion is an expression depicted in Qohelet's teaching that summarizes a worldview deriving from the Old Testament Scriptures. This claim can be attested in the parallels of Scripture such as Deut 10:12, stating, "And now, Israel, what does the Lord your God require of you, but to fear the Lord your God, to walk in all his ways, to love him, to serve the Lord your God with all your heart and with all your soul." This Scripture, directed to the nation of Israel, can be taken as a summary of Qohelet's teaching, whereby Qohelet takes the principle of this command a step further and elevates it to the application of all humanity. Suppose, as advocated earlier, the "fear God" concept in Qohelet is the same as the "fear of God" or "fear of the Lord" concepts running throughout the Old Testament. In that case, the biblical worldview of wisdom (i.e., biblical wisdom) is further depicted. Although holding a sense of pessimism, Longman states, "The book thus ends on a strong orthodox note, one that is in keeping with the dominant teaching of the rest of the OT, and one that is

---

37. Longman, *Book of Ecclesiastes*, 66.
38. Lee, "Vitality of Enjoyment," 33.

PART I. BACKGROUND ANALYSIS

positive, at least for the faithful. It is thus correct to characterize the book as positive and orthodox, while maintaining the dubious nature of Qohelet's own thinking."[39] Longman's statement is agreeable. However, the last part could be better characterized not as dubious but as artistic. Hence, while the book of Qohelet is indeed orthodox and positive, it reflects the mind and wisdom of a biblical worldview. Furthermore, there is an anticipation of judgment in Qohelet that can be depicted as eschatological, accompanied by an implicit hope of messianic salvation and a redemptive "world to come."[40] Qohelet explicitly mentions the judgment twice in his teaching, whereby Eaton, speaking of H. C. Leupold's observation of Qoh 11:9, states, "Leupold is probably right to argue that the definite article ('*the* judgment') points to a single specific event, not merely to God's general judicial activity. It is true that 'the judgment' is used elsewhere in the latter sense (e.g. 3:16, Heb.), but here the context points to a definite event."[41] If Leupold is correct, then it is safe to assume that Qohelet is a teaching of a theological worldview with a vertical perspective. Within the Old Testament, Qohelet's theology fits right in with the one story of the Bible, whereby its contribution to the metanarrative of the Bible becomes more evident and its canonicity is better recognized. For instance, the allusions to a fallen world and humanity in the horizontal view are also vertical in that they reflect the account of Genesis, whereby Barry G. Webb states,

> In Ecclesiastes God is supremely the creator, and the particular ways in which his relationship to the world and to humankind are understood throughout the book appears to draw heavily on the early chapters of Genesis. . . . In particular, he made human beings upright, though they have gone in search of many schemes (7:29). This is probably an allusion to the creation of human beings in the image of God and their subsequent fall, as in Genesis 1–3.[42]

---

39. Longman, *Book of Ecclesiastes*, 283.

40. For more clarity on the "world to come" concept in Qohelet, refer to the Targum translation. The targumim are Aramaic translations of the Hebrew Scriptures derived from the Babylonian exile. They are good sources for understanding how the ancient Hebrews interpreted the Scriptures. The targumim citations used here are from the English translation of Targum Onqelos, also called the Babylonian Targums. According to Ernst Würthwein, "Targum Onqelos is characteristically a relatively literal translation, almost consistently following the MT" (Würthwein, *Text of the Old Testament*, 134). For more details on the targumim, refer to the following reference: Würthwein, *Text of the Old Testament*.

41. Eaton, *Ecclesiastes*, 165.

42. Webb, *Five Festal Garments*, 103.

Furthermore, there are allusions to the sustainment of God's grace for humanity amid the fallenness, whereby the joy and gift passages (2:24; 3:12, 22; 5:17; 8:15; 9:7–9; 11:9, 10; 12:1) function as an exhortation to embrace life as a gift from God, whereby a person can find enjoyment in the rewards of their toil and not have to go through life consumed with the inevitable death.

An eschatological allusion also points to a future hope for standing in judgment. It may be safe to say that Qohelet's theology of eschatological judgment stems from his theology of the expected messiah. While messianic expectations varied among the Israelites, which described the characterization and mission of the messianic figure differently, they all agreed that the messiah would have an authoritative (of royal stature) and divine (of priestly stature) characteristic.[43] According to Dodson and Smith, "The term 'messianism' is a modern term used to describe a variety of Jewish expectations of a figure (or figures) who would act on behalf of or in tandem with God's dramatic, mostly end-time action."[44] Hence, while the concept of a messianic hope is more implicit in the Masoretic Text of Qohelet, there is a more explicit allusion in the targumim, whereby an added motif of a "world to come" is revealed. For instance, Qoh 1:3 of the Tg. Onq. translation states, "After he dies, what surplus does a person have from all his toil which he undertakes beneath the sun in this world except to occupy himself with the Torah in order to receive before the Master of the World a complete reward in the *world to come*." Is it feasible that Qohelet had in mind his expectation of messianic redemption and hope in his reflections and admonitions? It may be safe to assume so. Hence, Qohelet's worldview is unmistakably an attestation of the one story of the Bible and the progression of God's redemptive program, which inevitably points to the eschatological worldview of the New Testament.

One of the fullest New Testament allusions to Qohelet is found in Paul's letter to the Roman church. According to Webb, "The clearest link comes in Paul's classic exposition of the gospel in the letter to the Romans, especially 8:19–24 . . . . There is no quotation from Ecclesiastes here, but the structure of thought is very similar: creation, the fall, the divine imposition of 'frustration,' and the universal experience of it, by unbelievers and

---

43. For more background on *messianism*, see Dodson and Smith, *Exploring Biblical Backgrounds*.

44. Dodson and Smith, *Exploring Biblical Backgrounds*, 189.

believers alike, right up to the 'present time.'"[45] Paul's theology on creation in Rom 8:19–24 becomes an even more evident allusion to Qohelet with Paul's use of the Greek word *mataiotēs* (ματαιότης) in verse 20. *Mataiotēs* is the Greek equivalent in the LXX for the Hebrew word *hevel* (i.e., *vanity* in most English translations). Furthermore, Paul links an eschatological hope of freedom from corruption for the earthly creation and humanity (i.e., those who are the children of God).

According to Rom 8:20–21, "For the creation was subjected to futility, not willingly, but because of him who subjected it, in hope that the creation itself will be set free from its bondage to corruption and obtain the freedom of the glory of the children of God." The eschatological freedom Paul is referring to is the state of glory, whereby all things (i.e., all of creation, including humanity) will no longer be *hevel* (Gr. *mataiotēs*). Paul's and Qohelet's theology is the same, deriving from the same biblical worldview handed down through the generations of the Israelite nation. Hence, the rhetoric of Qohelet was intended to persuade his audience to righteous living and eschatological hope with an appeal to a reverential fear of God. Qohelet's appeal is as universal as the new covenant that is inclusive of all nations. It is an appeal that points to a future state of glory, whereby the God-fearer (an Old Testament referent equivalent to the New Testament referent of "the righteous") will stand on the day of judgment and receive the reward of entry into the world to come (i.e., the new Earth). Hence, Qohelet's appeal characterizes the person who has the "fear of the Lord" as one who lives in worship of God through living out the righteousness of God. That is, they live in faith and obedience under the lordship of God, and to live under the lordship of God is to live under his authority and abide in his commandments. Hence, Qohelet's theological worldview is seamlessly depicted throughout the one story of the Bible, whereby its canonicity is rooted. Although presented with the negative connotations of reality "under the sun," the teaching of Qohelet has always been a positive attestation to the joy and hope of the God-fearer, a *sustaining joy* in the temporal life of *"hevel" under the sun* and a *hopeful joy* for redemption in the *world to come*.

Although scholars such as Murphy see the worldview of wisdom literature as trademarked by daily human experience, scholars such as H. D. Preuss have argued for the recognition of wisdom literature's influence deriving from the theology of sacred national traditions.[46] Both scholars

---

45. Webb, *Five Festal Garments*, 107.
46. Murphy, *Ecclesiastes*, 141.

are correct in their observations of wisdom's influence, but perhaps the trademark is best recognized as a synergistic view of human experience and sacred cultic tradition. This view is undoubtedly the kind of depiction that can be seen in Qohelet's framework, whereby Qohelet paradoxically appeals to living wisely in the reality of human experience "under the sun," only to appeal to the hope and pursuit of reality of God's justice in the redeeming participation of the God-fearer in the "world to come." Referring to Israel, Gerhard von Rad states, "The experiences of the world were for her always divine experiences as well, and the experiences of God were for her experiences of the world.[47] In other words, although God's transcendence is separate and distinct from the world, human experiences correlate with the divine. Hence, for Israel, in the divine covenant with Yahweh, wisdom is an expression of human experiences deriving from a life of infinite and finite correlation. That is the experience of an infinite God intervening and working out his redemptive plan in relationship with finite human beings. Hence, all this is to say that Qohelet is in correlation with the one story of the Bible that testifies to the realities of human experience, the intervention of God, and the anticipated justice of those who fear God. There is no contradiction between the Bible's redemptive story, future anticipation of glory, and Qohelet's theology and worldview. On the contrary, Qohelet may be assumed to be the most relevant witness of the wisdom corpus to the fallenness of creation (the sinful plight of humanity), sustainment of humanity (God's grace), and anticipated judgment (the eschatological judgment and redemption) of salvation history and its future. In other words, Qohelet is a universal appeal to the redemptive plan of God unfolding as a unified program and metanarrative of one story witnessed through all of Scripture.

---

47. Von Rad, *Wisdom in Israel*, 62.

Chapter 3

The Universality of Qohelet's Message

THE UNIVERSALITY OF QOHELET'S message is best explained in the acceptance of Solomon as the author and teacher of Qohelet. If Solomon be the author and teacher, then the premise is not only that Solomon, being the wisest man who ever lived and a teacher of nations, was the most qualified person to teach with such artistic rhetorical strategy but that his message was presented with a universal appeal, whereby those who came from the ends of the earth to hear his teaching were able to receive it as a shared wisdom tradition between nations. In other words, to speak of the universality of Qohelet is to speak of its message as an admonition and call to all people in all times and spaces. Establishing Solomonic authorship is an added basis for approaching Qohelet in the search for coherency. With allusions pointing to Solomon as the most qualified king in Jerusalem to be Qohelet, the authority of Qohelet's wisdom and rhetorical strategy makes more sense than the view of an anonymous author. However, this theory does not hinge on Qohelet's internal allusions to Solomon alone but also on the canonical allusions of Solomon that point to Qohelet. In other words, the life and wisdom of Solomon parallel the life and wisdom of Qohelet expressed in his message. With Solomonic authorship, Qohelet's wisdom and teaching span a vast spectrum of universal appeal. This chapter suggests the Solomonic authorship view and the universality of Qohelet's teaching, whereby the theological trajectory of Qohelet can be charted along the canonical spectrum.

THE UNIVERSALITY OF QOHELET'S MESSAGE

SOLOMON AS THE AUTHOR AND TEACHER OF QOHELET

Perhaps the most appealing allusion to Solomon as the most likely person to be the author and teacher of Qohelet is in the superscription of Qohelet 1:1, stating, "The words of the Preacher, the son of David, king in Jerusalem." The allusions to Qohelet as a preacher (or teacher), the son of King David, and a king in Jerusalem function as descriptive attributes hinting at the identity of Qohelet. The Targum translation, in fact, explicitly tells us that Solomon is Qohelet, which seems like a perceivable implication of the mainstream Jewish community's acceptance of Solomon as the Qohelet. Hence, Qoh 1:1 of the Targum translation states, "The words of prophecy, which *Qohelet—who is Solomon* (קהלת הוא שלמה), the son of King David, who was in Jerusalem—prophesied."[1] According to Robert Gordis, "It is worth noting that the author himself never specifically calls himself 'the son of David.' The phrase in the superscription (1:1) is an addition by the editor, who goes beyond the author's statement in 1:12, 'I, Koheleth, was king over Israel in Jerusalem.'"[2] Gordis is suggesting that the credibility of Solomonic authorship is in the frame narrator's use of the title Qohelet. In other words, in Gordis's argument for Solomonic authorship, if the editor had intended to give the allusion that Solomon was the author, he would have done so by explicitly using the name Solomon as has been done in numerous pseudepigraphal works. Still, it is evident in Qohelet that the author is not so concerned with implying Solomonic authorship. Instead, it is through the experience expressed in Qohelet's teaching that unintentionally implies the authorship of Solomon. Hence, in examining the various points of Qohelet's teaching where allusive language points to a descriptor of Solomon, there is no need to accuse Solomon of referring to himself in the third person or the frame narrator of using a Solomonic personality. In the voice of the frame narrator, the author's identity is legitimized. The frame narrator's voice attests to Solomonic composition in the same manner that Prov 25:1 attests, "These also are proverbs of Solomon which the men of Hezekiah king of Judah copied." According to Gordis, "This same view underlies a succeeding statement in the same Baraita, which reads: 'And who wrote them? . . . Hezekiah and his group wrote Isaiah, Proverbs, Song of Songs and Ecclesiastes.' . . . On the basis of this notion, the Talmud assigns to Hezekiah and his group the 'copying out' or editing of all of

---

1. Clem et al., *Targum Onkelos, Jonathan*, Eccl 1:1.
2. Gordis, *Koheleth, the Man and His World*, 40.

PART I. BACKGROUND ANALYSIS

Solomon's books, i.e. *Song of Songs* and *Ecclesiastes*, as well as *Proverbs*."[3] In other words, although Hezekiah's group led the editing and copying of Solomon's compositions in the wake of a Jewish revival, the compositions were still of Solomonic authorship. Whether Solomon had composed Qohelet in old age as a melancholic reflection on the vanity of life or a wise sage skilled in rhetorical persuasion, Qohelet is filled with descriptors pointing to Solomon as the only king qualified of such expression and experience based on the biblical record.

Although more focus will be given to Solomon's wisdom in the following section, it is essential to the view of Solomonic authorship to recognize the wisdom statements in Qohelet that allude to Solomon. For example, Qoh 1:16 states, "I said in my heart, 'I have acquired great wisdom, surpassing all who were over Jerusalem before me, and my heart has had great experience of wisdom and knowledge.'" According to the biblical record, Solomon's wisdom was measureless, surpassing all people of the East and Egypt (cf. 1 Kgs 4:29-34). No other king in Jerusalem was endowed with the wisdom that God gave Solomon. Solomon's wisdom was so great that it became the most defining attribute of his life and reign as king. Walter Brueggemann states, "Indeed, his reputation as wise king was, in the end, more important than even his accomplishment as a temple builder."[4] Regarding accomplishments, Qohelet's list in Qoh 2:4-8 is closely associated with Solomon. For instance, Qoh 2:4-5 states, "I made great works. I built houses and planted vineyards for myself. I made myself gardens and parks, and planted in them all kinds of fruit trees." This statement alludes to Solomon's accomplishments recorded in 1 Kgs 7:1-12 and Solomon's vineyard recorded in Song 8:11, stating, "Solomon had a vineyard at Baal-hamon; he let out the vineyard to keepers; each one was to bring for its fruit a thousand pieces of silver."

Additionally, Qoh 2:7 is an allusion to Solomon's abundant provisions recorded in 1 Kgs 4:21-23, stating, "Solomon ruled over all the kingdoms from the Euphrates to the land of the Philistines and to the border of Egypt. They brought tribute and served Solomon all the days of his life. Solomon's provision for one day was thirty cors of fine flour and sixty cors of meal, ten fat oxen, and twenty pasture-fed cattle, a hundred sheep, besides deer, gazelles, roebucks, and fattened fowl." Qohelet 2:8 also alludes to Solomon's treasure of gold and silver recorded in 1 Kings, stating,

3. Gordis, *Koheleth, the Man and His World*, 39-40.
4. Brueggemann, *Solomon*, 104.

And they went to Ophir and brought from there gold, 420 talents, and they brought it to King Solomon. . . . Then she gave the king 120 talents of gold, and a very great quantity of spices and precious stones. Never again came such an abundance of spices as these that the queen of Sheba gave to King Solomon. . . . Now the weight of gold that came to Solomon in one year was 666 talents of gold . . . . All King Solomon's drinking vessels were of gold, and all the vessels of the House of the Forest of Lebanon were of pure gold. None were of silver; silver was not considered as anything in the days of Solomon. (1 Kgs 9:28; 10:10, 14, 21)

It is difficult to deny the similarities between the descriptive attributes of Qohelet and Solomon. Qohelet claims that his greatness surpassed all who were before in Jerusalem (Qoh 2:9), just as 1 Chr 29:25 records, "And the Lord made Solomon very great in the sight of all Israel and bestowed on him such royal majesty as had not been on any king before him in Israel." Commenting on the splendor of Qoh 2:9, Michael A. Eaton states, "The picture progresses to the splendour attained by Solomon. *I became great* refers to his wealth (cf. 1 Kgs 10:23). *I . . . surpassed* (RSV) or 'increased' (Heb.) repeats the vocabulary of the previous section. As he increased in wisdom (1:16, 18), so he increased in riches (cf. 2 Chr. 9:22)."[5] Although Qohelet is never explicit in revealing his identity, close ties and associations to King Solomon are nonetheless explicitly present in his accomplishments.

Furthermore, Qoh 7:27–28 gives us a descriptor alluding to Solomon's wives and concubines. Here, again, Qohelet is not explicit, leading scholars to ask the question of what exactly Solomon was looking for as he states, "Behold, this is what I found, says the Preacher, while adding one thing to another to find the scheme of things—which my soul has sought repeatedly, but I have not found. One man among a thousand I found, but a woman among all these I have not found." Longman comments on these verses, concluding that Qohelet is a "misogynist"[6] who dislikes women, which leads him to characterize Qohelet "as a confused wise man whose voice is not to be identified with the teaching of the canonical book."[7] In other words, according to Longman, these types of tensions in Qohelet's teaching, whereby he speaks well of women in Qoh 9:9 and then negatively of women in Qoh 7:28, are not reflective of the man Solomon was and therefore should not be taken as Solomonic authorship. Contrary to Longman's

---

5. Eaton, *Ecclesiastes*, 79.
6. Longman, *Book of Ecclesiastes*, 206.
7. Longman, *Book of Ecclesiastes*, 207.

view, however, if Qohelet is Solomon teaching from his experience, then it seems all the more plausible that he would impose such a view on women considering 1 Kgs 11:3 records that "he had 700 wives, who were princesses, and 300 concubines. And his wives turned away his heart." There are two points worth considering in Qohelet's frame of thought here. One, as expressed in the NIV and NLT Bible translations, Solomon is reflecting on the quality and attribute of virtue and righteousness (Qoh 7:28). Two, Solomon is also reflecting on a specific kind of woman that he describes as "the woman whose heart is snares and nets, and whose hands are fetters" (Qoh 7:26). Perhaps in all of Solomon's relationships, most strongly as a reflection on his one thousand romances, which have taken his heart away from Yahweh to the foreign gods of his wives and concubines, Qohelet is making a qualifying statement of observation that only Solomon would have been able to attest. Just before Qoh 7:27–28, Qohelet states in 7:26, "And I find something more bitter than death: the woman whose heart is snares and nets, and whose hands are fetters. He who pleases God escapes her, but the sinner is taken by her." If Qohelet is reflecting on his life, this strongly alludes to Solomon and his apostasy as recorded in 1 Kgs 11:4–6:

> For when Solomon was old his wives turned away his heart after other gods, and his heart was not wholly true to the Lord his God, as was the heart of David his father. For Solomon went after Ashtoreth the goddess of the Sidonians, and after Milcom the abomination of the Ammonites. So Solomon did what was evil in the sight of the Lord and did not wholly follow the Lord, as David his father had done.

As the biblical record of Solomon's life shows that he did not end his reign over Israel well, it makes the most sense to attribute Solomon as the author and teacher of Qohelet, which may very well be an exhortation of wisdom reflection on his life experiences and pursuit of knowledge. The form of Qohelet, thus, takes on a discourse of reflection wisdom by a royal figure who has traditionally been accepted as Solomon in his old age. Hence, the basic structure of Qohelet is a reflection on the life of Qohelet whereby M. A. Sweeney observes that "the subsequent body of the book (Eccles 1:12–11:6) includes a series of discourses on Qohelet's experience in life, a meditation on the life's experiences and their times, oppression, toil and indolence, companionship, religious duties, wealth, the relations between rulers and subjects, divine action, death, chance, wisdom and folly, and risk."[8] No royal figure in the biblical record other than Solomon was attributed such experiential knowledge. Thus, the qualifying characteristics of Solomon testify to the traditional view of Solomonic authorship whereby the Targum states in Qoh 12:10, "Solomon, who was called Qohelet, sought by his own wisdom to execute judgments on the thoughts of man's heart and without witnesses." Furthermore, Qoh 12:9 states, "Besides being wise, the Preacher also taught the people knowledge, weighing and studying and arranging many proverbs with great care." If Proverbs is accepted as Solomonic authorship, the allusion to Qohelet's arranging of proverbs is an association of the same wisdom and literary composition. This association provides more reasons than not to believe Solomon is the most qualified and likely person to be the author and teacher of Qohelet.

What has been presented thus far in this section is the internal evidence of Solomonic authorship in the allusions to Solomon in Qohelet's reflections. The following two sections will focus more on Solomon's qualifying attributes revealed in the record of 1 Kings. By implementing the discussions of Solomon's wisdom and ministry as a teacher of nations, the reliability of Qohelet's Solomonic allusions becomes more objective. Hence, with Solomon likely to be the first-person voice of Qohelet (i.e., the original author and teacher), the following two sections will solidify the Solomonic authorship position and further the argument to show that with Solomon as the author and teacher of Qohelet, there is a universality in Qohelet's message that appeals to all people in all times and spaces, whereby the attribute of Solomon's wisdom confers his ministry as Qohelet.

SOLOMON'S WISDOM

While the previous section focused primarily on descriptors in the text of Qohelet that allude to Solomon as the most likely author and teacher of Qohelet, this section will focus on the attribute of Solomon's wisdom as a qualifying agent for the authorship of Qohelet. In addition to the allusions that are indicative of the person of Qohelet as Solomon, there is an inherent attribute of wisdom that qualifies and complements the person of Qohelet as Solomon, endowed with measureless wisdom from God. According to 1 Kgs 4:29–30, "And God gave Solomon wisdom and understanding beyond measure, and breadth of mind like the sand on the seashore, so that Solomon's wisdom surpassed the wisdom of all the people of the East and

---

8. Sweeney, "Form Criticism," 238–39.

all the wisdom of Egypt." Commenting on Solomon's wisdom endowed to him in 1 Kgs 4:29–34, Walter Dietrich states, "Here his wisdom is given prominence. We have come full circle since the opening passage in 3:1–15. This time Solomon's wisdom is not that of a king or a judge, but of an academic. It is said that he simply knew a very great deal, much more than any other person. The geographical horizon opens unexpectedly: science was international even then."[9] The following section will discuss the geographical horizons open to Solomon's influence. Still, it is worth noting that such a vast influence of wisdom also contributes to the likelihood of the Solomonic authorship of Qohelet. Indeed, Solomon's wisdom defined his reputation even more than his accomplishments. Because Solomon asked the Lord to give him an understanding mind to govern his people (1 Kgs 3:9), the Lord tells Solomon, "Behold, I now do according to your word. Behold, I give you a wise and discerning mind, so that none like you has been before you and none like you shall arise after you" (1 Kgs 3:12). If we are taking this biblical record as literal and true then there is a solidifying attestation in Qoh 1:16 stating, "I have acquired great wisdom, surpassing all who were over Jerusalem before me, and my heart has had great experience of wisdom and knowledge." No other king throughout Israel was endowed with such wisdom as was given to Solomon. According to Brueggemann, "Once it was established, on the basis of 1 Kings 4:29–34, that Solomon could be utilized as an ongoing source of wisdom for subsequent generations (as was evidently the case in emerging Judaism), it was apparently not problematic to assign belated literature to that remembered, imagined, wise king."[10] Although stated in the negative view of Qohelet as an unauthentic work of Solomonic authorship, I would contend with Brueggemann that 1 Kgs 4:29–34 is not a solid basis for an excuse of pseudonymity, but rather a more substantial basis for a redactional compilation of a collective work already composed by the wise king (i.e., Solomon). Additionally, perceiving the Solomonic allusions in Qohelet as a mere persona of a later author creates many problems in establishing a real audience. According to Daniel C. Fredericks and Daniel J. Estes, "Believing the Solomonic allusions are fictional commends the writer for writing this speech in a style and vocabulary so similar to Solomon's traditionally ascribed texts and narratives about him. This pseudonymous writer, depending on how late in Israel's

---

9. Walter Dietrich, "1 and 2 Kings," in Barton and Muddiman, *Oxford Bible Commentary*, 237.

10. Brueggemann, *Solomon*, 201–2.

history he has composed this work, has also recreated the setting with great precision."[11] Although the name of Solomon might be easy to attribute to a piece of literature composed by an unidentified author, on the basis of 1 Kgs 3:9 and 4:29–34 alone, the genuine attribute of Solomon's wisdom cannot be so easily and unmistakably attributed to any other person in history than Solomon. Hence, Solomon's renowned wisdom recorded in the Scriptures establishes a testimony to the wisdom of Qohelet.

Furthermore, in comparing Qohelet with Solomonic history and the works of Proverbs and the Song of Songs, which have been traditionally more definitively attributed to Solomonic authorship, conceptual and linguistic parallels are evident of shared Solomonic authorship. Although space does not allow for an exhaustive list of conceptual and linguistic similarities, several examples will be given here to show that the wisdom of Qohelet is not unorthodox but, rather, orthodox. For instance, the same language in the concept of *foolish hand folding* is used in Qoh 4:5 as in Prov 6:10; 24:33. Hence, Qoh 4:5 states, "The fool folds his hands and eats his own flesh," and Prov 6:10 and 24:33 state, "A little sleep, a little slumber, a little folding of the hands to rest." Regarding the concept of *life-giving wisdom*, Qoh 7:12 states, "For the protection of wisdom is like the protection of money, and the advantage of knowledge is that wisdom preserves the life of him who has it," while Prov 8:35 states, "For whoever finds me finds life and obtains favor from the Lord." Regarding *ensnaring women*, Qoh 7:26 states, "And I find something more bitter than death: the woman whose heart is snares and nets, and whose hands are fetters. He who pleases God escapes her, but the sinner is taken by her," while Prov 7:25–27 states, "Let not your heart turn aside to her ways; do not stray into her paths, for many a victim has she laid low, and all her slain are a mighty throng. Her house is the way to Sheol, going down to the chambers of death" (cf. Prov 5:3–14; 9:13–18). A linguistic parallel spanning the Solomonic works of Proverbs and the Song of Songs is in the use of the word תענוגת (taʿanugot) in the concept of delight in Qoh 2:8, Prov 19:10, and Song 7:7.[12] These parallels evidence a

---

11. Fredericks and Estes, *Ecclesiastes and The Song of Songs*, 36.

12. For a more exhaustive list of conceptual and linguistic parallels between Qohelet, Proverbs, the Song of Songs, Solomonic history, and other areas of the Bible, see Fredericks and Estes, *Ecclesiastes and The Song of Songs*, 34–36. While Fredericks and Estes provide an exhaustive list, they note that their list represents the strongest of D. Johnston's *Authorship of Ecclesiastes*, 1880, stating that these parallels "are especially close in thought and reflect a common tradition permeated with characteristic vocabulary and phraseology. Many of these examples are words or phrases used exclusively by the

commonality in the language and concepts of knowledge and understanding in Qohelet's wisdom. These parallels solidify the statement of Qoh 12:9: "Besides being wise, the Preacher also taught the people knowledge, weighing and studying and arranging many *proverbs* with great care." There is no logical explanation apart from the Solomonic authorship view for the masterful wisdom expressed in Qohelet compared to the orthodox tradition of wisdom in Proverbs, as the verses already examined show that the Bible clarifies that Solomon's wisdom cannot be paralleled. In essence, Qohelet represents the wisdom that is thematically, conceptually, and linguistically equivalent to the biblical record of Solomonic history. Gordis states, "There was sufficient basis for the growth of a tradition of Solomonic authorship."[13] Hence, now that we have examined Solomon's wisdom in some of the parallels pointing to a common Solomonic authorship, it is only appropriate to examine Solomon's wisdom from the epistemology of Solomon's wisdom, that is, Solomon's wisdom in the context of his environment, whereby religion, society, and politics influence his worldview. On the basis of accepting the Solomonic authorship of Qohelet, the theological trajectory of Qohelet can be traced back to the origins of Solomon's upbringing. From this context, the trajectory of Qohelet's framework is best understood.

It is important to remember that Qohelet was an Israelite who was the last king to reign over the united kingdom of Israel. Although Solomon had foolishly failed in keeping the covenantal commands of Yahweh, causing the kingdom to be stripped from him, beginning with his son (cf. 1 Kgs 11:11–14), Solomon was nevertheless remembered as the wisest king who ever lived. Contrary to what some scholars have said regarding the supposed unorthodoxy of Qohelet, there is a worldview that can be heavily depicted from the life of Solomon that proves Qohelet's orthodoxy. In other words, a biographical analysis of Solomon and his environment gives insight into a worldview that is identifiable in the worldview of Qohelet. Since a person's understanding of wisdom is influenced by their worldview and worldview is influenced by religion and societal experience, it is essential to recognize the development of Solomon's worldview beginning from his childhood. In doing so, fewer tensions may be perceived in Qohelet's content with a more rational understanding of his frame of thought stemming from his life experiences as king and a man endowed with divine wisdom. Brueggemann states regarding the accumulation of wisdom, "We may, as a

---

Solomonic literature, but the rest show the preponderant use by Solomonic literature."

13. Gordis, *Koheleth, the Man and His World*, 41.

beginning point, characterize wisdom as *sustained critical reflection on lived experience in order to discern the hidden shape of reality that lives in, with, and under the specificities of daily life.*"[14] For Qohelet, this has undoubtedly been the expression of his teaching.

Parallels between Qohelet and Solomon's life have already been briefly discussed. However, there is another purview to consider in the accumulation of Solomon's wisdom. The first and most influential element of Solomon's wisdom is his upbringing in the fear of God. It is from within the confines of the covenant inaugurated at Sinai that Solomon's wisdom derived. Raised as an Israelite kid whose father was the most admired king devoted to Yahweh (cf. 1 Sam 13:14; Acts 13:22), it was natural that Solomon would have been reared in the fear of God.

Contrary to the critical view of Qohelet's worldview and theology, there is a purview to the fear of God expression in Qohelet that points to the identity of Solomon's wisdom. Gordis states, "The modern reader might expect that Koheleth would be led by his views to deny the existence of God, but that was impossible to an ancient mind, and especially to a Jew. . . . Koheleth, a son of Israel, reared on the words of the Torah, the Prophets and the Sages, could not doubt the reality of God for an instant."[15] Qohelet reveals an aspect of Solomon's life amid the foolishness of his ways. It reveals the undoubted perception of God in Solomon's wisdom. In other words, if Qohelet is a reflection of Solomon's life experiences, it would appear that amid all his observations, he has come to terms with his failures. Perhaps the most significant level of wisdom Solomon has accumulated is expressed in Qohelet, whereby he finds himself reflecting on the very element that makes life purposeful: the covenantal relationship in which he was reared as a child and the fear of God.

Furthermore, Solomon's position as king allowed him to pursue the conquest of wisdom. To consider wisdom, madness, and folly to such a degree as Qohelet and to make such broad claims about the value and vanity of life would require someone with access to a broad societal and political stream. Perhaps this is the reason for Qohelet's statement, "For what can the man do who comes after the king? Only what has already been done" (Qoh 2:12b). In this verse, Qohelet is stating his qualification for what he has claimed in the previous verses of 1:12—2:12a and his credibility for what he continues to say in his expressed observations. Hence, it is the expressed

---

14. Brueggemann, *Solomon*, 105.
15. Gordis, *Koheleth, the Man and His World*, 122.

wisdom of Qohelet that testifies to the acquired wisdom of Solomon. Although God endowed Solomon's wisdom, it was accumulated and sustained in Solomon's life by ongoing awareness and application. According to Brueggemann, "'wisdom' is an ongoing work bringing life into concrete conformity to the 'really real' that is not subject to human pressure, whether that pressure takes the form of wealth, of power, or of learning."[16] Although Qohelet rightly observed the vanity and vexation of life, he was able to discern concrete conformity in reality under the sun in the God-fearing element that sustains humanity with joy and hope. Perhaps Solomon, in his quest for knowledge and understanding, was taking a necessary endeavor to acquire what was needed to politically govern his society as 1 Kgs 3:9 states, "Give your servant therefore an understanding mind to govern your people, that I may discern between good and evil, for who is able to govern this your great people?" Solomon's request for wisdom was to discern right from wrong in order to govern God's people. In response, the Lord not only endows Solomon with wisdom to discern but also both "riches and honor" (1 Kgs 3:12–13). D. R. Jackson states,

> According to 1 Kings, Solomon's wisdom covered, specifically, the domains of politics (1 Kings 1:52–53; 2:6, 9), building (1 Kings 3:1–3; 5–7; 9:10; 10:14–22), dreams and visions (1 Kings 3:5–15; 6:11–13; 9:1–9; 11:9, 11–13), judicial decisions (1 Kings 3:16–28; 5:7, 12), academic and scientific research and literary composition (1 Kings 4:29–34), as well as the ability to solve the most difficult questions. It was his wisdom that attracted the attention of the Queen of Sheba (1 Kings 10:1–22) and others (1 Kings 10:24).[17]

These domains support the purview of Solomonic authorship and identity in Qohelet. Rationally, there is no other king fit to meet the demands of wisdom required in the life of Solomon and his depicted identity as Qohelet. Hence, it is from the demands of wisdom in the life of Solomon that he honed the authority to take on the role of Qohelet, the convener and assembler who gathers the people to impart his wisdom. Qohelet is more than a sage; he is Solomon, the teacher of nations, whose presence the whole earth sought to hear his wisdom (cf. 1 Kgs 10:24).

---

16. Brueggemann, *Solomon*, 106.
17. Jackson, "Solomon," 733.

THE UNIVERSALITY OF QOHELET'S MESSAGE

SOLOMON, THE TEACHER OF NATIONS

Up to this point, we have discussed allusions found in Qohelet pointing to Solomon as the most likely person to be the author and teacher of Qohelet and the attribute of Solomon's wisdom as a qualifying agent for the authorship of Qohelet. Perhaps the most fundamental feature of Solomon's life pointing to the identity of Qohelet, however, is the universality of Solomon's ministry as a teacher of nations. This attribute is significant in that it testifies to the universality of Qohelet's message. In other words, a vast spectrum in Qohelet's message spans all people in all spaces, thus pointing to Solomon as the only qualified king and son of David to have such influence. According to C. F. Keil and F. Delitzsch, "The widespread fame of his wisdom brought many strangers to Jerusalem, and all the more because of its rarity at that time, especially among princes. The coming of the queen of Sheba to Jerusalem (1 Kings 10) furnishes a historical proof of this."[18] More will be said about the reason for the Queen of Sheba's visit to Solomon and her testimony of his wisdom later in the section. First, it is essential to examine the vastness of Solomon's wisdom. First Kings 4:29–30 states, "And God gave Solomon wisdom and understanding beyond measure, and breadth of mind like the sand on the seashore, so that Solomon's wisdom surpassed the wisdom of all the people of the east and all the wisdom of Egypt." It may be safe to correlate the statement of Solomon's mind as being "like the sand on the seashore" to the expansive seashore surrounding the Earth. As the seashore encapsulates the Earth, so does the mind of Solomon encapsulate wisdom. Solomon's wisdom was so great that 1 Kgs 4:30 says Solomon's wisdom "surpassed the wisdom of all the people of the east and all the wisdom of Egypt." This statement succinctly places Solomon's wisdom in the context of the ancient Near East. Gary Inrig states, "Wisdom was a much-prized pursuit in the ancient world, and it often took the form of proverbs, songs, or nature observations. Solomon excelled in all of these, so much so that his fame spread to all the surrounding nations."[19] Hence, amid the world's wisdom traditions, most notably of the ancient Near East, Solomon's influence surpassed even those nations whose wisdom traditions had long existed before Israel. According to 1 Kgs 4:33, Solomon "spoke of trees, from the cedar that is in Lebanon to the hyssop that grows out of the wall. He spoke also of beasts, and of birds, and of reptiles, and of fish."

---

18. Keil and Delitzsch, *Commentary on the Old Testament*, para. 5954.
19. Inrig, *I and II Kings*, 30.

Solomon was an expert not only in the proverbs but also in the sciences, both shown to correlate in the totality of human experience in the message of Qohelet. On the one hand, Qohelet speaks of proverbs deeply rooted in philosophical, sociological, and theological thought. On the other hand, Qohelet speaks on the sciences deeply rooted in nature's physical and metaphysical realms.

As mentioned earlier, the queen of Sheba's visit to Solomon is significant because it testifies to Solomon's breadth of influence as a teacher of nations throughout the earth. First Kings 10:1 states, "Now when the queen of Sheba heard of the fame of Solomon concerning the name of the Lord, she came to test him with hard questions." The queen of Sheba traveled from afar to test Solomon, as she ruled in Sheba (Saba), southwest of Arabia, approximately at the southeast point of the Red Sea. In the New Testament writings of Matt 12:42 and Luke 11:31, Jesus refers to the queen as the *queen of the South*. According to J. Arthur Thompson, "The ancient kingdom of Saba, the South Arabic name of the old SABEAN state, lay in the Southwest corner of the Arabian peninsula, roughly the area of modern Yemen."[20] Hence, her travel to Solomon would have been very long, but she was willing because of what she had heard of Solomon's fame *concerning the name of the Lord*. The queen of Sheba had many questions she wanted to ask Solomon. But with what could a non-Israelite possibly be concerned with an Israelite king and his God, other than trade interest? Although the queen came to Solomon with extraordinary gifts, 1 Kgs 10:2 tells us that she had much on her mind that she felt compelled to discuss with Solomon. The queen of Sheba's time was so well spent with Solomon that 1 Kgs 10:3 states, "And Solomon answered all her questions; there was nothing hidden from the king that he could not explain to her." Some scholars have speculated as to whether this visit actually occurred. Still, the evidence is mentioned in the Bible and in the Ethiopian text of *Kebra Nagast*, which suggests that she bore a child from Solomon named Menelik. According to William H. Barnes, "In Ethiopian tradition she is famously depicted as a most noble queen who ended up being seduced by Solomon, and giving birth to a son Menelik, the founder of the Ethiopian dynasty."[21] Although speculative, the point is that the queen's visit to Solomon is a testimony to his influence throughout the nations. If there was a witness to Solomon's wisdom external to Israel, it is the queen of Sheba, whose distance in travel

20. Thompson, s.v. "queen of Sheba," 5:7.
21. Barnes, *1–2 Kings*, 101.

testifies to the breadth of his territory of influence. The queen of Sheba came to Solomon as a student seeking answers from the wisest teacher on earth. She was left breathless after seeing all his wisdom, not only in the answers he had given her regarding her concerns but also in his mastery reflected in "the house that he had built, the food of his table, the seating of his officials, and the attendance of his servants, their clothing, his cupbearers, and his burnt offerings that he offered at the house of the Lord" (1 Kgs 10:4–5). First Kings 10:6 reveals her reason for her visit, which was not for trade interest, although that may have been her excuse. Instead, her visit was compelled by what she had heard in her own land about Solomon's wisdom, whereby she concludes by stating, "but I did not believe the reports until I came and my own eyes had seen it. And behold, the half was not told me. Your wisdom and prosperity surpass the report that I heard" (1 Kgs 10:7). Here, again, is a testimony of Solomon's universal influence, whereby even the peoples of many far-off nations would come to gather in Jerusalem to learn from the great and wise teacher, Solomon.

The Bible asserts that Solomon, in his wisdom, was a teacher of nations. In this case, it may be safe to speculate that Solomon's teaching ministry may have been facilitated in many different contextual settings. While the Bible depicts Solomon's teaching to the queen of Sheba as a one-on-one conversation, there is no reason not to believe that Solomon may have taught groups of people gathered in one setting. It may have been in one or more of these group settings that Solomon taught the lessons of Qohelet. The power, wisdom, influence, and the person of Qohelet are strongly linked to the person of Solomon. Commenting on 1 Kgs 4:29–34, Paul R. House states, "This notation indicates that Solomon's skill in judgment and speech was matched by his artistic gifts. Finally, Solomon possessed knowledge of botany and biology. This type of encyclopedic knowledge was highly valued in the ancient Near East, so it is no wonder his fame spread to other countries."[22] Still, it may suffice to say that although Solomon was knowledgeable in the sciences, much of his teachings also incorporated sociological, philosophical, and theological appeal; this is evident in both the Proverbs and Qohelet. It may also be likely that the rhetoric of scientific, sociological, and philosophical appeal in the teachings of Solomon is the universal foundation for appealing to the pagan nations with rhetoric that subtly appeals to his theological worldview rooted in the covenant and Torah. Hence, what seems contradictory in Qohelet may, in fact, be

---

22. House, *1, 2 Kings*, 118.

complementary. In other words, as Qohelet involves the appeal of life's experience under the sun, it is only to establish an appeal to righteousness in the fear of God. In the study of Solomon's wisdom, Brueggemann observes, "The ground of Solomon's reputation is that the king is said to be enormously imaginative and energetic in the production of proverbs and songs, thus processing not only insight (as in 1 Kings 3:16–28) but also an artistic flair for aesthetic utterance."[23] In its narrative form, the book of Qohelet best demonstrates this artistic flair Brueggemann is speaking of, making Solomon's reputation and influence a universal appeal. The universality of Solomon's lessons goes beyond scientific, sociological, and philosophical lines, stretching to the universality of the creator. When Solomon reaches this climax, the listener is drawn to his God, just as the queen of Sheba was, as she states in 1 Kgs 10:9, "Blessed be the Lord your God, who has delighted in you and set you on the throne of Israel! Because the Lord loved Israel forever, he has made you king, that you may execute justice and righteousness." To reiterate, the significance of the story of Solomon and the queen of Sheba is that it is a testimony to Solomon's wisdom and the universality of his teachings as the only qualified king of Jerusalem and son of David with whom Qohelet can be justly identified.

Furthermore, there is an even greater testimony to the greatness of Solomon's wisdom and teaching in Jesus's own words, testifying to the universal appeal of salvation in Solomon's teaching to the queen of Sheba. As mentioned earlier in this section, Matt 12:42 and Luke 11:31 also testify to the universality of Solomon's wisdom as an appeal to the universal God, creator of all things (cf. Col 1:16). Jesus states in Matt 12:42, "The queen of the South will rise up at the judgment with this generation and condemn it, for she came from the ends of the earth to hear the wisdom of Solomon" (Luke 11:31 parallels with Matt 12:42). According to Michael J. Wilkins, "Solomon's wisdom was so widely renowned that the queen went to question him and found his wisdom to be more than she had anticipated. She and the people of Nineveh had allowed the revelation of God to penetrate to their pagan hearts and so will be God's eternal witnesses against the Jewish religious leaders that they have not opened their heart to Jesus, the preeminent revelation of God."[24] If Solomon is Qohelet, then the universal appeal of Qohelet's wisdom is best understood from the view of Solomon's teaching ministry. Qohelet's message presents two aspects of life that appeal

---

23. Brueggemann, *Solomon*, 116.
24. Wilkins, "Matthew," 81.

to the ontological and metaphysical realities of human experience. First is the appeal to the experience of injustice and the fate of death in life under the sun. Second is the appeal to divine hope and justice in a life to come for those who fear God. These two aspects of human experience are correlated with what has been the teaching of Solomon through the proverbs. They are not contradictory but complementary. In other words, while the aspects of justice and hope are favored over the evils of injustice and death, the totality of human experience cannot negate the one for the other. This is a reality that every human being must come to terms with in some way or another. Hence, the universal appeal to Solomon's wisdom and influence is a testimony to the universality of Qohelet's message, whereby the appeal to God's righteousness is made to all the earth. In other words, Qohelet's message was not limited to an isolated reflection of the Jewish experience but was an experience relatable to all humanity.

Hence, what has been discussed in this chapter assumes the position of Solomonic authorship in the book Qohelet and aims to show how the universality of Qohelet's message in both the horizontal and vertical views can only make sense when understood from the universality of Solomon's reputation and influence of his wisdom and teaching ministry. The text of Qohelet objectively testifies to Solomonic authorship and the universality of his message in its reference to his kingship, his vast wealth and accomplishments, as well as the frame narrator's reference to Qohelet as a son of David and wise teacher, an arranger of proverbs. Fredericks and Estes state, "Qoheleth is placed on a pedestal as the model wise man in his teaching, study and writing. . . . Qoheleth was successful as a wise man, not only because of his knowledge but because of his application of that knowledge for the benefit of the people. He was a listener as well as a teacher."[25] Additionally, the objective evidence of the canonical record of Solomon's life in 1 Kings, the Targum interpretation of Qohelet, and the testimony of Jesus in Matthew and Luke establish witnesses to Qohelet's identity as most likely that of Solomon. What may be concluded from this chapter is that the objective evidence presented for Solomon as the author and teacher of Qohelet outweighs the subjective evidence of a later date assumed on the basis of language (briefly discussed in chapter 2). Hence, Gordis observes, "The Aramaic theory has, accordingly, won no adherence from any scholar except its original proponents, and may safely be pronounced

---

25. Fredericks and Estes, *Ecclesiastes and The Song of Songs*, 246.

unacceptable."[26] In this case, there is no better evidence than the record of Solomon's life, wisdom, and universal teaching ministry as a testimony to Solomon as the most qualified person for the identity of Qohelet. On this basis, a more coherent reading and understanding of Qohelet's universal appeal and teaching is more clearly depicted in the trajectory of its most prominent projectile themes.

---

26. Gordis, *Koheleth, the Man and His World*, 414.

PART II.

Analysis for Coherence

Chapter 4

Modern Scholarly Attempts to Find Coherency in Qohelet

As a segue into this study's thesis chapter (i.e., chapter 5), it is only necessary to discuss modern scholarly attempts already made in the search for coherence in Qohelet. As mentioned earlier, Qohelet has developed a broad interpretive spectrum over the centuries of church history with both satisfying and unsatisfying characterizations. But before advancing in the quest for coherency in Qohelet, we must first know where we currently are. While this study does not intend to solve the search for coherence, it certainly hopes to contribute by suggesting a reading of Qohelet that allows for a more balanced understanding of Qohelet's overall theological framework. Hence, the three modern scholarly approaches to Qohelet that this chapter will discuss all fall within different areas on the interpretive spectrum, all contributing to a unique understanding of Qohelet's intentions and flow of thought. While the leading proponents of these approaches aim to find coherency in Qohelet, they will nonetheless prove that coherency is still needed. By understanding these interpretive approaches, the main argument of this study that will be presented in chapter 5 will allow us to bridge gaps between the supposed contradictions of Qohelet, thus emphasizing the coherency in Qohelet's thematic trajectory guiding its theological framework. What is hoped to be accomplished in this chapter is that a line of distinction will be drawn between what has already been contributed to the study of Qohelet and what is to be presented in our advancements.

PART II. ANALYSIS FOR COHERENCE

COHERENCY IN PATTERNS OF TENSION

A leading proponent for coherency in patterns of tension in Qohelet is J. A. Loader, whose search for coherency in Qohelet takes a diachronic approach whereby his interpretation begins from a form and text-critical analysis. While the diachronic approach is valid, most scholars agree it is secondary to the synchronic approach, whereby canonical and narrative criticism take precedence. In other words, while the diachronic methods of interpretation consist of textual, source, and form criticisms, the synchronic methods consist of canonical and narrative criticisms. The method of interpretation used (i.e., diachronic or synchronic) is often a driving factor for the scholar's historical/historiographical genre and factual/imaginative history view of a particular book or the entire Bible. To be clear, historical and historiographical genres carry the same connotation that both are writings of history. However, what is denoted when these terms are more accurately defined is, on the one hand, that historical genre is that which is a written record of fact. Although the facts may not be completely accurate, there is a very minimal deviation from the events whereby its production is not motivated by a particular purpose of the historian. On the other hand, the historiographical genre is a compilation of historical sources, such as lists, inscriptions, annals, and accounts, that are manipulated by the motivation of a particular agenda of the historian, thereby allowing for an imaginative composition of recorded events in order to convey a particular message.

Closely related to historical and historiographical genres are the views of factual history, which deals with actual events throughout time and space, and imaginative history, which is associated with etiological history. Just like the historical genre, factual history focuses on elements of truth, whether the events recorded are of complete accuracy or not. On the contrary, imaginative history stems from the historiographical genre view. It focuses on elements of creative manipulation whereby a historian compiles historical sources and constructs a story to fit his etiological motive. An etiological motive is when an author seeks to explain the cause of present circumstances through historical events (whether they have taken place or not) to bring about a cultural reform. According to Steven L. McKenzie, "Etiologies, in fact, can be very imaginative."[1] The problem with the imaginative history approach is that it questions historical authenticity and reality, not in the sense of questioning the human experience through

---

1. McKenzie, *Introduction to the Historical Books*, 12.

image reality, which is common in the Bible, but in imaginative creativity whereby the motive is to create a message as seen fit for the influence of cultural reform and not an experience of factual reality. For Loader, however, his diachronic approach to Qohelet is guided by his compositional and authorship view of Qohelet. In other words, Loader believes Qohelet was composed and authored in the Hellenistic era, setting the basis for much of his interpretative approach. When it comes to Loader's reasoning for a diachronic approach to the interpretation of Qohelet, he states,

> Clear distinction should be made between text-immanent and historical perspectives in biblical criticism. As in linguistics, diachronic work may not precede synchronic work in literary analysis. Here I differ fundamentally from Braun, who, in his dissertation on Qohelet, starts from considerations of historical background. Instead, the literary product as it is should form the point of departure. Form and contents should first be analyzed in their own right and only then historical perspectives, like traditions and comparative material, should be brought to bear on the problems that present themselves.[2]

While this section does not intend nor permit to take up a detailed critique of Loader's interpretative analysis, it instead takes up a general analysis of Loader's interpretive approach whereby he finds coherency. With that being said, Loader's interpretation finds "neither a logical development of thought nor a loose compilation of aphorisms in a series of short collections."[3] Nonetheless, this is not to deny that the pericopes do not have a structure or that the structures do not interlink. Loader's interpretative analysis focuses on the text of Qohelet's form, which he sees as poetic, and the contents, which he sees as polar structures intended to create tension. Loader states, "By 'polar structures' I mean patterns of tension created by the counterposition of two elements to one another."[4] These counterpositions are, thus, thought patterns structured within the contents of Qohelet, whereby Qohelet's wisdom subtly climaxes to a polemical conclusion. These conclusions are developed throughout the pericopes in Qohelet, consisting of a pole, contra-pole, and tension. For example, a pole, though not always, might be an expression of general wisdom (often seen as deriving from a Hellenistic worldview), whereas a contra-pole, though not always, may be

---

2. Loader, *Polar Structures in the Book of Qohelet*, 1–2.
3. Loader, *Polar Structures in the Book of Qohelet*, 8.
4. Loader, *Polar Structures in the Book of Qohelet*, 1.

an expression of God's work, thus creating a tension with one another that draws a conclusion from Qohelet's wisdom and observation, also known as *Qohelet's wisdom*. Qohelet's wisdom differs from general wisdom in that it is specialized wisdom (my observation of Loader's distinction between general and Qohelet's wisdom). Hence, Qohelet's specialized wisdom is expressed as an attack on the general wisdom that polemicizes general wisdom's optimism. Regarding Qohelet's wisdom, Loader states, "In this way he poignantly polemizes against general *hokmā*."[5] In the polemics of Qohelet's wisdom, Qohelet acknowledges God's work in a world from which God is distant and far off. According to Loader, "He accepts God, but God is far—this is the ground for the polarity in his thought."[6] On the one hand, Qohelet recognizes the optimistic appeal to the general wisdom of the Hellenistic world. On the other hand, Qohelet recognizes the work of God that is incomprehensible and dominates general wisdom. While this assertion is appealing, Loader believes that Qohelet denies the doctrine of retribution and any relation between right and wrong deeds and good and bad consequences. Instead, Loader sees Qohelet's tension of right and wrong—good and bad as a result of the *hevel* (vanity) of the world. In a critique of Loader's interpretation of Qohelet, Michael V. Fox disagrees with this view of Loader by stating, "Qohelet sees the tension as a clash between two truths, neither of which he dismisses or ascribes to another form of wisdom. Nor does he reconcile the tension by abandoning belief in divine justice or by embracing theodicy."[7] While Fox's interpretation of Qohelet will be discussed in the next section, it can be said in this section that Fox does not see Qohelet as polemical but as a man in distress.[8] But Loader's view on Qohelet's denial of retribution is due to what he calls the *religio-historical developments* of Judaism. These developments include the idea that God is remote, creating an empty vacuum that needs to be filled with intermediaries, often in the form of a personification of God intended to draw him near. Loader states, "To sum up: Since the exile God becomes the distant God. While this is shown by circumlocutions for his name, these at the same time have the polar function (together with the angels) to bring the far-off God 'near' again. So the emptiness is filled with intermediaries,

---

5. Loader, *Polar Structures in the Book of Qohelet*, 52.
6. Loader, *Polar Structures in the Book of Qohelet*, 129.
7. Fox, *Time to Tear Down*, 68.
8. Fox, *Qohelet and His Contradictions*, 112.

and therefore no tension can be observed in the situation."[9] Loader, however, does not see Qohelet as able to fill the empty vacuum created by a far-off God whereby tension is non-existent. Instead, Qohelet accepts the idea that God is far off and distant while simultaneously explaining the tensions in his polar structures (e.g., God-*hevel* creates a polar tension). In other words, according to Loader's interpretation, Qohelet's view of a far-off God (cf. Qoh 5:2) denies that God practices retribution and, instead, believes that God "merely acts."[10] However, God's acts are not incumbent upon any particular person. For Loader, Qohelet's polarity in his frame of thought is thus placed in the religio-historical development of Judaism and not only by Greek elements. Within the confines of Judaism's religio-historical development and Hellenistic elements, Loader makes the case for Qohelet's frame of thought as fully Jewish amid the Greek influences surrounding the Hellenistic era in which the composition and authorship of Qohelet are rooted.

While Loader's contribution to the search for coherency in Qohelet is commendable, his diachronic approach fails to satisfy a coherent reading. For one, Loader's diachronic approach enforces a historical reconstruction of the text that deviates from the actual claims of Qohelet and its frame narrator. As mentioned earlier, Loader's method of interpretation is driven by his view of authorship, which is closely tied to his view on date and composition. Loader denies the traditional view of Qohelet's authorship and composition for the same reasons as the critical scholars who hold to the language arguments briefly discussed in chapter 2. Hence, this brings Loader to a conclusion that "since Solomon was known as the sage par excellence it is not hard to understand why the author (1:12—2:11) and the editor (1:1), follow Egyptian usage, put the wisdom of an unknown teacher of the third century B.C. into the mouth of the great king who lived in the tenth century B.C."[11] This conclusion leads Loader to a development of historical reconstruction that now places Qohelet in a compositional background of the Hellenistic era. Hence, the opposition of Qohelet and his frame narrator's claims of being king over Israel in Jerusalem (1:1, 12), a son of David (1:1), with wisdom surpassing all who were over Jerusalem before him (1:16), and an arranger of many proverbs (12:9) is perhaps the most significant tension that Loader has developed in his quest for coherency in Qohelet.

9. Loader, *Polar Structures in the Book of Qohelet*, 128.
10. Loader, *Polar Structures in the Book of Qohelet*, 128.
11. Loader, *Ecclesiastes*, 4.

PART II. ANALYSIS FOR COHERENCE

One keynote regarding Loader's interpretation of Qohelet is his view of Qohelet as a polemic against what he called general *hokmā* (i.e., general wisdom), which can be thought of as human wisdom grounded in a secular worldview. Although a polemic appeal is indeed evident in Qohelet, Loader's polar structure interpretation remains challenging. According to Eunny P. Lee,

> Some scholars argue for an overarching architectonic design, whether in the form of a palindrome, polar structures, or elaborate structures governed by refrains and numerological patterns. In the end, however, these intricate proposals have failed to be persuasive. The convoluted diagrams and outlines that accompany such proposals are often difficult to follow and are overly dependent on the particular rubrics assigned to the discrete units. Even multiple readings do not allow such intricate structures to emerge naturally.[12]

Biblical coherency does not require such difficult and unnatural reading. But this is the risk of beginning with a diachronic approach. Still, Loader does not deny that an organizational structure is depicted in Qohelet, whereas other scholars, such as F. Delitzsch, "have considered it to have virtually no structure whatsoever."[13] Recognizing a purposeful structure in Qohelet is essential to the search for coherency in Qohelet, especially for taking a synchronic approach. Hence, Loader's analytical diagram connecting stichoi of counterposing poles is helpful in seeing the unity of Qohelet's content. However, this can be seen even without the necessity of religio-historical development and Hellenistic influence.

Ultimately, Loader concludes that when form and content are analyzed in relation to each other, "a coherent picture emerges"[14] when the history of religious developments and wisdom traditions are investigated. According to Loader, "Form and contents fit each other in delicate detail as well as in general. And this in turn fits the historical situation."[15] For Loader, it is in the overlap of what he calls the *chokmatic* (i.e., wisdom) and *religio-historical* developments that the tensions in Qohelet are explained. Hence, for Loader, there are no contradictions, just purposeful and polemic tensions.

12. Lee, "Vitality of Enjoyment," 15.
13. Garrett, *Proverbs, Ecclesiastes, Song of Songs*, 268.
14. Loader, *Polar Structures in the Book of Qohelet*, 132.
15. Loader, *Polar Structures in the Book of Qohelet*, 132.

While there are certainly influences in Qohelet that are rooted in the wisdom traditions of both the Israelite and ancient Near Eastern cultures, to say that Qohelet's influences are of a later religio-development of Judaism and Hellenistic era, particularly its Hellenistic philosophy, is to place Qohelet in a dated era that diminishes the integrity of Qohelet and its frame narrator. Hence, a satisfying approach to Qohelet must maintain fidelity to the integrity and authenticity of Scripture on all levels of criticism, including textual, literary, source, form, narrative, and canonical criticisms. Nonetheless, aspects of Loader's contribution to the search for coherency in Qohelet have stirred up valuable and thought-provoking considerations in the ongoing quest. Like other contributions on the interpretative spectrum of Qohelet, Loader's interpretation involving *Polar Structures in the Book of Qohelet* is a plausible attempt at laying out a reasonable option for reading and understanding Qohelet.

COHERENCY IN HARMONIZATION

Michael V. Fox is a scholar who has written extensively on the book of Qohelet in modern scholarship. Fox's study of Qohelet began in 1972 when he wrote his dissertation on "The Book of Qohelet and Its Relation to the Wisdom School."[16] In addition, Fox has contributed scholarly attempts to provide a more coherent reading in scholarly journals such as the *Journal of Biblical Literature* 105 (1986), *Hebrew Union College Annual* 58 (1987), and *Journal for the Study of the Old Testament* 42 (1988).[17] One might expect a change in conclusions through many years of investigation. Still, Fox notes, "While my main conclusions are unchanged, my interpretations of specific passages and meanings have occasionally departed from those published in the above articles."[18] Hence, Fox's take on Qohelet from the most basic reading is summarized as "everything in life is vanity. There is no point in striving too hard for anything, whether wealth or wisdom. It is best simply to enjoy what you have when you have it and to fear God."[19] Even within the entanglement of contradictions in Qohelet, Fox believes this clear understanding of Qohelet's message cannot be suppressed and therefore disagrees with the interpretations that seek to harmonize Qohelet by excising

---

16. Fox, *Qohelet and His Contradictions*, 7.
17. Fox, *Qohelet and His Contradictions*, 7.
18. Fox, *Qohelet and His Contradictions*, 7.
19. Fox, *Qohelet and His Contradictions*, 9.

its contradiction (i.e., explaining away the contradictions). Hence, Fox's method and approach to his search for coherency in Qohelet is only appropriate to examine as it provides a different angle of understanding to Qohelet's intentions and frame of thought.

Fox's approach to Qohelet begins with an analysis of contradictions. Fox's view on the contradictions in Qohelet is that they are not unintended contradictions, whereby Qohelet contradicts himself, but contradictions of the world observed by Qohelet in his pursuit of knowledge. To Fox, the contradictions in Qohelet are real and intended. As discussed earlier, neither are the contradictions a polemic against what Loader calls general *hokmā* (wisdom). Hence, interpretations of Qohelet scholars are governed by their views on how the contradictions function in Qohelet. According to Fox, "To interpret Qohelet's contradictions we must clarify their terms and context and determine as precisely as possible what conclusions he draws from them. This task requires us to describe systematically and abstractly ideas that Qohelet expresses unsystematically and concretely."[20] Hence, in approaching Qohelet, Fox notes a few preliminaries when dealing with the contradictions. However, only the three most essential preliminaries to Fox's approach to his interpretation of Qohelet will be discussed. To begin, as the first preliminary, Fox uses language in his understanding of Qohelet's contradictions that he has observed from an apparent relationship between Qohelet and Albert Camus, a French philosopher of the twentieth century. Although Fox admits that Camus's ideas cannot be fully transferred to Qohelet and their distinctions are significant, he recognizes a fundamental correspondence between them. According to Fox, "For both, a dogged pursuit of the consequences of their beliefs and observations produces contradictions, some accidental, some the deliberate products of honest observation, most of them well-recognized by their respective interpreters."[21] Hence, Fox commends both thinkers (i.e., Qohelet and Camus) for their resilience in accepting such contradictions of reality, whereby they can still find virtue in affirming values amid the contradictions of life. Fox rejects the view that Qohelet accepts the contradictions of reality as paradoxes and tensions. Instead, Fox states, "Qohelet uses contradictions as the lens through which to view life; it is appropriate, then, that we use his contradictions as the angle of approach to his thought."[22] That said, part of Fox's

---

20. Fox, *Time to Tear Down*, 3.
21. Fox, *Qohelet and His Contradictions*, 14.
22. Fox, *Qohelet and His Contradictions*, 11.

approach is to examine concepts through words, such as the prominent motif *hevel*, which Fox interprets as absurd, and the significant themes communicated by these words while concentrating less on the terminology.

A second preliminary Fox presents is that of Greek parallels. Fox recognizes a similarity in Qohelet's affirmation of individual experience of pleasure with Hellenistic philosophy, whereby a distinction is also drawn between the anthropological question of Qohelet on the "profitability of human experience"[23] and the "philosophical anthropology in Greek thought."[24] In this distinction between Qohelet and Greek anthropology, Loader has argued for tensions in polar structures. Fox, however, does not advocate for such a Hellenistic influence on Qohelet and instead views these philosophically anthropological distinctions as common concerns shared among scholars in the Hellenistic era. According to Fox, "Particularly significant are Qohelet's affinities with Epicureanism, which regarded sensory experience as the ultimate source and arbiter of knowledge, and which affirmed pleasure (intellectual as well as physical) as the only good for man."[25] It is essential to note that Fox's perception of Greek Hellenistic parallels in his reading also establishes his view on the dating of Qohelet. In addition to the linguistic influences discussed in chapter 2, Fox recognizes these parallels as evidence for the contemporary and intellectual context in which Qohelet was composed.

As a third preliminary, Fox distinguishes between the terms "wisdom" and "the wise," and "wise man/woman" and "sage." These critical distinctions help guide his readers through his interpretation before getting into a more interpretive meaning of these terms. Beginning with the term "wisdom," Fox makes the distinction that wisdom (with the lowercase *w*) pertains to the attribute of wisdom that is "praised by Wisdom Literature."[26] This attribute, however, is not the same as the genre of wisdom, which Fox distinguishes as *Wisdom* (with the uppercase *W*). This *Wisdom* Fox defines as "the literary genres that comprise what modern scholars call Wisdom Literature, as well as the ideas, assumptions, goals, and attitudes characteristic of such works."[27] Although there are no typographical distinctions between the attribute and literary genre of wisdom in this study, there is

---

23. Fox, *Qohelet and His Contradictions*, 16.
24. Fox, *Qohelet and His Contradictions*, 16.
25. Fox, *Qohelet and His Contradictions*, 16.
26. Fox, *Qohelet and His Contradictions*, 17.
27. Fox, *Qohelet and His Contradictions*, 17.

PART II. ANALYSIS FOR COHERENCE

undoubtedly a distinction between these two concepts that are agreeable with Fox.[28] Additionally, Fox distinguishes that a *wise man/woman* pertains to anyone possessing the common attribute of *wisdom*. However, the *wise man/woman* is not to get confused with the *sage*, whom Fox describes as "one of the creators and teachers of Wisdom."[29] While the term "sage" is not used often in this study, neither in the general sense nor as a direct identifier of Qohelet, it is agreeable between most scholars that Qohelet, being a practitioner of Wisdom teaching, is indeed a sage. Hence, as Fox frequently references these terms, it is with setting this preliminary that Fox's interpretation of Qohelet is more accessible.

In addition to his preliminaries, in his search for coherency in Qohelet, Fox discusses his approach to three interpretive approaches and considerations: harmonization, additions, and quotations. The approach to these elements is critical for understanding Fox's method of finding coherency in the overall harmonization of Qohelet. Hence, beginning with Fox's approach to harmonization, Fox states, "A certain measure of harmonization is a proper and necessary part of the reading process, for a reader must attempt to construct a coherent picture of an author's thought by interpreting one statement in light of another. The goal of a coherent reading makes the reader strive to discover coherency in the text."[30] That said, Fox's approach to harmonization does not attempt to explain away the contradictions or to arbitrate the opposing statements. In the traditional method of harmonization, Fox references the attempts of scholars to explain away the contradictions by interpreting the use of words differently as they pertain to different situations. Fox references Loader's harmonization method, whereby an arbitrary approach is taken to balance the tensions. Fox agrees with the concept Loader poses in that the patterns of tension are always in the works of God that produce negative and unfavorable results. However, Fox believes that Loader forces this concept on the entire book of Qohelet, thus disagreeing by stating, "I do not always find both 'poles' of a contradiction in a single passage. Moreover, even if Loader's conclusion is right, I do not think his analysis of specific passages leads to it."[31] Although Fox agrees with Loader that passages in Qohelet formulate into an unsubordinated

---

28. Refer back to ch. 1.
29. Fox, *Qohelet and His Contradictions*, 17.
30. Fox, *Qohelet and His Contradictions*, 22–23.
31. Fox, *Qohelet and His Contradictions*, 20.

"*zwar-aber*"[32] relation, still, for Fox, these harmonistic approaches are disputable and unjust to passages often imposed with arbitrary explanations.

The interpretive approach of additions is a hypothetical approach to Qohelet that James L. Crenshaw follows. According to Crenshaw, "In light of editorial activity in the Bible and in parallel sources, it is certainly possible that a work as controversial as Ecclesiastes would have been subjected to editorial glosses. That conclusion seems inevitable when one takes into account the two epilogues that refer to Qoheleth in the third person."[33] This approach views some context within Qohelet as being editorially added by scribes intent on presenting various perspectives of an issue. In other words, these editorial additions to Qohelet were not intended to remove contradictions but to dampen Qohelet's worldview. Fox, however, finds a dilemma with this approach to Qohelet. To Fox, the element of editorial additions blurs Qohelet's thoughts and the content considered authentic material. In essence, these blurs lead to a perception of an entirely different book, whereby Fox states,

> To a scholar who excludes certain passages as containing unauthentic ideas, any interpretation that uses them in reconstructing Qohelet's thought is, at best, addressing a later stage in the book's development, one in which the author's thought had been superseded if not entirely undermined. Conversely, to an interpreter who maintains the authenticity of the disputed passages, any reading that excludes key passages has large gaps that leave the reconstruction not only incomplete but irreparably distorted. The two interpreters are talking about different books.[34]

In relation to the hypothesis of additions is the concept of excisions. In Fox's harmonizing approach, excisions do not establish consistency in Qohelet for several reasons. First, the most frequently removed material is syntactically linked to the original unorthodox material. Although syntax can be replicated, ideas cannot, thus being unsuccessful in dampening the tensions by adding unoriginal orthodox ideas. Second, excisions do not fulfill the purpose of Qohelet but render the scribe's assertions ineffective. Third, rather than the scribe's intent of dampening tensions by making editorial

---

32. The term "*zwar-aber*" is German and pertains to the conjunction of two opposing statements. For further background on the uses of *Zwar . . . aber* in concessive patterns in interaction, see Günthner, "Concessive Patterns in Interaction."

33. Crenshaw, *Qoheleth*, 26.

34. Fox, *Qohelet and His Contradictions*, 23.

additions and excisions to the text of Qohelet, the pessimistic character remains unresolved. Hence, Fox states, "The addition-hypothesis requires us to assume that a scribe (or several) who fundamentally disagreed with Qohelet undertook to copy the work, then inserted additions that were supposed to counterbalance Qohelet's skepticism and yet manifestly fail to do so."[35] Finally, also related to the editorial additions hypothesis, Fox sees passages passing to later additions as unsuccessful in establishing consistency in Qohelet's frame of thought. Particularly to the passages of retribution, Fox points out that most scholars agree with the verses of Qoh 5:5b and 7:17 as being attributed to the originality of Qohelet but are no less distinct from the passages scholars excise as being later additions from glossators or redactors. According to Fox, "If we leave the book with any significant inconsistencies in central matters such as wisdom and justice, we are undercutting the criteria whereby the putative additions were discovered."[36] For Fox, approaching Qohelet with the interpretive element of editorial additions does not give justice to the harmonization of Qohelet but instead leaves inconsistencies where scholars such as Crenshaw would attempt to mediate with such a hypothetical approach.

One last hypothesis Fox recognizes as inconsistent in the search for coherency in Qohelet is the quotation hypothesis. This approach to Qohelet, which Robert Gordis follows, attempts to identify unmarked quotations parallel to traditional wisdom to prove that the traditional wisdom statement is wrong. Fox states, "In my view, there very likely are quotations in the book, but identifying them is not crucial. If the author considered it important that we recognize that another person is speaking this or that sentence, he could have let us know. But he does not."[37] Hence, although Fox recognizes that the mention of another person may mark quotations, an introduction of a quotation of another person's speech (i.e., *verbum dicendi*), or a shift in singular and plural pronouns, he believes that none of the scholars holding to the quotation hypothesis have been successful with identifying quotations that are rational and logical. For Fox, the quotation hypothesis is too quickly used to eliminate significantly complex difficulties, leading Fox to conclude that there is no natural line of reasoning to Qohelet's relation between the quotations and the views they express. Fox, therefore, states, "Thus, unless we also assume that Qohelet rejects the ideas

---

35. Fox, *Qohelet and His Contradictions*, 25.
36. Fox, *Qohelet and His Contradictions*, 25.
37. Fox, *Time to Tear Down*, 20.

he is quoting, the quotation hypothesis in itself takes us nowhere. We have yet to determine which view is Qohelet's, just as if we never assumed the presence of quotations at all."[38] Hence, while Fox realizes the many interpretive challenges of Qohelet, he does not presume to have succeeded nor attempted to solve the issues raised by the contradictions.

Fox's preliminaries and considerations of the different approaches to interpreting Qohelet have guided his harmonistic approach. Rather than attempting to eliminate the contradictions like other scholars, Fox believes that describing the entire layout of Qohelet's diverse landscape is a faithful task. According to Fox, "A life with a strict correspondence between deed and consequence, virtue and reward, vice and punishment, would make sense. But Koheleth sees that this does not happen, and he is weighed down by the collapse of meaning, as revealed by the contradictions that pervade life. These are antinomies, contradictory propositions that seem equally valid."[39] It is here in the equally valid antinomies that Fox finds harmony. It is not a harmony strained by an interpretation of explaining away the contradictions but a harmony that is accepting of the contradictions with an interpretation that targets the author's intention. For Fox, coherency in the author's intent is found in the variant use of words in their different contents. In other words, it is in the choice and frequency of especially repeated words used in Qohelet that the thoughts of Qohelet are harmonistically complementary.

COHERENCY IN RHETORICAL CONTRADICTION

Eunny P. Lee offers a relatively balanced interpretation of Qohelet by acknowledging Qohelet's contradictions as an art of rhetoric. While she agrees with both Loader and Fox that the contradictions were intended, Lee's view of the contradictions contrasts with Loader and Fox in that they are not intended to polemicize general wisdom of the Hellenistic era, nor are they, as Fox would interpret, observations of a man in distress. Instead, for Lee, the contradictions of Qohelet are an expression of reality that is entirely accepted and embraced in the mind of the sage. In other words, for Qohelet, the conflicting contradictions of life are part and parcel of the human condition and, thus, should be interpreted as an interplay of the *hevel*, joy, and fear of God motifs. Lee argues "that the contradictory strains

---

38. Fox, *Qohelet and His Contradictions*, 28.
39. Fox, *Ecclesiastes*, xxx.

in Ecclesiastes are integral to Qohelet's discourse; they are part and parcel of the author's observations concerning the human condition. If the text is read as a unified composition, then neither the commendations of enjoyment nor the injunction to fear God may be dismissed as a secondary or peripheral concern."[40] Therefore, Lee's primary emphasis is on the theme of enjoyment and its interplay with the fear of God motif. Where other scholars have commonly interpreted the enjoyment and fear of God passages as peripheral to the leitmotif of *hevel* in Qohelet, Lee's interpretation brings the motifs of joy and fear of God to the forefront of Qohelet's frame of thought. For Lee, there is a unification in the discourses of Qohelet that purposely uses a strategy of catchwords and linking devices, connecting Qohelet's ideas. Hence, Lee's search for coherency in Qohelet identifies hinges between individual units that segue from one unit to the next, often functioning as both a retrospect and introduction. Although it is not intended to extrapolate the scholar's interpretations discussed in this section, one example can be given from Lee's interpretation of a hinge connecting a previous reflection with a subsequent thought. According to Lee,

> Many commentators take 3:1–15 to be a coherent unit. The Catalogue of Times (3:1–8) and the subsequent prose commentary (3:9–15) are bound together by their common concern with the determination of all times and events. Then, a new unit seems to be signaled at 3:16 with the introduction of a new subject matter, that of social injustice. Yet the introductory statement in 3:16 *zveöd raiti* "furthermore I saw" suggests an association with the preceding remarks, specifically harking back to *raiti* "I saw" in 3:10. The particle *weöd* "furthermore" suggests a shift in focus, but all the while maintaining a connection with the previous reflections.[41]

From this strategy of Qohelet's catchwords and linking devices, Lee finds a coherently unified harmony of the text that allows for a balanced interplay of life's tragic and joyous dimensions. It is not that Qohelet is polemicizing or expressing distress, but instead, using a strategy of rhetoric that can be synthesized with the realities of life for an admonition toward ethical stewardship of life under the sun.

Lee's approach to the joy and fear of God passages in Qohelet leads her to a conclusion that offers three syntheses of Qohelet's theology of enjoyment. For Lee, the joy and fear of God passages correlate, thus suggesting

---

40. Lee, "Vitality of Enjoyment," 12.
41. Lee, "Vitality of Enjoyment," 29.

implications of an ethical dimension. The first synthesis presented in Lee's interpretation of Qohelet is "The Normativity of Enjoyment." The normativity of enjoyment entails the mark of the human attribute of joy, in which God has designed humanity to function. The normativity of enjoyment is the continuous practice of joy in human life. It is a function whereby life can be lived to the fullest. For Lee, Qohelet's admonitions are a rhetorical strategy imploring people to live morally by doing ethically right and avoiding what is ethically wrong. In this, humanity has the strength to persevere and prosper in a world of *hevel*. Lee states, "On the one hand, Qohelet's conception of normative humanity is undergirded by a theology of God's inscrutable activity. . . . On the other hand, Qohelet derives the normativity of enjoyment from what he 'sees' in the world."[42] The first conception relates to the religious duty of humanity toward God to embrace life in all its troubles and limitations. In other words, although it is impossible to understand God's activity done under the sun entirely, it is nonetheless God's design for humanity to find enjoyment in life. The second conception noted by Lee relates to the human experience that is common to all people. For Lee, the human experience of reality under the sun is where Qohelet derives his rhetorical strategy, aiming to compel his listeners to a life-changing condition of enjoyment. But he can only do this by appealing to the human state he observes in the world. Hence, according to Lee, "Qohelet's commentary on his social world, then, is precisely what contemporary society needs to hear. The disease of dissatisfaction that Qohelet observes in his world in fact takes on a heightened virulence in today's culture, shaped by its sophisticated technology of mass communication in service to a consumerist ethos."[43] In other words, the normativity of enjoyment is counterintuitive to the culture of Qohelet's world and modern-day society. While cultural norms and expectations advocate for mass consumption and jealous behavior, Qohelet advocates for joy in contentment and generosity. Lee perfectly states, "Qohelet's ethic of enjoyment, then, is a recuperation of the norm. Enjoyment is emphatically not about the pursuit of more—not even the pursuit of joy—but the glad appreciation of what is already in one's possession by the gift of God. It means that the human becomes free not to grasp, not to possess, not to know."[44] Hence, for Lee, the synthesis of Qohelet's theology of enjoyment in the normativity of enjoyment entails the God-honoring

---

42. Lee, "Vitality of Enjoyment," 191.
43. Lee, "Vitality of Enjoyment," 194.
44. Lee, "Vitality of Enjoyment," 194–95.

pursuit of stewardship, which is fixed on living life in pious joy as both a divine responsibility and a gift of divine grace.

The second synthesis presented in Lee's interpretation of Qohelet is "The Ethic of Joy and Life in Community." The view of Qohelet as an ethical message of joy and life in the community opposes the commonly misconstrued idea that Qohelet does not contain community concerns. For Lee, Qohelet includes a message of communal appeal in his lament of the oppressed with no one to comfort them (Qoh 4:1–4) and his call to a rewarding life of companionship whereby it is asserted that two are better than one (Qoh 4:9; 9:9). According to Lee, "Qohelet commends enjoyment because it is what promotes the well-being of the individual. But the benefits of enjoyment are not limited to the personal level, because the individual's practice of enjoyment also has ramifications for the health of a much wider circle of humanity."[45] In other words, a practice of enjoyment that suits piety and stewardship to the God-given gift of life will always entail a communal overflow pouring out into the community and people in close proximity. Without the pious practice of enjoyment, the threats of *hevel* overrun the social arena, leading to tragic consequences of greed and selfish discontentment. For Lee, Qohelet's ethic of joy and life in the community counteracts the commination against the created order and sustains it through the joys experienced in charity and communal servitude. Lee compares and contrasts Qohelet's approach to social change to the effect of a prophet. For Lee, "The sage's approach to social change may differ from the prophetic model, but it has the same goal of effecting positive societal changes, albeit from a different angle. Qohelet's teachings combat social injustices, not by calling his audience to political or social activism, but rather by addressing the fundamental human vices that lie at the root of societal maladies."[46] Hence, there is an ethical dimension in the communal practice of joy when stewarded correctly in each individual. For Lee, the ethical aspect of joy in life and community was common among the Israelites. Lee reflects on the Old Testament concepts of community depicted in the festive meals and celebrations that are especially inclusive of those who have no portion of their own. Although Lee recognizes that Qohelet does not explicitly speak of inclusiveness in the communal meals as do the festal regulations of Israel, she observes that "the rhetoric of his admonitions concerning eating, drinking, and the proper use of food suggests that

---

45. Lee, "Vitality of Enjoyment," 199.
46. Lee, "Vitality of Enjoyment," 200.

an individual's enjoyment must never come at the expense of the neighbor, but must instead promote the same possibilities for the neighbor."[47] Hence, Qohelet's theology of enjoyment entails the synthesis of ethical enjoyment in life and community. The ethical aspect of enjoyment in life is not meant to be an isolated individual experience, as it cannot be ethical if it is isolated. Instead, the ethical aspect of enjoyment in life is to be a communal interaction that fosters the good and well-being of others.

The third synthesis presented in Lee's interpretation of Qohelet is "Enjoyment and Double Agency." Double agency refers to the divine and human agency. On one hand, the divine agency regards God as the giver of joy. On the other hand, the human agency is responsible for stewarding the commendation and command to be joyful. For Lee, enjoyment is a gift available to everybody, though not every person appropriates enjoyment as they ought. To become a recipient of joy, they must participate in the occasions of enjoyment God provides. According to Lee, "To be sure, God gives the means. But this divine giving always calls for a taking up on the part of the human beneficiary. Whenever the divine agent gives an occasion for enjoyment, the human recipient must actively and willingly take up that opportunity and enjoy to the full, with all that it entails."[48] In Lee's interpretation of Qohelet, there is an ethical call to participate in the God-given gift of enjoyment. In this participation, both the divine and human agency make up the entire nature of joy. While joy is granted to all people, the effort of the human agency never conjures it. Instead, joy is only given by the divine agency of God. According to Lee, "The gift of joy is given to those who are somehow—mysteriously and graciously—already approved of God (2:24–26; 9:7), for God gives according to God's own economy. By the same token, that grant may be taken away just as inexplicably by some absurd circumstances of life (2:20–21, 26; 5:12–13; 6:1–2). Human beings cannot possess anything inalienably."[49] Hence, for Lee, Qohelet's theology of enjoyment entails the synthesis of double agency. God grants enjoyment, and the human chooses to partake in good stewardship or immorally dispose of it. But when the human agent takes up enjoyment, they are reflecting the image of the divine agent, God. The divine gift of enjoyment also functions as a sustaining force for the human agency. Despite the vexation of *hevel* in life under the sun, enjoyment can nourish the soul and give the strength and

---

47. Lee, "Vitality of Enjoyment," 202.
48. Lee, "Vitality of Enjoyment," 206.
49. Lee, "Vitality of Enjoyment," 207.

fortitude to live life to the fullest. Lees states, "If it is true that ethics should never be completely independent of what human beings deeply need and desire, then Qohelet has hit upon a salutary point of orientation for his theological ethics. Joy is both the end and the means of human agency. It is both the substance and the driving force of his ethic."[50] In other words, in Qohelet's theology of enjoyment, the synthesis of enjoyment and double agency offers an ethic of joy realized in a puzzling world. For Lee, this concept of joy is an intricate attribute of pious living and moral uprightness. Qohelet is, therefore, a peculiar book that "addresses the deepest human needs and confronts the most perplexing problems of human life."[51]

Lee's interpretation of Qohelet's contradictions as a rhetorical strategy has come later to the interpretative spectrum of Qohelet than the interpretations of Loader and Fox discussed in the previous sections. Lee has sought to further the search for coherency in Qohelet by adding to the spectrum some new dimensions to reading Qohelet. With each approach to Qohelet, conceptual overlap is inevitable. However, with moderate nuances, each interpretation contributes enormously to offering different angles for thinking through the complexities of Qohelet. While Loader understands the contradictions of Qohelet to be a rhetoric aimed at polemicizing the wisdom of Hellenistic thought, Lee understands the contradictions of Qohelet to be a rhetoric aimed toward the appeal to living in ethical piety. While Fox understands the contradictions of Qohelet to be real and intended, he nevertheless sees the contradictions of Qohelet as an expression of a man (i.e., Qohelet) in distress. On the contrary, while Lee would agree with Fox that Qohelet's contradictions are intended and real, she would differ in the understanding that Qohelet's contradictions are not an expression of Qohelet's distress but a rhetorical appeal to living life to the fullest. Hence, the following chapter seeks to continue the journey to understanding the framework of Qohelet and his intentions. While there is expected to be conceptual overlap, the slight nuances of this study will further the search for coherency and add another dimension to the interpretative spectrum of Qohelet.

50. Lee, "Vitality of Enjoyment," 210.
51. Lee, "Vitality of Enjoyment," 210–11.

Chapter 5

Coherency in the Theological Trajectory of Qohelet's Projectile Themes

CHARTING THE THEOLOGICAL TRAJECTORY of Qohelet can be done by examining Qohelet's three most prominent and overarching themes. These themes are carried along by the literary motifs that convey either implicitly or explicitly the theological message of Qohelet, whereby fallenness, sustainment, and judgment cohere with the overall biblical message of sin, grace, and redemption. As derived from the surface structure of Qohelet, the three themes of fallenness, sustainment, and judgment set the basis for tracing the lines of trajectory that function as a guide to Qohelet's theological framework in the premise that humanity enters a fallen world, God sustains humanity amid the fallenness, and God preserves the lives of those who fear him on the day of judgment. Like any other trajectory a projectile follows, so is the theological trajectory of Qohelet, followed by themes functioning as projectiles guiding the frame of thought in Qohelet's teaching. Projectile momentum is given by the motifs of vanity, striving after wind, and vexation in the theme of fallenness; joy, gift, and eternity in the theme of sustainment; and the deeds of the wicked and the righteous, death, and the hope of the God-fearer in the theme of judgment. In taking a synchronic methodological approach, the inconsistencies of Qohelet take on a function of thematic underpinning, whereby coherence in the course, followed by the projectile themes of fallenness, sustainment, and judgment, form a framework guiding a theological trajectory aiming at an appeal to righteous living and eschatological hope.

PART II. ANALYSIS FOR COHERENCE

FALLENNESS

The first premise consists of the theological implication that humanity enters a fallen world. This premise can be traced in Qohelet's horizontal view of all things under the sun, expressed in the motifs of vanity, striving after wind, and vexation. Most essential to the theme of fallenness is understanding the motif of vanity. Deriving from the Hebrew word *hevel*, the meaning of vanity is the most consistent description Qohelet uses for all things under the sun. An analysis of the Hebrew word *hevel* shows that it is used thirty-eight times in Qohelet, more than in any other book of the Bible. According to the BDB lexicon, *hevel* means "*vapour, breath.*"[1] This meaning is often taken figuratively, which the *NIDOTTE* translates as "vain, empty, void, worthless, profitless."[2] Hence, figuratively speaking, *hevel* connotes a lack of worth and value. The Greek equivalent of *hevel* rendered in the LXX is *mataiotēs*, which, according to BDAG, is the "state of being without use or value, *emptiness.*"[3] Additionally, the LEH *Septuagint Lexicon* provides the meanings of "*emptiness, vanity.*"[4] Moreover, the *NIDNTTE* places the word *mataiotēs* in the semantic domains of "Worthless, Vain, Empty."[5] Often, depending on the Bible translation used, *hevel* is rendered in the English language as "futile," "meaningless," or "vanity." Although "futile" and "meaningless" are not entirely inappropriate words for translating *hevel*, an analysis of the English word "vanity" shows it to be the best word translated for *hevel*, taking an omnivalent approach. In the English ESV, NRSV, and KJV translations, and the Latin Vulgate, "vanity" (*vanitas* in the Latin Vulgate) conveys Qohelet's rhetorical message and strategy most significantly. Hence, when defining the English word "vanity," *Merriam-Webster's Collegiate Dictionary* provides several meanings, but the most appropriately aligned meaning with *hevel* and *mataiotēs* is "something that is vain, empty, or valueless; from Latin *vanitat-, vanitas* quality of being empty or vain."[6] Significantly, this definition of vanity falls within the same semantic domain as the original Hebrew word *hevel*, which is figuratively defined as "a value lacking." Qohelet's use of the word *hevel* also reveals the

---

1. BDB, s.v. "הֶבֶל," 210.
2. Johnston, s.v. "הֶבֶל, הָבַל," 1:981.
3. BDAG, "ματαιότης," 621.
4. LEH, "ματαιότης,-ητος," 386.
5. Silva, "Worthless," 1:83.
6. *Merriam-Webster's Collegiate Dictionary*, s.v. vanity.

COHERENCY IN THE THEOLOGICAL TRAJECTORY

rhetorical strategy that he is using to describe several earthly activities that are summarized in his premise that "All is vanity" (Qoh 1:2). Speaking of Qohelet's rhetorical strategy in using what he calls veiled language, James L. Crenshaw states,

> His teachings are twice encoded in an inclusion that indicates a superlative. "Utter futility," they teach, "utter futility. Everything is futile" (1:2 and a shorter version in 12:8). In the same way that the Hebrew title of the exotic scroll Song of Songs and the expression "holy of holies" mean "the very best song" and "the holiest one of all," *habal habalim*, which I have translated as "utter futility," connotes the supreme emptiness.[7]

In a fallen world, the figurative implications of *hevel* are best understood as conveying a "lack of value." Vanity, therefore, is the most consistent description that Qohelet gives for everything under the sun. It is the description of a fallen state, whereby there is a fallen world filled with fallen beings. Greg W. Parsons states, "The theme of 'vanity' for every activity 'under the sun' indicates that life on this horizontal plane without input from God (above the sun) has no lasting meaning."[8] In other words, everything under the sun is as good as an affliction, which lacks the wholeness of life and the reality of perfection. For Qohelet, the word *hevel* hearkens back to the fall of creation in Genesis, whereby Barry G. Webb states,

> In Ecclesiastes God is supremely the creator, and the particular ways in which his relationship to the world and to humankind are understood throughout the book appears to draw heavily on the early chapters of Genesis. . . . In particular, he made human beings upright, though they have gone in search of many schemes (7:29). This is probably an allusion to the creation of human beings in the image of God and their subsequent fall, as in Genesis 1–3.[9]

Instead of going straight to the point and explicitly stating that the world and humanity are fallen from the state of glory, Qohelet implicitly makes this point in the hyperbolic language of all things *hevel under the sun*. For Crenshaw, "The main reason for the hidden aspects of reality is the absence of rationality in the universe."[10] That is to say, though implicit,

---

7. Crenshaw, *Qoheleth*, 23.
8. Parsons, "Guidelines for Understanding and Proclaiming," 173.
9. Webb, *Five Festal Garments*, 103.
10. Crenshaw, *Qoheleth*, 29.

the contextual element of fallenness in Qohelet is the plot by which Qohelet captures his audience's attention with the logical relationship of cause and effect. Because of the fall, all things under the sun have become *hevel* and reduced to a state of affliction where all things lack value, worth, and perfection; it is the imposition of the curse. The motif of vanity is, thus, the basis and starting point of Qohelet's theological trajectory. With the inclusio of *all things vanity* set at the bookends of Qoh 1:2 and 12:8, and its repetitive use emphasizing the *all* in the passages in between (e.g., Qoh 1:13–14; 11:8), there is a clear projection in view that is identifiable to every human being living under the sun. When there is a combination of vanity (*hevel*) and *under the sun*, there is a reality of every activity in life as being a "striving/chasing after the wind" (ESV, NASB, NRSV) or a "breaking of the spirit" (Targums).

Striving after the wind is an inherent consequence of the fall that has reduced the "business that God has given to the children of man to be busy with" (Qoh 1:13) to a pursuit that lacks value. *Striving after the wind* is a human experience that can never be objectively resolved in life under the sun. The *striving after wind* phrase, in fact, is directly correlated to the motif of vanity. For Qohelet, it is the endless cycle of unresolved pleasure and achievement. According to the *Dictionary of Biblical Imagery*, "The image of appetite, though mentioned only a few times, is another informing metaphor for the book. In particular it is the voice of unsatisfied desire: 'The eye is not satisfied with seeing' (1:8), 'his eyes are never satisfied' (4:8), 'yet his appetite is not satisfied' (6:7)."[11] The Hebrew word for "striving" is *re' ut* (רעות), which has the semantic range of "break, companion, keep company with, devour, eat up, evil entreat, feed, use as a friend, make friendship with."[12] When *re' ut* is used with the word רוח—*ruach* ("wind"), either of these meanings can connote the pursuit of something that lacks substance and value.

Hence, Qohelet uses descriptive rhetoric that hearkens back to the literal meaning of *hevel*. In other words, the element of wind can be likened to the element of vapor or breath, a diffused matter that lingers for a short moment in the wind yet can never be grasped. The idea of *hevel* as vapor or breath connotes the idea of an intangible or transient substance. Qohelet states, "I hated all my toil in which I toil under the sun, seeing that I must leave it to the man who will come after me, . . . because sometimes a person

---

11. Ryken et al., *Dictionary of Biblical Imagery*, 228.
12. Strong, *Strong's Hebrew and Chaldee Dictionary*, para. 7488.

who has toiled with wisdom and knowledge and skill must leave everything to be enjoyed by someone who did not toil for it. This also is vanity and a great evil. What has a man from all the toil and striving of heart with which he toils beneath the sun?" (2:18, 21–22). Qohelet associates the endless toil and the rewards thereof with an evil that is vain and striving of heart. Qohelet has observed that the daily striving of humanity to survive in life only succumbs to death and a loss of all that has been acquired, including the wisdom and knowledge it took to achieve such rewards of the toil. The Aramaic Targums translation uses the phrase "breaking of the spirit," which takes a more descriptive approach to the effect of *striving after the wind*. In other words, Qohelet recognizes an effect on the daily business of humanity that is much more than a stress on the physical body, but rather a breaking of the inner spiritual being of humanity. The *breaking of the spirit* testifies to the fallenness of creation whereby evil has befallen the condition of humanity. This fallen condition diminishes the quality of life and forces humanity to question its value. Kathleen A. Farmer states, "Qohelet tells us what his experimentations and his wisdom helped him discover: human effort cannot create anything which may be relied upon to endure."[13] For Qohelet, both the *vanity* of life and the *striving* after wind activity lead to vexation that leads to sorrow. Hence, continuing to develop his frame of thought, Qohelet emphasizes the theme of fallenness with words that describe the intricate effects of a life and a world that lacks wholeness.

Vexation is another case in point. The Hebrew word for vexation is *kaʿ as* (כעס), which can carry the meanings of "to grieve, to anger, to irritate, to offend."[14] According to Norbert Lohfink, "The root always denotes 'a sense of exasperation, a bad temper,' a 'very intense emotion.' Almost always—most of the exceptions being in Ecclesiastes—there is an interpersonal context: *kaʿ as* is evoked by others and leads to a reaction against them."[15] The exception Lohfink refers to in Qohelet is that Qohelet's observation of *vexation* is not evoked by others but by the *vanity* and *striving* of life. In wisdom, there is *vexation* (Qoh 1:18); in toil, there is *vexation* (Qoh 2:23); in eating (i.e., the provision and reward of toil) there is a *vexation* (Qoh 5:17). Qohelet is using irony in the idea that the very elements that describe a life of an established person (e.g., a person who has acquired an abundance of intellect, a successful career, and a surplus of material necessities) are accommodated by an

---

13. Farmer, *Who Knows What Is Good?*, 158.
14. *HALOT*, s.v. "כעס," 2:491.
15. Lohfink, s.v. "כַּעַס כָּעַס," 7:284.

intense emotion of exasperation, anger, and grief. In other words, *vexation* is an inevitable result of humanity's striving to live life. According to John D. Currid, "Heaping up worldly wealth and having the expectation of finding meaning in it is folly (v. 7). No matter how much we toil to fill our bellies and to get things, our cravings are never satisfied. Natural yearnings return day after day; sinful desires are insatiable, and they are never quenched."[16] Hence, Qohelet states, "For all his days are full of sorrow, and his work is a vexation. Even in the night his heart does not rest. This also is vanity" (Qoh 2:23). This is the experiential reality of life under the sun, which is an inescapable result of the fall (Gen 1–3).

The projectile theme of fallenness hearkens back to the sinfulness of humanity that has brought on the condition of a life of diminished value. In Qohelet's observations of *vanity, striving after wind, and vexation* of life, he is not speaking as a man in despair but as a man whose aim is to appeal to a reality beyond what most people can discern. Qohelet is, therefore, making bold claims with an aim that must begin with the reality and acknowledgment of sin and the fallen condition of all of creation, including humanity. Such negativity in his teaching begs the question of who Qohelet is speaking to and what he is trying to say. By taking the Solomonic view of Qohelet, it may be asserted that he was speaking to people from different nations, most of which held to pagan ideologies. With the Solomonic view, it may also be asserted that Solomon is taking on the role of an evangelist whose aim is to impart a message of wisdom and knowledge that is not solely horizontal but vertical. Hence, the theme of fallenness functions as a strategy of rhetoric that allows Qohelet to disrupt the common views of society so that he may redirect the minds of his listeners to a new perspective. Where secularism views wealth and knowledge as worth seeking, Qohelet's emphasis on *vanity, striving after wind, and vexation* takes a different view on wealth and knowledge as lacking value. However, Qohelet does not leave his audience in despair but imparts hope rooted in divine wisdom stemming from a theological worldview of the Torah. But before Qohelet can impart hope, he must begin with an appeal to the fallenness of creation, which functions as a projectile theme setting the framework for his overall message.

---

16. Currid, *Ecclesiastes*, 87.

SUSTAINMENT

Premise two is the theological implication that God sustains humanity amid the fallenness. This premise can be traced in Qohelet's use of the motif of joy, gift, and eternity. Although enjoyment in a fallen world has its limitations and lack of value, Qohelet, nonetheless, sees the reward and rejoicing of one's labor as a sustaining gift of God (cf. Qoh 3:13; 5:19). In other words, to have joy in a world of *hevel* and affliction is a God-given gift of sustainment. Qohelet implicitly appeals to the grace of God to sustain humanity in the theme of joy, whereby he states, "For apart from him who can eat or who can have enjoyment? For to the one who pleases him God gives wisdom and knowledge and joy; but to the sinner he gives the work of gathering and heaping, only to give to one who pleases God. This also is vanity and a chasing after wind" (Qoh 2:25–26). While some scholars have seen the theme of joy as a peripheral to Qohelet's message, it is, in fact, more central to Qohelet's message than might appear—five different Hebrew words in Qohelet appeal to the element and sense of joy. Beginning with the element of joy, Qohelet uses the Hebrew noun word *simchah* (שמחה). *Simchah* is the element setting the basis for the overall motif of enjoyment and the theme of sustainment. *Simchah* conveys the state of gladness in the heart of a person and is accommodated by a type of wisdom and knowledge that is only given to those who please God (Qoh 2:26). *Simchah* is the element of joy that preoccupies the one who pleases God, whereby the person with *simchah* is sustained and does not worry about or regret the past but looks forward to the future with vision (Qoh 5:20). *Simchah* is the joy that Qohelet commends, and more importantly, it is the joy that God approves for living (Qoh 8:15; 9:7). Four additional Hebrew words convey the sense of enjoyment throughout Qohelet. The Hebrew noun word *chutz* (חוץ) conveys the lack of enjoyment or inability to have joy (*simchah*) apart from God (Qoh 2:25). *Chutz* also conveys the inability to experience *tov* (טוב), which is an adjective conveying enjoyment that is "to the taste, *good, sweet, agreeable for eating.*"[17] When *tov* is used in Qohelet to convey the sense of enjoyment, it is often related to eating and drinking, giving the expression of satisfaction in the provision of one's toil (Qoh 2:24; 9:7). Furthermore, the Hebrew word *'ekhol* (אכל), when used to convey enjoyment, carries

---

17. BDB, "טוב," 373.

the connotation "of peaceful enjoyment of results of labour; figurative of receiving consequences of action, good or bad."[18]

For instance, Qoh 5:19 conveys the positive aspect of ' *ekhol* by stating, "Everyone also to whom *God has given wealth and possessions and power to enjoy them*, and to accept his lot and rejoice in his toil—this is the gift of God." On the contrary, Qoh 6:2 conveys the negative aspect of ' *ekhol* by stating, "a man to whom God gives wealth, possessions, and honor, so that he lacks nothing of all that he desires, yet *God does not give him power to enjoy them*, but a stranger enjoys them. This is vanity; it is a grievous evil." Last but certainly not least in the semantic range of the enjoyment motif is the Hebrew word *ra' ah* (ראה). *Ra' ah* conveys a positive sense of enjoyment that is often juxtaposed with the Hebrew word רעה (*ra' ah*), which is pronounced the same but means "evil" and is often seen as the counterpart of the *good* and *evil* in the world. *Ra' ah* (ראה) in the motif of joy is, therefore, the sense of enjoyment that is experienced in the interest of the heart with good and joyful pleasure. To *ra' ah* (ראה) is to "*gaze at* with apprehension; with exultation, triumph = *feast eyes upon*."[19] For Qohelet, it was *ra' ah* (ראה) whereby he sought to find out what is good by testing his heart with pleasure (Qoh 2:1). And it was in the eating and drinking of one's toil that Qohelet determined to be *ra' ah* (ראה), thus suggesting *ra' ah* (ראה) be a communal experience (Qoh 5:18; 9:9). Hence, joy in Qohelet is best conveyed not as the enjoyment of labor under the sun but enjoyment in the contentment of life. The motif of joy in Qohelet is, thus, a sustaining element of grace that is a gift of God to the God-fearer.

The more significant theological reflection surrounding the context of joy is the paradox of joy in a world of affliction. In other words, humanity is afflicted with the burden of toiling all of their days, yet to enjoy the rewards of their toil is considered a *gift* of God (Qoh 5:19). The Targums explain this paradox clearly in Qoh 2:24, stating, "There is nothing suitable for man except that he eat, drink, and show himself good before the children of man by doing the commandments of the Lord and by walking in right paths before Him so that it will go well for him because of his toil. I also saw that (when) a person is prosperous in this world, it is from the hand of God, who has decreed what would become of him." Zack Eswine defines *gift* by stating,

18. BDB, "אָכַל," 37.
19. BDB, "רָאָה," 908.

A gift isn't earned, it is given. When someone gives us a gift, we do not purchase it, we receive it. A gift is not deserved or obligated; it is bestowed out of the kindness and desire of the giver. We are prone to complain about the gifts someone gives us. Entitlement, discontentment, and ingratitude cause us publicly to mock it or to attempt to return it privately for something more desirable. But the Preacher reorients us. To taste the sweetness of ordinary joys, we learn to enter each day with a conviction about the givenness of all things.[20]

The Hebrew word translated as "gift" is *mattat* (מתת). *Mattat* is used only twice in Qohelet, and both times it denotes the meaning of a "reward" or "gift." The motif of reward and gift is inherent to the motif of joy, whereby Qohelet perceives that "there is nothing better for them than to be joyful and to do good as long as they live; also that everyone should eat and drink and take pleasure in all his toil—this is God's gift to man" (Qoh 3:12–13). According to Kathleen A. Farmer, "Qohelet is convinced that God intends for us to 'take pleasure' in what we do during our brief lives on earth (vv. 12–13). This is not to say, however, that anything which gives pleasure would be approved of by God. Qohelet clearly draws some conditions around the nature of the 'pleasure' God intends for us to have, by referring in vv. 16ff. to righteousness and wickedness."[21] Life, therefore, even in the context of fallenness, is a precious *gift* of God and, thus, should be stewarded with care and gratitude. The *gift* of enjoyment is grounded in the *gift* of joy (*simchah*) that can only be experienced in a *God-fearing heart*, whereby the *God-fearing heart* finds satisfaction and contentment in the rewards of his toil. Qohelet argues for this very point by stating, "If a man fathers a hundred children and lives many years, so that the days of his years are many, but his soul is not satisfied with life's good things, and he also has no burial, I say that a stillborn child is better off than he" (Qoh 6:3). To the person that beholds the *gift* of *joy* there is the ability to enjoy life in all that God does whether in the day of prosperity or the day of adversity (Qoh 7:14). Amid the curse bestowed upon creation is God's grace to sustain humanity. Hence, in the view of Solomonic authorship, it can be deduced that while Qohelet hearkens back to the fallenness of creation through the motif of vanity (*hevel*), he also hearkens back to God's act of grace and providence in covering the shame of Adam and Eve with

---

20. Eswine, *Recovering Eden*, 104.
21. Farmer, *Who Knows What Is Good?*, 161.

garments of skin. In other words, as God's providence was given to Adam and Eve so as to give them sustenance for living without the burden of shame, God also gives his providence through the gift of joy so as to give humanity sustenance for living in a fallen world (cf. Neh 8:10). Eswine states, "We hear him tell us that 'God made man upright, but they have sought out many schemes' (Eccl. 7:29). But though our many schemes sabotaged life under the sun, the gift of having a place to dwell, a thing to do, sustenance to cultivate, and a people to enjoy it with has not left us. God, and this witness to him, remains."[22] Hence, God did not leave humanity in the vexation of their toil but has graciously *gifted* the ability to enjoy the rewards of their toil by placing a preoccupation of *sustaining joy* in the heart of the God-fearer (Qoh 5:20). On the one hand, the concept of *vanity* sets the basis for Qohelet's thoughts toward the misfortunes of humanity, particularly the righteous (Qoh 9:2). On the other hand, the concept of *joy* also runs throughout the entire text of Qohelet, setting the trajectory for the idea that even in a world and life of vanity, God provides sustainability for those who fear him and live in righteousness. God's grace has given humanity responsibilities while also placing *eternity* in their hearts, whereby joy can be expressed in the partaking of the rewards of their toil (Qoh 3:10–12), which God has approved (Qoh 9:7). Qohelet states, "I have seen the business that God has given to the children of man to be busy with. He has made everything beautiful in its time. Also, he has put eternity into man's heart, yet so that he cannot find out what God has done from the beginning to the end. I perceived that there is nothing better for them than to be joyful and to do good as long as they live" (Qoh 3:10–12). Qohelet is appealing to the reality that God is so infinite in wisdom and action that no human can fully comprehend the work of God. Nonetheless, God gives the heart of humanity the desire to live, whereby death, although a reality, is not cumbersome. Instead, humanity is given a desire that sustains them in a world full of uncertainties.

Woven in between the uncertainties of life and the certainty of death is the concept of *eternity*. The concept of *eternity* is expressed by Qohelet in the passages of Qoh 3:10–12, 5:20, and 12:5–7. Contrary to the view that Qohelet's message ends at death with no view of the afterlife, an ongoing state of existence beyond the grave is presupposed; otherwise, no meaning could be made of his reference to the judgment. While some scholars view Qoh 3:11 as a negative connotation that is interpreted with the meaning

---

22. Eswine, *Recovering Eden*, 16.

that Qohelet was frustrated with the limitations of humanity's ability to discover what God is doing, on the contrary, there is a positive connotation that appeals to the grace of God that sustains the sanity of humanity with the business of responsibility and the desire to understand the mysteries of the world. The concept of *eternity* in Qoh 3:11, thus, connotes the idea that God has busied humanity with a desire to know and understand the mysteries of the world and beyond the world. Although vexing, it is also joyful and rewarding that the business of responsibility and the desire to seek knowledge keeps the human mind preoccupied with purposeful living rather than death (Qoh 5:20). Hence, inherent to the projectile theme of sustainment is the correlation between *eternity* and *joy*. According to Eswine, "Humanity still has Eden in its veins. We have 'eternity' in our hearts (Eccl. 3:11). Our souls instinctively yearn for a purposed life without end under this time-chained sun. The Preacher teaches us how to speak humanly and honestly about our longing for purpose, the tension we experience, and the reality of handling time with our neighbors."[23] Significantly, the Hebrew word for "eternity" is *'olam* (עלם), which also connotes the *futurity of the world*.[24] For Qohelet, while understanding the finite limitations of humanity to know the work of God fully, there is still a joyful desire that God has given to humanity to know not only the mysteries of the world under the sun but also the mysteries of what is to come beyond the sun. The theme of *sustainment* is therefore proven to be a prevalent thought in the teaching of Qohelet, whereby his theological trajectory aims beyond the reality of a fallen world to the reality of a merciful and graceful God who is sustaining the one who fears him until he vindicates them. The projectile theme of *sustainment*, thus, points forward to a hope of sustainment not only in life under the sun but also in the day of judgment. While realizing the fallen state that made all things *hevel* (vanity) under the sun, Qohelet also recognizes the sustaining grace of God that carries humanity through life with purpose and hope. Just as King Solomon wrote in Prov 29:18, "Where there is no vision, the people perish" (KJV), Qohelet teaches that God has given a desire to every person that is beyond the mere existence of themselves. That is to know, to understand, to live, and to enjoy. In this, humanity is consumed with a desire that they will never be able to grasp fully. Nevertheless, they are sustained with the ability to live joyfully in a world of vanity and vexation. With the projectile theme of sustainment,

---

23. Eswine, *Recovering Eden*, 126.
24. BDB, "עלם," 762–63.

the preacher Qohelet is, thus, developing a framework that aims at a reality beyond the sun. This reality is carried further along in the projectile theme of *judgment*, which every human will face. Together, the projectile themes of *fallenness* and *sustainment* highlight the significance of the projectile theme of *judgment* in the theological framework charted in Qohelet's theological trajectory. The premise that humanity enters a fallen world and that God sustains humanity amid the fallenness is not the be-all and end-all for the human creation but instead is the catalyst to a hopeful future, whereby Qohelet prophetically exhorts his audience to live righteously in anticipation of future redemption. Considering the vast wisdom of Qohelet that has drawn the attention of people from all over the earth, it is not surprising that in his rhetoric he would appeal to the negative before drawing a conclusion that ends on a positive note. In other words, Qohelet has just set the groundwork for the apex of his message that functions as a final point. The realities of *fallenness* (sin) and *sustainment* (grace) in life under the sun culminate in a reality that is inevitable for every human. Hence, Qohelet segues from the horizontal reality of life under the sun to the vertical reality of life that every human will face in judgment.

JUDGMENT

Premise three consists of the theological implication that God preserves the lives of those who fear him on the day of judgment. This premise can be traced in Qohelet's use of the motif of the deeds of the wicked and the righteous, death, and the hope of the God-fearer. The concept of judgment, thus, does not always carry a negative connotation. While Qohelet ends his teaching with the statement, "For God will bring every deed into judgment" (Qoh 12:14), he also makes clear that God will judge to determine whether the deeds of a person are good or evil. If there was one eternal fate destined for all humanity, what is the use of distinguishing between good and evil? Using irony in Qoh 8:12–13, Qohelet implicitly appeals to an enteral state beyond the life under the sun. The implication is that there is an eternal state specifically rewarded for the God-fearer (i.e., the person who has lived righteously while under the sun).[25] First, Qohelet appeals to the current reality that is identifiable under the sun by saying that a *sinner prolongs his life* even though they do evil, but that it will go well for the person who fears God (Qoh 8:12). Then Qohelet says that the *wicked person will*

25. Refer back to ch. 1 for the theological implications of the God-fearer.

not prolong his days because he does not fear God (Qoh 8:13). The Targums translates the second part of Qohelet 8:12, "And I know that there will be good *in the world to come* for those who fear the Lord, who fear before Him and do His will" (Targums). On the one hand, for Qohelet, his statement in 8:12–13 does not present a contradiction, but instead presents two realities, whereby Qohelet *knows* (a statement of fact) that it will be well for those who fear God in a life beyond the sun, even though while under the sun the wellness of the sinner may seem better than the wellness of the God-fearer. On the other hand, contrary to the leitmotif of *hevel*, Qohelet 8:12b provides a glimmer of hope for the God-fearer amid the reality that, while under the sun, the same events happen to both the righteous and the wicked, the good and the evil (Qoh 9:2). Qohelet's reference to the deeds of the righteous and the wicked are centered around the origins of sin that began in the garden. In the garden, man's nature became corrupt, and every generation inherited the sinful nature. Depraved humanity rebels against God, living a life full of evil and madness, affecting the order of the cosmos and the reality of human relations, and causing chaos whereby "there are righteous people to whom it happens according to the deeds of the wicked, and there are wicked people to whom it happens according to the deeds of the righteous" (Qoh 8:14). Qohelet points out that this is an evil under the sun, whereby the wicked live as though they are invincible, perhaps even as though they are gods, having no regard for life, except to satisfy their own passions. Nevertheless, like those they oppress, they also go to the grave. However, where justice is turned upside down in Qoh 8:14 and 9:2, Qohelet turns justice right side up in Qoh 8:12, as Craig G. Bartholomew states, "In v. 12 Qohelet confesses what he 'knows' about God's justice despite the prolonging of sinners' lives. Even though a sinner sins continually and lives a long life, Qohelet knows that it will be well with the one who fears God."[26] For this reason, Qohelet exhorts his audience to righteous living. Reflecting on his observations from the previous chapters, Qohelet concludes in 9:1 that "the righteous and the wise and their deeds are in the *hand of God*. Whether it is love or hate, man does not know; both are before him." This statement is a comforting reminder of God's love for his holy people as written in Deut 33:3. Hence, for Qohelet, living righteously before God is living in fear of God.

There is still a reality under the sun, however, that does not hold the righteous exempt from experiencing the effects of evil. The experiences of

---

26. Bartholomew, *Ecclesiastes*, 290.

love and *hate* are figurative for *good* and *evil*, over which the righteous and the wicked have no control or knowledge of what they will get. Qohelet states, "It is the same for all, since the same event happens to the righteous and the wicked . . . . As the good one is, so is the sinner" (Qoh 9:2). These are the commonalities of all people living under the sun. Although the righteous have a differentiating peace and joy that comes from fearing God, they, like the wicked, share in the detriments of a fallen state, not knowing from one day to the next whether *love* (good) or *hate* (evil) will be their experience. According to Christopher J. H. Wright, "Our own death is unpredictable as to *when* it will happen, though it is utterly certain *that* it will."[27] This reality is yet another consequence of the fall, which every person will give an account, as before the judgment comes death.

Although death is an inevitable experience for every human, neither the righteous nor the wicked are exempt. Qohelet teaches in 7:16–18 that a person should not be overly righteous as to think that they are exempt from death, whether death comes at a mature or premature time (Qoh 7:16). Nor should a person be overly wicked as to be led to the likelihood of premature death (Qoh 7:17). Instead, a person should live with the understanding of life's limitations and the detriments to those who live in excess of both wickedness and righteousness. Farmer states,

> Since this is the case, Qohelet offers two bits of advice to the reader. On the one hand he says, "Be not righteous overmuch, and do not make yourself overwise" (v. 16). No matter how piously or righteously you act, you will not be able to guarantee your prosperity. On the other hand, "Be not wicked overmuch, neither be a fool" (v. 17). Overzealousness toward either extreme can have negative consequences. Qohelet apparently believes that if you act without moderation, you risk either destroying yourself or dying "before your time" (vv. 16–17).[28]

There is a paradoxical human experience of good and evil recognized by Qohelet that is set in the broader context of fallen humanity. While it is chaos that the same events would happen to both the righteous and the wicked, these events stem from man's heart. "This is an evil in all that is done under the sun, that the same event happens to all. Also, the hearts of the children of man are full of evil, and madness is in their hearts while they live, and after that they go to the dead" (Qoh 9:3). While there is no control

---

27. Christopher J. H. Wright, *Hearing the Message of Ecclesiastes*, 112.
28. Farmer, *Who Knows What Is Good?*, 178.

over the paradoxes of human experience, however, all a person can do is trust in the provision of God to sustain life and seek to live in honor of God as if it were their last day on earth.

Regardless of the shared fate of the wicked and the righteous, Qohelet makes a stark contrast between the two, whereby the righteous are those who live in a future hope (cf. Qoh 8:12) and the wicked are those who live with no regard for anything beyond the sun (cf. Qoh 5:12). Qohelet states, "He who is joined with all the living has hope, for a living dog is better than a dead lion" (Qoh 9:4). Qohelet sees value in the hope of those still alive. Theologically, hope is always tied to the God-fearer, whereby a sense of peace and joy that makes life worth living is experienced. Furthermore, *dogs and lions* are figurative of those regarded as low in stature and of humble state (dogs) and those regarded as high in stature and of prideful state (lions). These can be contrasted as the poor and rich, the powerless and powerful, and the oppressed and oppressors. Although the rich and powerful may have lavish lives in this life, their reward perishes with them when they die. However, those of low stature are better off than the dead lions who died in their greed. While the dead have no consciousness of thought, the living do and thus exist. The hope of the living is in their time and opportunity to enjoy the life God gifted them by making the best of their time by glorifying God while under the sun and with the understanding that their promise, which lies ahead, is redemption. The God-fearer, thus, is hopeful through life with an eschatological hope of prolonged days in a world to come.

The climax of Qohelet's message is his explicit appeal to the eschatological hope of redemption, whereby the righteous will stand, vindicated, liberated, and redeemed in judgment. In the Old Testament, the anticipation of an eschatological judgment is typically accompanied by the hope of messianic salvation and a redemptive "world to come." Qohelet mentions the judgment twice in the book (Qoh 11:9; 12:14), whereby Eaton states, regarding Qoh 11:9, "Leupold is probably right to argue that the definite article ('*the* judgment') points to a single specific event, not merely to God's general judicial activity. It is true that 'the judgment' is used elsewhere in the latter sense (e.g. 3:16, Heb.), but here the context points to a definite event."[29] Hence, with judgment comes justice, and with justice, liberation. Qohelet's explicit appeal to the consequential deeds of humanity and the reality of a succumbing death for all people has carried along the projectile

---

29. Eaton, *Ecclesiastes*, 165.

theme of judgment. Although it can be inferred that Qohelet understood the fallenness of humanity (Gen 3) and believed that all men would give an account of their deeds to God in judgment (Deut 11:12), as stated earlier, the concept of judgment does not always carry a negative connotation. On one hand, it is negative in that the judgment will be to the detriment of the wicked. On the other hand, the judgment will be a time of vindication for the righteous. Wright states, "In that sense, the Hebrew *mishpat* ('judgment') in the last verse of the book can have its positive meaning of an action that brings longed-for rectification—putting things right."[30] The element of a positively hopeful outcome of death and judgment is implied more explicitly in the targumim, where an added motif of a "world to come" is revealed. For instance, Qoh 1:3 states, "After he dies, what surplus does a person have from all his toil which he undertakes beneath the sun in this world except to occupy himself with the Torah in order to receive before the Master of the World a complete reward in the *world to come*" (Tg. Onq.). Furthermore, Qoh 2:10 in the targumim states, "And I did not prevent my mind from experiencing all the joy of the Torah because my mind was free, rejoicing in the wisdom that was given to me from before the Lord and from all the children of men. I rejoiced in it more than all my labor, and this was my good portion for which was prepared for me to receive a complete wage in the *world to come* because of all my burden" (Tg. Onq.). The *world to come* motif is explicitly stated in the targumim a total of twenty-eight times, making it a significantly essential element to understanding the rhetoric of Qohelet. Taken together, the inter-dependency between the contextual elements of a fallen world, sustaining joy, and the eschatological appeal to the *world to come*[31] present not an enigmatic mystery but a redirecting of the heart and mind to a salvific appeal in the hope of glory that is tied into the messianic hope and expectation flowing throughout the entire canon.[32] This *world to come* is a hopeful outlook that is central to the vertical view

---

30. Christopher J. H. Wright, *Hearing the Message of Ecclesiastes*, 137.

31. Although the *world to come* motif in the targumim is not explicit in the Masoretic Text, it is essential to how the ancient Hebrews interpreted Qohelet. The point is to show how this motif reveals an eschatological appeal presupposed in the Masoretic Text and implicit in the theological trajectory of Qohelet. For further insight, a copy of the English translation of the Babylonian Targums can be found in the Accordance Bible Software program.

32. Bruce Waltke agrees with this view in his work *Old Testament Theology*. Waltke states, "The doctrine of the afterlife in Ecclesiastes is consistent with the Old Testament in general" (Waltke and Yu, *Old Testament Theology*, 965).

of an eschatological reality that was shared among the ancient Israelites. In essence, Qohelet is taking on the role of an apologist who appeals to the providence of God through earthly observations inherent to the creation and the fall. In other words, Qohelet uses a rhetorical strategy that begins with disrupting the minds and hearts of his listeners with the heightened perception of evil, only to redirect their minds and hearts to a just God who sustains humanity with a hope of a redemptive future. Farmer said, "It is not Qohelet's opinion that 'everything goes.' Rather, Qohelet advises his audience to relax and enjoy their brief lives on earth (vv. 12–13), trusting that the God who has 'appointed a time for every matter, and for every work,' will also appoint a time to 'judge the righteous and the wicked' (v. 17)."[33] Hence, in the projectile theme of judgment, Qohelet has arrived at the end of the matter, which is validated in the voice of the frame narrator. "The end of the matter; all has been heard. Fear God and keep his commandments, for this is the whole duty of man. For God will bring every deed into judgment, with every secret thing, whether good or evil" (Qoh 12:13–14). The God-fearing person lives under the lordship of God, and to live under the lordship of God is to live under his authority and abide in his commandments. This is the worldview of Qohelet and is evident in the joy and hope of the righteous. In other words, the eschatological hope of the God-fearer is a sustaining joy in the temporal life of *hevel* under the sun and a hopeful joy for redemption in a world to come. Qohelet's theological trajectory is, thus, a culmination of thematic underpinning inherent to the projectile themes of fallenness, sustainment, and judgment. The supposed contradicting motifs, such as vanity and vexation, joy and gift, and judgment, take on a function of thematic grain carried along by the projectile themes guiding Qohelet's frame of thought aimed at an appeal to righteous living and eschatological hope. Taking on the role of an evangelist, apologist, and *preacher*, Qohelet's message is a universal appeal for all nations. In his message, Qohelet coheres with the messianic vision of the Old Testament and the eschatological hope of the gospel.

---

33. Farmer, *Who Knows What Is Good?*, 161–62.

PART III.

Qohelet's Theological Affinity to the Metanarrative of the Bible

Chapter 6

The New Testament and the Trajectory of Qohelet's Theology

THE PROJECTILE THEMES OF fallenness, sustainment, and judgment in Qohelet are rooted in salvation history, aiming at a messianic and eschatological vision revealed in the New Testament. This chapter will discuss three points of aim regarding Qohelet's trajectory and what the New Testament reveals about Qohelet's theology on sin (fallenness), grace (sustainment), and redemption (judgment). As stated in the introductory chapter, by focusing on three points of discussion relating to the theological trajectory of Qohelet's projectile themes, the realities of life in the fallen state of humanity, life in the sustaining grace of God, and life in the imminent judgment inform our understanding of how humanity ought to live in the world while under the sun. These three points of aim not only correlate with the fallenness, sustainment, and judgment themes of Qohelet but are also inherent to the unfolding themes of the Bible leading up to the New Testament revelation of Messiah/Christ and the eschatological hope of redemption. According to Iain Provan, "Ecclesiastes, as part of the Scripture that is given us for shaping faith and life, offers us such advice, correlating as it does so with extensive sections of the New Testament that also touch on such themes."[1] Hence, by examining the message of the New Testament in correlation to Qohelet's projectile themes, the coherency argument of this study is strengthened, whereby salvation history culminates in Christ's call to repentance, grace, and redemption. Furthermore, in synthesizing the

1. Provan, *Ecclesiastes, Song of Songs*, 42.

PART III. QOHELET'S THEOLOGICAL AFFINITY

trajectory of Qohelet with the New Testament teachings, it becomes apparent that Qohelet has always been a vision of glory and redemption, whereby understanding the applicability of Qohelet's theology to Christian living testifies to the themes of fallenness, sustainment, and judgment alluded to in the New Testament's universal appeal to righteous living in fear of God.[2]

THE NEW TESTAMENT ON THE FALLEN STATE OF CREATION AND HUMANITY

Qohelet's projectile theme of fallenness corresponds to the New Testament's doctrine of sin in that the New Testament presupposes the fallen state of creation as a result of Adam's sin. One of the most significant verses in the New Testament that corresponds to the theme of fallenness in Qohelet is Rom 8:20, which states, "For the creature was made subject to vanity, not willingly, but by reason of him who hath subjected *the same* in hope" (KJV). Interestingly, Paul would use the very same Greek word for vanity (i.e., *mataiotēs*—ματαιότης) rendered in the LXX translation of Qohelet. Just like Qohelet, Paul understood the vanity of creation as a depreciated condition, whereby the wholeness that was once existent in the world is no longer the reality. For Paul, the vanity of creation is affected by the corruption that humanity has become bound to by sin (Rom 8:20), whereby the fallen state of creation and humanity has brought significant suffering into the world, diminishing the quality of life on earth. Even when humanity is too blind and calloused to realize the agony of imperfection, there is nonetheless an inward groaning that yearns to be whole again (Rom 8:23). Paul states, "For we know that the whole creation has been groaning together in the pains of childbirth until now" (Rom 8:22). "Until now" (ἄχρι τοῦ νῦν—*achri tou nun*) conveys a motion that is spatial with movement from one point to another, such as *from past to present*. Hence, the implication of Rom 8:22 is that Paul reflects on the fallenness of creation and humanity that originated in the garden of Eden. It is, thus, no coincidence that Paul would describe the agony of the fallen creation in the same manner as the consequence befallen Eve. God states to the woman in Gen 3:16, "I will surely multiply

---

2. This premise requires a canonical view and analysis of Qohelet and its contribution to the metanarrative of the Bible. This premise is further developed in this chapter by focusing on Qohelet's theological affinity to the New Testament. For a pre-discussion on Qohelet's canonicity refer to ch. 2: "The Canonicity of Qohelet in the Wisdom Corpus and the Bible."

your pain in childbearing; in pain you shall bring forth children." Victor P. Hamilton describes the birth pangs of a woman with two emphasizing words when he states, "For the woman who is destined to conceive (v. 15) will give birth in *agony*. At the point in her life when a woman experiences her highest sense of self-fulfillment (according to OT emphases), she will have some physical *anguish*."[3] For Paul, *agony* and *anguish* are the effects of sin that have befallen all creation and not just the woman (Eve). When Paul uses the birth pangs of childbearing as a metaphor for describing the condition of fallen humanity and creation, he is describing the effects of the depreciated state of *mataiotēs*—ματαιότης (vanity) as the imposition of sin and the outcome of righteous judgment (Rom 8:20).

The fallen state of creation and humanity is not just an attestation of the apostle Paul. In 1 Pet 1:18, the apostle Peter tells us that the condition of vanity was inherited from our forefathers (i.e., Adam and those who followed him). While 1 Pet 1:18–19 testifies to the redemption from the *emptiness* of life through the shed blood of Jesus Christ, it, nonetheless, alludes to a condition that is *mataios*—μάταιος (vain). According to Thomas R. Schreiner,

> The "emptiness" (*mataias*) of life is a theme mentioned often in Ecclesiastes. In the Old Testament it is often associated with the idolatry of pagans. Similarly, in the New Testament the word group depicts pre-Christian existence (Acts 14:15; Rom 1:21; Eph 4:17). The life of unbelievers before their conversion is futile, empty, and devoted to false gods. Such a way of life has been handed down from the forefathers, from generation to generation.[4]

Throughout the Old Testament, there has been a prophetic message of idolatry, whereby idolatry, resulting from the corruption of humanity, was a significant issue the prophets contended against in the Old Testament. Idolatry was not only to the detriment of those who made the idols but also to those who worshiped and trusted the idols. The sin of idolatry stifles its worshipers from hearing and seeing the conditions of the fallen state to thinking they are sinless. Hence, the detriment of becoming deaf and blind, just like the idols they worship, befalls the idolator, which becomes especially evident in the parallel between the lifelessness of idols in the passage of Ps 115:4–8 and the repeated references to Jesus's statements in the Gospels and Revelation. Hence, Jesus states, "Having eyes, do you not see?

3. Hamilton, *Book of Genesis, Chapters 1–17*, 200, emphasis added.
4. Schreiner, *1, 2 Peter, Jude*, 84.

and having ears, do you not hear?" (Mark 8:18), and "The one who has ears, let him hear" (Matt 13:9; Rev 2:7, 11, 17, 29; 3:6, 13, 22). Because of the rebellion of humanity toward the Creator, the fallen nature has driven humanity away from the worship of the only true living God to the worship of false gods.

Interestingly, the Old Testament translates the all-familiar word of Qohelet, *hevel*, as "idols" six times in the ESV Bible. According to the *Hebrew and Aramaic Lexicon of the Old Testament*, *hevel* can also connote "idols, things that do not really exist."[5] According to G. K. Beale, "The point is that our lives become vain and empty when we commit ourselves to vain idols of this world, since 'there is no such thing as an idol in the world'" (1 Cor 8:4).[6] In essence, Qohelet's message is an idol killer in that Qohelet's theological trajectory takes the projectile theme of fallenness and admonishes against idolatry in the earthly experience of life itself. Qohelet appeals to the vanity of life under the sun to point out that all of life's pursuits in and of themselves are meaningless and empty. In Matt 16:26, Jesus states, "For what will it profit a man if he gains the whole world and forfeits his soul?" Jesus is alluding to the fallen state of creation and the idolatrous hearts of humanity. Although idolatry in the New Testament may not be as explicit as in the Old Testament, the worship of false gods was still a common practice in the Greco-Roman era, including the pursuits of life that exalt oneself before God.[7]

For this reason, Paul admonishes, "Put to death therefore what is earthly in you: sexual immorality, impurity, passion, evil desire, and covetousness, which is idolatry" (Col 3:5). Furthermore, 1 John 2:15–17 states, "Do not love the world or the things in the world. If anyone loves the world, the love of the Father is not in him. For all that is in the world—the desires of the flesh and the desires of the eyes and pride of life—is not from the Father but is from the world. And the world is passing away along with its desires, but whoever does the will of God abides forever." Like Qohelet, the apostles testified to their knowledge and understanding that there are two paths to living. On the one hand, there is the pursuit of the world, which implies pursuing all things pleasurable to the flesh (i.e., idolatry). On the

---

5. *HALOT*, s.v. "הֶבֶל," 1:237.

6. Beale, *We Become What We Worship*, 308.

7. For background on the topic of idolatry in the Greco-Roman era see the sections on "Hellenistic-Roman Religion" and "Economic Life" in Ferguson, *Backgrounds of Early Christianity*. Also see the section on "Purity" in Archie T. Wright, *World of the New Testament*.

other hand, there is the pursuit of God, which implies a life lived with the reverential fear of God. In Matt 7:13–14, Jesus states, "Enter by the narrow gate. For the gate is wide and the way is easy that leads to destruction, and those who enter by it are many. For the gate is narrow and the way is hard that leads to life, and those who find it are few." According to Craig L. Blomberg, "'Wide' versus 'narrow' may refer not only to the majority versus the minority but also to relative levels of difficulty or ease. 'Narrow' in v. 14 comes from the verb *thlibō*, meaning *to experience trouble or difficulty*, while 'broad' in v. 13 can have overtones of *prosperous*."[8] In other words, the pursuit of a fallen world, which can be summed up as the pursuit of all things that do not glorify God, only leads to death. Although a person may experience material wealth and prosperity in life under the sun, they will ultimately face a judgment that leads to death. Hence, Jas 4:4 states, "You adulterous people! Do you not know that friendship with the world is enmity with God? Therefore whoever wishes to be a friend of the world makes himself an enemy of God." Hence, throughout the New Testament, explicit and implicit allusions to the fallenness of creation and humanity exist, testifying to the message of idolatry in the Prophets of the Old Testament and the message of idolatry in the theme of fallenness in Qohelet.

However, the most explicit New Testament allusion to the fallen state of creation and humanity is its allusion to death. Like Qohelet, the New Testament sees death as an evil imposition impartial to all life (Qoh 8:8; 9:2–3; Rom 5:12; Heb 9:27). Death is the foremost evidence of the curse resulting from sin and is strongly depicted in God's warning against touching and eating of the tree of the knowledge of good and evil (Gen 2:17; 3:3). It was about death that the serpent deceived Eve in Gen 3:4, stating, "You will not surely die." Furthermore, in Gen 3:19, the Lord says, "By the sweat of your face you shall eat bread, till you return to the ground, for out of it you were taken; for you are dust, and to dust you shall return." As Qohelet recognizes the curse of death as a consequence of the fall and a factor of the diminishing value of life under the sun, the New Testament not only testifies to the physical reality of death but also further unfolds the curse's detriment to a spiritual reality referred to as the second death. Jesus states, "He who has an ear, let him hear what the Spirit says to the churches. The one who conquers will not be hurt by the second death" (Rev 2:11). The second death refers to eternal separation from God and final punishment

---

8. Blomberg, *Matthew*, 132.

for the wicked. Commenting on the meaning of the "second death" in Revelation, G. K. Beale states,

> In contrast, the wicked have "their part in the lake burning with fire and brimstone, which is the second death" (21:8b). This figurative portrayal of punishment indicates that there is additional suffering besides the anguish of separation from God. As observed already, the antitheses of old vs. new and first vs. second contrast the partial and temporal with the consummate and eternal. So here "second death" refers to a perfected and eternal punishment.[9]

For Qohelet, death is a vain consequence of sin and rebellion, whereby the New Testament testifies that "the wages of sin is death" (Rom 6:23). In other words, death is inherent to the root cause of the fall (i.e., sin) from which no man can save himself. The concept of death in Qohelet is an allusion to the human rebellion against the sovereign God and the diminishing value of its result. In light of the New Testament, however, the concept of death in Qohelet is an acknowledgment of humanity's doom and need for salvation. From the Gospels and Acts to the Epistles and Revelation, the message of the New Testament reveals the Savior as Jesus Christ. It inaugurates the redeeming promises of God prophesied throughout the Old Testament. Like Qohelet, who sees the inevitable experience of life in a fallen world that burdens humanity with strife and vexation, Jesus states in Matt 18:7, "Woe to the world because of *its* stumbling blocks! For it is inevitable that stumbling blocks come; but woe to the person through whom the stumbling block comes!" (NASB20). Nonetheless, the fallen state of humanity and creation is not the be-all and end-all for those who are in Christ. Instead, the New Testament testifies to the grace of God that sustains humanity amid the fallen condition with a hope that has been unfolded and recorded throughout human history, beginning with Moses and all the prophets (Luke 24:7).

THE NEW TESTAMENT ON THE SUSTAINING GRACE OF GOD

Qohelet's projectile theme of sustainment provides insight into his theology of grace, teaching that amid the fallenness of creation, humanity has been gifted with the ability to live in joy, contentment, and hope. No matter how vexing life can be, God has made everything beautiful in its time (Qoh

---

9. Beale, *Book of Revelation*, 1061.

3:11) and life is, therefore, worthy of being rejoiced in. Just as God's grace is depicted in the joy passages of Qohelet as sustainment for humanity amid the vanities and vexation of life, the New Testament testifies to a joy in Christ Jesus that is sustaining for those who trust in him amid the trials and tribulations of life. Joy is significant in the New Testament because it is a direct attribute of Jesus, who states in John 15:11, "These things I have spoken to you, that my joy may be in you, and that your joy may be full." Furthermore, the author of Hebrews speaks of this joy as being an enduring strength to Jesus while suffering on the cross. Hebrews 12:2 states, "Looking to Jesus, the founder and perfecter of our faith, who for the joy that was set before him endured the cross." According to Donald Guthrie,

> The linking of *joy* with suffering in this verse echoes a constant New Testament theme. Indeed on the eve of his passion Jesus spoke of his joy and of his desire that his disciples should share it (John 15:11; 17:13). It is highly probable that the disciples remembered this remarkable fact when they later reflected on the passion of Jesus. The writer here does not consider it necessary to enlarge on the theme of joy, but he attaches some importance to the fact that it was *set before him* which suggests that it took precedence over everything else.[10]

The connotation of verses such as John 15:11 and 17:13 is that Jesus is the beholder of joy, and his joy fills a void in the person who trusts him. Jesus's joy is the type of joy that gives strength (Neh 8:10), and it is the type of joy that gives peace (Rom 15:13). Hence, Jas 1:2–4 states, "Count it all joy, my brothers, when you meet trials of various kinds, for you know that the testing of your faith produces steadfastness. And let steadfastness have its full effect, that you may be perfect and complete, lacking in nothing." Jim Samra states, "The Greek word order emphasizes the words 'joy' and 'trials.' It is not intuitive that trials should cause joy, so James asks his readers to make a deliberate effort to set aside their natural inclinations of fear, discouragement, and anger and choose to be joyful in the midst of trials."[11] For Qohelet, joy is an expression of hope in God and contentment in life, recognizing that although the business that God has given humanity to be busy with is vanity, it is also, nonetheless, a gift. To have the joy of the Lord is to have peace. Peace is an aspect of joy that sustains the believer (God-fearer) in their journey through life under the sun. The apostle Peter describes this

---

10. Guthrie, *Hebrews*, 252.
11. Samra, *James, 1 and 2 Peter, and Jude*, 6.

PART III. QOHELET'S THEOLOGICAL AFFINITY

joy as inexpressible and filled with glory, stating, "Though you have not seen him, you love him. Though you do not now see him, you believe in him and rejoice with joy that is inexpressible and filled with glory, obtaining the outcome of your faith, the salvation of your souls" (1 Pet 1:8–9). In other words, the sustaining joy of the Lord is unexplainable, yet it is real and recognizable. Amid the vanities of a fallen world and the vexation of the human curse, it is the joy of the Lord that sustains the believer.

Jesus refers to the concept of a servant who enters into his master's joy in the parable of the talents (Matt 25:21–23). In Matt 25:21, the master speaks to his servant with five talents and says, "Enter into the joy of your master." Again, in Matt 25:23, the master speaks to his servant with two talents and says, "Enter into the joy of your master." In the case of both of these servants they were rewarded for their stewardship over the little they were given by their master. As a result, not only did the servants double their master's interest in the talents, but they were invited to share in their master's delight. Considering the phrase "enter into the joy of your master" in parallel with the phrase of Jesus in John 15:11 stating "that my joy may be in you," there is an implied impartation of joy from the master (i.e., Jesus) to the servant that brings delight and pleasure in its purest form. Hence, the apostle Paul often refers to joy as part of the fruit of the Spirit (Gal 5:22) in association with the Holy Spirit. With joy that is of the Holy Spirit of God, there is the accompaniment of peace, which is an essential attribute of the sustaining grace of God for the believer. C. Marvin Pate states, "Paul uses three nouns—'righteousness,' 'peace,' and 'joy'—to characterize the blessings of the kingdom of God, all of which proceed from the Holy Spirit (cf. Rom 5:1–5)."[12] Paul's characterization of the kingdom of God's blessings, all of which proceed from the Holy Spirit, is indicative of joy being an inner component of the righteous person (i.e., God-fearer). In other words, joy, being of the Holy Spirit and the Holy Spirit indwelling in the heart of every believer, is an inner attribute that sustains a person with a peace that "surpasses all understanding" (Phil 4:7). Hence, the sustaining grace of God is rooted in joy and gives the believer every reason to rejoice in what Douglas Sean O'Donnell calls "trembling trust," defined as "those who, in the midst of all the hard truths and awful troubles of this fallen world, come before the Lord with trembling trust [and] are given by him the gift of grateful obedience, steady contentment, and surprising joy."[13] In other words, the

12. Pate, *Romans*, 274.
13. O'Donnell, *Ecclesiastes*, 9.

sustaining gifts of peace and contentment that accompany the joy of trusting in the grace of God are essential to living amid a world filled with vanity and vexation.

It is not a coincidence that Qohelet discusses the concept of joy in close relationship to the concept of contentment. Qohelet encourages his audience to enjoy the portion of their toil that God has given them, recognizing that while not everyone is allotted a great deal of wealth or longevity of life, those who fear God have been given the ability to be joyful with the little (Qoh 5:19; 9:9). Contentment is also a message of God's grace, whereby the New Testament teaches to be content not only in material wealth but in every situation. Fredericks and Estes state,

> The commoner can sleep deeply and be quite satisfied with the modest pleasures that should be adequate for anyone's contentment. These simple sources of enjoyment are more easily renewed, though they are deemed inferior by those addicted to a possibly non-renewable "higher standard of living." But, whether one is blessed with minimal or optimal wealth, the advantage to one's labour is the wonderful ("beautiful"; *yāpeh*) condition of contentment with God's rewards and the labour that sets the table with food and drink which at least sustains, if not indulges, one's small span of life.[14]

Hence, the New Testament teaches in Heb 13:5, "Keep your life free from love of money, and be content with what you have, for he has said, 'I will never leave you nor forsake you.'" Additionally, Jesus stated, "Therefore I tell you, do not be anxious about your life, what you will eat or what you will drink, nor about your body, what you will put on. Is not life more than food, and the body more than clothing?" (Matt 6:25). The Father and the Son express comfort and provision over the God-fearer. God's word taking on flesh in Jesus (John 1:14) knows the needs of humanity, and he identifies with the experience of life under the sun and is compassionate toward his creation (Heb 2:17–18). Jesus goes on to say, "Look at the birds of the air: they neither sow nor reap nor gather into barns, and yet your heavenly Father feeds them. Are you not of more value than they?" (Matt 6:26). The rhetorical question Jesus is asking is more explicitly stated in Matt 10:31, stating, "Fear not, therefore; you are of more value than many sparrows." If humanity is more valuable than the birds of the sky, how much more will God provide to sustain humanity in every circumstance of life? Whether it

---

14. Fredericks and Estes, *Ecclesiastes and The Song of Songs*, 157.

PART III. QOHELET'S THEOLOGICAL AFFINITY

be daily bread for nourishment or strength to endure and overcome temptation or persecution, the Lord's grace spans the entire spectrum of human experience amid the fallenness of creation. The person who believes God's word is the truth is sustained by the joy and peaceful contentment of their believing (Rom 15:13), whereby the peace that surpasses all understanding rests on their heart and mind because they are set on Christ Jesus (Phil 4:7). Hence, the apostle Paul, in his bondage of being jailed and persecuted for the sake of the gospel, states, "For I have learned in whatever situation I am to be content" (Phil 4:11). Furthermore, he states, "For the sake of Christ, then, I am content with weaknesses, insults, hardships, persecutions, and calamities. For when I am weak, then I am strong" (2 Cor 12:10). According to Richard L. Pratt Jr., "From this understanding of his weakness, Paul concluded that he would delight in weaknesses rather than abhor them. Insults, hardships, persecutions, and difficulties were causes for joy because in these times of weakness, Paul was strong in the power of God."[15] For Paul, the sufferings of this world did not compare to the glory that is to be revealed at the second coming of Christ (Rom 8:18). Paul's belief in the redeeming glory that is set before those who put their trust in the Lord and endure through the sufferings of life was a reality to be reckoned. In other words, because Paul knew in his belief that the promises of God were true, he was strengthened with the power to endure his trials with joy. By the grace of God and the power of the Holy Spirit, Paul was sustained in the peace of God through every circumstance, which was his exhortation to the church.

The projectile theme of sustainment in Qohelet is lived out in the fear of God motif, pointing to a joyful and glorious hope of redemption (Qoh 8:12). Paul understood this hope to be an eternal reality beyond the world under the sun. Nonetheless, Qohelet had a theology of grace that understood God shows no partiality (Qoh 3:17; Rom 2:11). The very gift of life itself is a gift of God's grace, and the lot given to each person is a gift undeserved to which no one is entitled. However, for those who fear God, grace upon grace is given (John 1:16). But how does a person show appreciation for God's graceful gifts? It is by stewarding life well, being joyful and content, living in righteousness to God's glory, honor, and praise, and looking to the future redemption of a wholesome state in which death, mourning, crying, and pain will no longer exist (Rev 21:4). Hence, God has delegated a responsibility to humanity that keeps them consumed with life rather than

---

15. Pratt, *I and II Corinthians*, 427.

death. Qohelet states, "I have seen the business that God has given to the children of man to be busy with. He has made everything beautiful in its time. Also, he has put eternity into man's heart, yet so that he cannot find out what God has done from the beginning to the end. I perceived that there is nothing better for them than to be joyful and to do good as long as they live" (Qoh 3:10–12). The message of the New Testament also points to an eternal hope and redemption filled with joy and peace in Christ Jesus. The apostle John states, "But to all who did receive him, who believed in his name, he gave the right to become children of God, who were born, not of blood nor of the will of the flesh nor of the will of man, but of God" (John 1:12–13). Furthermore, in the Gospel of John, Jesus states, "I have said these things to you, that in me you may have peace. In the world you will have tribulation. But take heart; I have overcome the world" (John 16:33). In believing these words of Jesus, the believer (i.e., God-fearer) has been given the ability to be joyful in his promise of sustainment and redemption. In other words, believing in the gospel of Jesus and knowing that his word is true gives peace to the believer and joy to endure in the temporal circumstances of the human condition. However, Jesus says, "Come to me, all who labor and are heavy laden, and I will give you rest. Take my yoke upon you, and learn from me, for I am gentle and lowly in heart, and you will find rest for your souls" (Matt 11:28–29). Jesus sets a condition that one must trust him to find sustainment through life's circumstances. Moreover, to trust in him, one must know him with reverential fear. God has never desired for humanity to live apart from a relationship with him, so he has sent his Son Jesus as a reconciliation between humanity and himself (Rom 5:11; 2 Cor 5:18–19). Only because of God's grace is humanity sustained in a world of vanity and vexation. Though there is much suffering now under the sun, the apostle Paul teaches that through repentance and faith in Jesus, humanity becomes reconciled and heirs to God and co-inheritors with Christ who will one day share in his glory (Rom 8:17; Eph 1:11; 1 Pet 1:3–5).

THE NEW TESTAMENT ON THE ESCHATOLOGICAL JUDGMENT AND HOPE OF GLORY

While the Old Testament has been a vision of Messianic redemption, the New Testament has been an eschatological vision of Christ, who is the hope of glory (Col 1:27). The hope of glory is the eschatological redemption referred to by the apostle Paul as the revealing of the sons of God, the adoption as sons, and the redemption of our bodies, which is the promise and hope of the believer (Rom 8:23–24). This hope was embedded in the messianic vision highly anticipated throughout the Old Testament covenants and has now been revealed in the covenant of the New Testament. Throughout the Gospels and Acts, the Epistles, and Revelation, messianic fulfillment is revealed, and a continued vision of eschatological hope persists. Often described as the reality of the *already but not yet*, there lies a present and future duality. The Gospels and Acts reveal the good news of Christ's first coming, his redemptive work on the cross, his resurrection, and his continued mission through the commission of the church. The Epistles exhort the church to eagerly await in anticipation for Christ's return in the second coming, whereby the elect, both living and dead, will also be raised in bodily resurrection. The apocalyptic book of Revelation is an admonition and exhortation of divine judgment on the *Day of the Lord* and restoration in the new heaven and new Earth established as the kingdom of God. As a whole, the New Testament is the testimony of God concerning his Son Jesus Christ (1 John 5:9). It is a testimony that gives assurance of salvation in the now (present) and salvation in the eschaton (future/end) to every believer. The New Testament is the eschatological vision of Christ that reveals and anticipates the hope and praise of his glory. Qohelet's projectile theme of judgment aims at not only the future damnation of the wicked but also the future redemption of the God-fearer (Qoh 3:17; 8:12–13; 12:14). Collectively, the inter-dependency between the contextual elements of a fallen world, sustaining joy, and judgment do not present an enigmatic mystery but a redirecting of the human heart and mind to a salvific appeal in the hope of glory that is tied into the messianic hope and expectation that runs throughout the entire canon.

The eschatological judgment and hope of glory are testified to in the New Testament eschatological vision of Christ. Beginning with the Gospels and Acts, the Gospels are the revelation of Christ and his work of redemption that laid the foundation for the apostles' teaching. Written as a biographical-historical account of Jesus's birth, ministry, death, and resurrection, the Gospels not only reveal the first coming of Jesus but establish the promise of eschatological redemption and restoration for the entire creation in anticipation of his return. Beginning with the genealogy of Christ, Matthew and Luke show how Christ was the promised seed of Abraham by which all the world would be blessed (Matt 1:2–17; Luke 3:23–38). They also give an account of Jesus's conception (Matt 1:18–25) and birth (Luke

2:1–7) that affirms the prophet Isaiah's prophecy of a child born of a virgin, who would bring order and peace to the nation of Israel (Isa 7:1–17; 9:6–7). In all four Gospels, Jesus's divine ministerial works from his teachings, healings, casting out demons, and various other miracles testify to his divinity, which becomes apparent to those witnessing these events. However, the most revealing testimony of Jesus as Messiah/Christ is the authority in which he spoke. In Luke 4:18–21, Jesus reads from the scroll of Isaiah, proclaiming that the prophecy has been fulfilled on that day in him. This moment is significant because Jesus is portraying himself not just to be a prophet but the Messiah whom the prophets had prophesied.

In John 8:12–30, Jesus bears witness to himself as the light of the world who judges in truth by the Father, who also bears witness to him. Jesus also begins to establish his passion, whereby he will be put to death and resurrected back to life (Matt 16:21–23; 17:10–13; Mark 8:31–33; 9:11–13; Luke 9:22). In John 14:1–6, Jesus gives the eschatological hope whereby he will return to take his disciples with him to a place that he is preparing in the house of the Father. In this eschatological return, all disciples must take heart and not be troubled. However, before that time comes, there is still work to be done in the mission of God, whereby Jesus is crucified and resurrected on the third day. In all of his events up to his resurrection, the eschatological vision of Christ is inaugurated. His appearances to the disciples before his ascension testify to his word and promise, whereby he then commissions the disciples to carry on his mission of making more disciples and teaching them what he has taught them while promising to always be with them through the promise of the Father, sealed by his Holy Spirit (Matt 28:16–20; Mark 16:15–19; Luke 24:44–53). Hence, the book of Acts records the account of God's ongoing mission of Christ through his Holy Spirit working through his disciples to build the church through the testimony of his Son, Jesus Christ. Elwell and Yarbrough state, "Everyone agreed that Jesus had died. But for Christians it did not end there."[16] In other words, the eschatological vision of Christ continues in the promised hope of glory for all who receive Christ through the testimony of his word. The New Testament Gospels and Acts urge the lost to be reconciled to God, in Christ, whom all will one day give an account to in judgment (Acts 17:31).

Often serving different purposes for different audiences, the Epistles appeal to holy and righteous living in persevering faith in Christ while anticipating his return. In the epistles of the Pauline corpus, we learn that the

---

16. Elwell and Yarbrough, *Encountering the New Testament*, 190.

PART III. QOHELET'S THEOLOGICAL AFFINITY

gospel is the power of God for salvation to those who believe (Rom 1:16; 1 Cor 1:18) and that being justified by his grace through faith in Christ, we are heirs to eternal life (Titus 3:7; Eph 2:4–7). Paul reminds us that the Holy Spirit has been given to us as a seal and guarantee of Christ's promise (2 Cor 1:22; Eph 1:13). Hence, Elwell and Yarbrough state, "Paul's view of things to come has profound implications for the way life is to be lived now."[17] To Paul, the eschatological resurrection is an imminent reality of our being united with Christ at his second coming (Rom 6:5) and, therefore, should be a motivation to live in righteousness to God's glory, honor, and praise. Furthermore, in the General Epistles, we learn of a living hope that is in the resurrection of Christ (1 Pet 1:3) and that by persevering in faith there is an entrance into the eternal kingdom of the Lord Jesus Christ (2 Pet 1:11), which is Christ's promise to every believer (1 John 2:25; 5:11). Additionally, Jude exhorts the church to "keep yourselves in the love of God, waiting for the mercy of our Lord Jesus Christ that leads to eternal life" (Jude 1:21). Hebrews exhorts the church to not be sluggish in their walk but to encourage one another as the day draws near for the eternal promise given to us in Christ (Heb 10:25), whereby the reward of our confidence in the promise of Christ will be received in doing the will of God (Heb 10:35–36). In James, saving faith is confident and professing and enduring faith that *works* (Jas 2:24). It is in the gift of faith that God has made way for salvation through his Son Jesus, whereby all who believe in him and persevere in his will as they are enduring through trials will receive the crown of life (Jas 1:12). Hence, every message conveyed in the Epistles carries a common appeal to Christ as the justifier and redeemer, who will one day come back for his faithful bride (the church). The foundation of the church that the apostles laid centered on the promise of God to establish his kingdom, whereby those who are justified will be co-heirs with Christ. Commenting on 1 Peter, Elwell and Yarbrough state, "Christian believers can look forward to an unfading, eternal inheritance in heaven (1:3–6). This includes the salvation of their souls, and for this reason they should be filled with profound and persistent joy (1:8–9)."[18] In essence, the eschatological vision of Christ depicted in the Gospels is a universal appeal to the whole world, whereby the eschatological vision of Christ depicted in the Epistles functions as a reminder and exhortation to the church (i.e., those who have become

---

17. Elwell and Yarbrough, *Encountering the New Testament*, 250.
18. Elwell and Yarbrough, *Encountering the New Testament*, 346.

justified by God's grace through faith in Jesus Christ) to remain hopeful in the redemption anticipated at the return of Christ.

The eschatological appeal of the Epistles is an extension of the eschatological vision of Christ in the Gospels and is further extended in the eschatological vision of Revelation. Elwell and Yarbrough state, "It is with good reason that the New Testament ends with the book of Revelation.... It also shows in a marvelous, symbolic way the two elements of Christ's messianic ministry: that of Suffering Servant (the Lamb) and that of ruling Sovereign (the Lion)."[19] In other words, the vision of Christ's work on the cross and resurrection is depicted in the metaphor of the Lion and the Lamb. The duality of this metaphor is that Christ, although slain and put to death on the cross, has conquered the enemy and the world and now sits in glory at the right hand of the Father. Hence, Revelation is an apocalyptic literature that depicts the Day of the Lord in vivid symbolism. Just as the Day of the Lord is depicted throughout the Old Testament judgment and redemption oracles, so is the Day of the Lord depicted in the New Testament admonitions and appeals to the return of Christ. The Day of the Lord will consist of a period whereby judgment, wrath, redemption, and restoration come to fruition, beginning with the triumphant entry of Christ, "coming with the clouds, and every eye will see him, even those who pierced him, and all tribes of the earth will wail on account of him" (Rev 1:7).

Hence, the eschatological series of events will consist of an outpouring of divine judgment, also referred to as the wrath of the Lamb (Rev 6:16–17) and a restoration of all things new (Rev 21:5). The eschatological vision of Christ for the believer is the complete restoration from the fallen state, whereby there is the destruction of chaos and restoration of order that will exceed that of the pre-fall state (Rev 21–22). The sinful inclination of humanity will cease, and those who stand in the judgment will inhabit the new Earth with no more curse. There will be a river of life flowing from the throne of God with the tree of life on both sides of the river (Rev 22:1–2). Where Adam was restricted from the tree of life in the garden of Eden, every inhabitant of the new Earth will have unrestricted access to the tree of life. Additionally, the Father and the Son will reign from the new city of Jerusalem, where God's throne will be established, and every inhabitant will see God face-to-face with unrestricted access to him. In this fulfillment, all order of creation will be restored to a more excellent Eden, whereby every believer who endured in faith will live in communal eternity with Christ.

---

19. Elwell and Yarbrough, *Encountering the New Testament*, 365.

PART III. QOHELET'S THEOLOGICAL AFFINITY

The book of Revelation gives us future insight into God's plan for creation and those who place their faith and hope in the Son, Jesus Christ.

The New Testament's eschatological vision of Christ extends through the Gospels and Acts, the Epistles, and Revelation, reminding the believer that a consummation with the Creator (John 1:3; Col 1:16) is still yet to come. The eschatological vision of Christ in the New Testament unfolds what has been anticipated throughout the Old Testament covenants. There is fulfillment and expectation in the revealing of Messiah/Christ (the first coming) and continued anticipation for a complete restoration of creation (the second coming). These events will take place on the eschatological Day of the Lord, consisting of *judgment* and *redemption*. For those who reject the gospel of Jesus Christ, there will be a great white throne judgment (Rev 20:11), but for the faithful God-fearer and righteous in Christ, there is a hope of glory and promised redemption. Hence, the New Testament vision of Christ gives the believer eschatological hope in the present reality of what Christ has already done and encouragement to persevere to the future reality of what Christ is still yet to do.

The reality of an eschatological judgment and hope of glory was not a new concept of the New Testament but the New Testament's revelation and fulfillment of the Old Testament messianic vision. Qohelet was very much attuned to this reality, which was passed down through the messianic vision of the covenants. Unfolded through the covenants, the Old Testament allusions and proclamations in the Law/Torah, Prophets/Nevi'im, and Writings/Ketuvim about Messiah are brought to fruition in the child born of a virgin, a Son of God and Son of Man, derived from the royal line of Judah and the offspring of David. His name has been revealed as Jesus (Luke 1:26–33), the name with the authority to judge people for their sins (John 5:22–27) and the name with the power to save and forgive people of their sins (Acts 4:12). According to Gentry and Wellum, "What the Old Testament anticipated, the New Testament says is now here. Although we still await our glorification, to be at present united to Christ and in the new covenant entails that one has been born of the Spirit and forgiven of his or her sin.... We wait for the consummation, but *at present* we enjoy what it means to be God's *new* people."[20] In other words, the eschatological vision of Christ in the New Testament is both a warning of imminent judgment and a promise of redemption. It is an appeal to righteousness and justification, whereby Qohelet admonishes that "God will bring every deed into

20. Gentry and Wellum, *Kingdom Through Covenant*, 808.

judgment, with every secret thing, whether good or evil" (Qoh 12:14). And it is hopeful, whereby Qohelet states, "Though a sinner does evil a hundred times and prolongs his life, yet I know that it will be well with those who fear God, because they fear before him" (Qoh 8:12). Hence, it is in the explicit appeal to judgment that Qohelet makes an implicit appeal to salvation. And it is Qohelet's projectile theme of judgment that follows a trajectory aimed at the revelation of the Messiah/Christ and the eschatological Day of the Lord entailing judgment and redemption.

Chapter 7

Qohelet as a Guide for Life in the Trajectory of Fallenness, Sustainment, and Judgment

Now that an analysis of Qohelet's correlation to the metanarrative of the Bible has been reviewed from its canonicity discussed in chapter 2 and its anticipation of redemption addressed in chapter 6, the applicability of Qohelet's theological trajectory can be better understood as a guide for life for every believer. Throughout the entirety of the Bible, there have been warnings against sin, the promise of sustainment in God's grace to persevere in righteousness, and the eschatological hope of withstanding in the final judgment for those who fear God and place their faith in the Son, Jesus the Messiah/Christ. Qohelet's theological trajectory of fallenness, sustainment, and judgment appeal to these core elements of the biblical message, thus making Qohelet a message of wisdom for guiding its reader to a life of righteousness and hope. Douglas Sean O'Donnell states, "I believe the best way to read Ecclesiastes is as (1) God's wisdom literature (2) with a unified message (3) that makes better sense in light of the crucified, risen, and returning Christ."[1] Hence, as mentioned previously, sensitivity and patience are crucial in the approach to Qohelet. If articulations of Qohelet's theological message are narrow, then conflict will inevitably arise between the interpretation and application of the text. It is only after analyzing all that has been discussed in the previous chapters that the applicatory

---

1. O'Donnell, *Ecclesiastes*, 4.

implications of Qohelet as a guide for life become coherent. By focusing on three points of discussion relating to the theological trajectory of Qohelet's projectile themes, the realities of life in the fallen state of humanity, life in the sustaining grace of God, and life in the imminent judgment inform our understanding of how humanity ought to live in the world while under the sun. While there is some overlap with the previous chapter, this chapter focuses on the applicability of Qohelet's theology to Christian living, whereby the universal appeal to righteous living in the fear of God functions as a guide for life that is correlated with the themes of fallenness, sustainment, and judgment.

LIFE AND THE FALLENNESS OF HUMANITY

The issue of sin has always been linked to the fallen state of humanity, whereby the wholesome nature and design in which God has created humankind have been depreciated and compromised by the effect of sinful disobedience. Daniel L. Akin and Jonathan Akin state, "When man rebelled against God's design (Gen 3), a frustrating curse was brought into the world. Now nothing works right, and we live in a broken world where we suffer the consequences of going our own way. Disease, death, poverty, evil, injustice, and more characterize our current existence."[2] This existence is strongly depicted in Qohelet as a primary emphasis for his teaching. While Qohelet understood that life is a gift from God, meant to be enjoyed in reverential fear of God, he nonetheless emphasized the reality of the fallen nature to bring a conscious awareness of sin to his audience. Theologically speaking, before Qohelet can appeal to righteous living in the fear of God, he must first appeal to the issues that war against humanity's ability to live righteously. Repeatedly, Qohelet uses the motif of "striving after wind" to depict a pursuit of selfish pleasure, a pleasure that is only meant to satisfy "the desires of the flesh and the desires of the eyes and pride of life" (1 John 2:16). According to the *Dictionary of Biblical Imagery*, "The most detailed account of the futility and disillusionment that attend an abandonment to pleasure occurs in Ecclesiastes 2:1–11, where the author decides to 'make a test of pleasure' by pursuing discreet sensuality, the acquisition of goods, sex and entertainment. But after keeping his 'heart from no pleasure,' he comes up empty: 'all was vanity and a striving after wind' (RSV)."[3] Hence, Qohelet

2. Akin and Akin, *Exalting Jesus in Ecclesiastes*, 7.
3. Ryken et al., *Dictionary of Biblical Imagery*, 653.

PART III. QOHELET'S THEOLOGICAL AFFINITY

teaches there is no gain in pursuing the false pleasures of sin. To chase after the sensual pleasures of sin and think that it will satisfy the desires of the flesh and the desires of the eyes and pride of life is like trying to take hold of wind and vapor as if it were something tangible. However, the pleasure of sin will never be enough to satisfy the void humanity has suffered from the fall. Depravation of the heart has become humanity's nature and reality from which moral virtue and principles have become impaired. This is not to say that humanity is unable to respond to God's appeal to righteous living, but that humanity is unable to do anything in and of themselves to be righteous and meet God's standards of glory (Pss 14:1–3; 53:1–3; Rom 3:10–12; 3:23). Millard J. Erickson states,

> Sin is inescapable. This fact is depicted in Scripture's frequent references to sinners as "spiritually dead" (Eph. 2:1–2, 5). This does not mean that sinners are absolutely insensitive and unresponsive to spiritual stimuli, but, rather, that they are unable to do what they ought. Unregenerate individuals are incapable of genuinely good, redeeming works; whatever they do is dead or ineffective in relationship to God.[4]

Consequently, the world becomes a vexation for the person striving after the pleasures of sin and self-indulgence. For this reason, Qohelet states, "What has a man from all the toil and striving of heart with which he toils beneath the sun? For all his days are full of sorrow, and his work is a vexation. Even in the night his heart does not rest. This also is vanity" (Qoh 2:22–23). Vexation is a state of unrest whereby the annoyance of greed and discontentment consumes the mind. Greed and discontentment lure people to chase after the false pleasures of sin by way of evil. However, Qohelet teaches that "evil will not save those who practice it" (Qoh 8:8 NASB20). In other words, sin has no regard for others and will lead a person to seek his gain by any means, even if it means hurting others (Qoh 8:9). At the heart of sin is rebellion that seeks to be like God and usurp his authority. According to 1 Sam 15:23a, "For rebellion *is as* the sin of witchcraft, and stubbornness *is as* iniquity and idolatry" (KJV). The Hebrew word used for stubbornness is פצר (*ptzr*). First Samuel 15:23a is the only place in the Bible that uses פצר (*ptzr*) in a sense conveying "rebellion against someone, arrogance."[5] In other words, when a person defies the word of God and thinks he knows better than God, he is being presumptuous, placing himself above God,

---

4. Erickson, *Introducing Christian Doctrine*, 206.
5. Baker and Carpenter, *Complete Word Study Dictionary*, 913.

which is sin and idolatry. Qohelet's theme of fallenness centers around this very issue of humanity's arrogance to fulfill his desires, teaching that all is vanity and a striving after wind (Qoh 1:2, 14).

What, then, is Qohelet really saying about sin in his projectile theme of fallenness? Zack Eswine states, "We remember Adam and Eve's season prior to their fall, and we learn again to long for that recovery while we are migrants here, worn out among the shanties."[6] In other words, Qohelet's theme of fallenness appeals to the pre-fall state of creation and humanity, whereby God establishes his human creation as his image bearers who are to function as his priest-kings. Peter J. Gentry and Stephen J. Wellum said, "Through this relationship, God's rule is extended in his people *and* to the creation, and we learn what it means to love our triune God and our neighbor."[7] Hence, Qohelet's teaching is not an expression of a man of distress or pessimism, as some might read it, but emphasizes the great curse imposed on creation due to sin. Qohelet's emphasis on the curse is meant to disrupt the ideologies of the world that have become rooted in the nature of humanity in order to guide them back to a life of righteousness that can only be attained in the reverential fear of God. To have the fear of God is to know the righteousness that comes from understanding the knowledge and wisdom of God while at the same time living in the righteousness of God. In other words, the person with the reverential fear of God lives according to the knowledge and wisdom of God, which results in righteousness. And the life lived in the fear of God is characterized by a life lived in worship of God through living out the righteousness of God in faith and obedience to God's commands. First Thessalonians 4:3–8 states,

> For this is the will of God, your sanctification: that you abstain from fornication; that each one of you know how to control your own body in holiness and honor, not with lustful passion, like the Gentiles who do not know God; that no one wrong or exploit a brother or sister in this matter, because the Lord is an avenger in all these things, just as we have already told you beforehand and solemnly warned you. For God did not call us to impurity but in holiness. Therefore, whoever rejects this rejects not human authority but God, who also gives his Holy Spirit to you. (NRSV)

Note how this passage starts with the phrase, "This is the will of God, your sanctification." Focusing on this phrase is very important because of

---

6. Eswine, *Recovering Eden*, 15.
7. Gentry and Wellum, *Kingdom Through Covenant*, 34.

the different semantic domains in which the Greek word ἁγιασμός—*hagiasmos* ("sanctification") can be used. In this phrase, "sanctification" is used as a noun in the domain of "consecration" and "dedication,"[8] to which the apostle Paul is attributing the will of God. In other words, the will of God is that to which the believer is consecrated and dedicated. It is the will of God by which he gives his Holy Spirit and the believer's sanctification is derived. It is the will of God that calls us to holiness, and the will of God is our sanctification.

All this is to say that it has never been God's will for his creation to live a meaningless life apart from him (Gen 1:26–31). But the reality is that life apart from God is meaningless and void of any absolute satisfaction, so that the human heart, consumed by its selfish desires, never finds rest. To this effect, Qohelet states, "This also, I saw, is from the hand of God, for apart from him who can eat or who can have enjoyment? For to the one who pleases him God has given wisdom and knowledge and joy, but to the sinner he has given the business of gathering and collecting, only to give to one who pleases God. This also is vanity and a striving after wind" (Qoh 2:24–26). Qohelet's evangelistic role of preaching to all nations aimed to win the hearts of his audience back to God. O'Donnell states, "The book was written to appeal to all nations (not just Israel), so that all people everywhere might recognize and return to the one universal Creator God (Gen. 1:1; cf. Eccl. 12:1)."[9] Hence, Qohelet's function as a guide for life is to first bring to the minds of his audience the reality of sin and the condition of creation and humanity. This is the first and necessary task of Qohelet's guide for life, in order that it may be shown how the grace of God has provided a way to navigate through the curse in righteousness, whereby joy in the hope and promise of redemption (i.e., to be made wholesome as in the pre-fall state) can be attained. The God-fearer does not seek to prolong his life in the world under the sun but instead seeks to live in glory and honor to God no matter the circumstances. In this, the God-fearer finds sustainment in the world of vanity. While no one has control over the paradoxes of human experience, all a person can do is trust in the provision of God to sustain life and seek to live in honor of God as if it were their last day on earth. Hence, life and the fallenness of humanity in Qohelet's theological trajectory is a warning against sin, functioning as a guide to fix our eyes on

---

8. Louw and Nida, *Greek-English Lexicon*, 538.

9. O'Donnell, *Ecclesiastes*, 36.

the Creator of heaven and Earth, who is unfolding his plans to restore the life corrupted by sin.

LIFE AND THE SUSTAINING GRACE OF GOD

Qohelet's projectile theme of sustainment orients his audience to God's providence, whereby hope in the Creator to fix what has been broken by the fall gives joyful strength to those who fear him. Although implicit, Qohelet hints at an appeal to God's merciful and graceful attributes, which are God's provision for sustaining humanity amid the fallen world so that they may persevere in righteousness amid the irony of human experience. In this appeal, the student who pays attention and listens closely to the words of Qohelet will find a guide for living in joyful contentment to the glory and honor of God. Hence, O'Donnell states,

> The idea of God's providence—his constant care of the world being *just*—comes from the final line: "and God seeks what has been driven away" (Eccl. 3:15), or, as the NIV translates it, "and God will call the past to account." This is a difficult phrase to translate and even more difficult to interpret. The sense seems to be that in the way God controls the times, he ends up balancing the scales of justice. For those who have lost out in life as the result of injustice, he redeems the time; and for those who have done injustice, he renders judgment in his time. On the last day, God will certainly call every action into account (11:9; 12:14)![10]

In other words, there is a sustaining effect in understanding God's providence and recognizing that all things on this earth and in life are in the hand of God (Qoh 2:24). Although the world is fallen and the heart of humanity is desperately sick (Jer 17:9), God's grace abounds (Rom 5:20). The frame narrator of Qohelet tells us that the words of Qohelet are wisdom and that "the words of the wise are like goads, and like nails firmly fixed are the collected sayings; they are given by one Shepherd" (Qoh 12:11). According to Tremper Longman III, "In brief, the frame narrator likens wisdom teaching to the goads that prod cattle into line and nails that are firmly fixed in their place. He also names their source as coming from a shepherd. In other words, the frame narrator uses figurative language to describe the origin and effects of wisdom teaching."[11] God has given humans access to

---

10. O'Donnell, *Ecclesiastes*, 78.
11. Longman, *Book of Ecclesiastes*, 278–79.

his wisdom, beginning with the reverential fear of God. Amid all the vexation, vanity, and strife in the human experience in the fallen world, Qohelet appeals to the fear of God, which is the beginning of wisdom (cf. Prov 1:7; 9:10) and the primary source for making the most out of life under the sun through righteous living and joyful contentment. Although Qohelet finds some issues with wisdom as a cause of vexation and a pursuit that can become a striving after wind, he also acknowledges that wisdom is better than folly and a gift to those who please God (Qoh 2:13, 25). In other words, despite the vexing effects of knowing too much, wisdom is, nonetheless, a thing to be grasped and valuable for preserving and sustaining life. Qohelet states, "Wisdom is good with an inheritance, an advantage to those who see the sun. For the protection of wisdom is like the protection of money, and the advantage of knowledge is that wisdom preserves the life of him who has it" (Qoh 7:11–12). In essence, Qohelet teaches that wisdom is a guide for good stewardship of life in the grace of God, which begins with wisdom that only comes from the reverential fear of the Lord. Commenting on Qoh 7:11–12, Iain Provan states, "Verses 11–12 sum up the value of wisdom for 'those who see the sun,' that is, for all human beings. It is like an 'inheritance' passed down through the generations so that those who now receive it may live well. It brings 'benefit' (*yoter*) to those who are its recipients."[12] Hence, Qohelet states, "Wisdom gives strength to the wise man more than ten rulers who are in a city" (Qoh 7:19). In parallel, Prov 21:22 states, "A wise man scales the city of the mighty and brings down the stronghold in which they trust." Speaking proverbially, Qohelet depicts wisdom as a vital tool and source for decision-making. Just as rulers are tasked with making decisions on a large scale of complex matters, the person who has been given wisdom is equipped to discern and deliberate issues of great matter for living. Longman states, "Qohelet here appears to give wisdom great value; he believes that a wise person is more capable and effective than a city's *ten leading citizens*."[13] Hence, the ability to discern and make wise decisions is vital to establishing a foundation of joy that strengthens the perseverance and sustainment of life. The concept of joy runs through the entire Bible, and it is no coincidence that Qohelet integrates the theme of joy with the theme of fallenness. The attribute of joy is integral to Qohelet's appeal to live in righteousness, whereby a person can find gladness in contentment. The Bible teaches that joy is an attribute of God, from which strength for

---

12. Provan, *Ecclesiastes, Song of Songs*, 141.
13. Longman, *Book of Ecclesiastes*, 197.

living derives. According to 1 Chr 16:26–27, "For all the gods of the peoples are worthless idols, but the LORD made the heavens. Splendor and majesty are before him; *strength* and *joy* are in his place" (emphasis added). Additionally, Prov 17:22 states, "A joyful heart is good medicine, but a crushed spirit dries up the bones." God's attribute of joy is not given to those who rebel against him but only to those who yield to him in faithfulness. On the contrary, those who rebel against God do not have joy and are constantly consumed with strife in trying to acquire more material and worldly gain (Qoh 2:26). But for the God-fearer, God has given a joy that endures and perseveres through every circumstance. Zack Eswine states, "With God, even amid the meaninglessness, the madness, the lament, and the cynicism, a human being 'will not much remember the days of his life because God keeps him occupied with joy in his heart' (Eccl. 5:20)."[14] Hence, for the life that is passing through under the sun, joy is a beautiful and wonderful gift that sustains those who fear God through the various trials of human experience. The apostle James exhorts the believer to "count it all joy when you meet trials of various kinds" (Jas 1:2). For James and the apostles, joy looked beyond life's current circumstances to a reward that lay ahead beyond the grave. First Peter 4:13 states, "But rejoice insofar as you share Christ's sufferings, that you may also rejoice and be glad when his glory is revealed." Qohelet's emphasis on joy shares the same vision of the apostles when he teaches the occupation of joy that God gifts keep the mind from being burdened with the strife and vexation of the fallen state. Instead, the beholder of joy is content with gladness and rejoices in their toil (Qoh 3:22; 5:19).

The ability to rejoice in one's toil is a gift of God's sustaining grace, whereby the responsibility of work is meant to preserve life. God has given the business to be busy in life to every human, but those who seek God find rest in the peace of his presence so that the God-fearer does not live consumed with vexation from the turmoil of life but in joy, gladness, and thanksgiving in the portion that has been given him under the sun (Qoh 3:9–13). The responsibility of work, although the imposition of the curse, is nonetheless an activity that consumes and diverts a person's mind from a constant pondering of life's futileness. Not only does a constant pondering of the futility of life enhance vexation, but it can also lead to depression, which is the opposite of joy. According to John D. Currid, "The unbeliever can easily be led into despair because he has no satisfactory answers.

---

14. Eswine, *Recovering Eden*, 33.

And, so, he often fills up his life with stuff. These are fleeting things that ultimately give no satisfaction. They are *hebel*."[15] On the contrary, the righteousness of the God-fearer stores up a treasure of inheritance and reward in heaven. Colossians 3:23–24 states, "Whatever you do, work heartily, as for the Lord and not for men, knowing that from the Lord you will receive the inheritance as your reward. You are serving the Lord Christ." Hence, it is this hope in God that sustains humanity. For Qohelet, apart from God, no one can find joy (Qoh 2:25). Joy only comes to the person who lets their garments always be white and oil not lacking on their head (Qoh 9:8). Enjoyment comes to those who recognize God as the giver and sustainer of life, being content and thankful to God for the rewards of their toil. Qohelet functions as a guide for life to the modern-day believer by teaching that no matter the circumstances life presents, there is still joy to be found amid the chaos of creation's fallenness. This joy is in the Lord and gives strength (Neh 8:10) that carries a person through the business of life, knowing that all things are in the hand of God (Qoh 2:24; 9:1). In essence, the presence of God in the Old Testament God-fearer had the same effect as the indwelling Spirit in the New Testament believer, whereby the apostle Paul states, "But we have this treasure in jars of clay, to show that the surpassing power belongs to God and not to us. We are afflicted in every way, but not crushed; perplexed, but not driven to despair; persecuted, but not forsaken; struck down, but not destroyed" (2 Cor 4:7–9). Speaking of the Holy Spirit in the Old Testament, Paul Jackson states,

> Not only did the prophets benefit from the influence of the Spirit, but also the Spirit will be shed upon the people of God (Isa. 44:3) and upon all the people (Joel 2:28). . . . The reception of the new Spirit, prophesied in Ezekiel and Jeremiah, is dependent upon repentance (Ezek. 18:31) and is associated with the creation of a new heart (Jer. 31:31–34). This prophetic foreshadowing, in light of the individual, sporadic, and temporary manifestation of the Spirit in the OT, looked forward to a time when the Spirit of God would revitalize His chosen people, empower the Messiah, and be lavishly poured out on all humankind.[16]

Hence, Qohelet's projectile theme of sustainment is a guide to life in its appeal to fear God and make the most out of life by remaining in the

---

15. Currid, *Ecclesiastes*, 56.
16. Paul Jackson, "Holy Spirit," in Brand et al., *Holman Illustrated Bible Dictionary*, 774.

constant state of enjoyment, whereby contentment is a motive for rejoicing. No matter how difficult life can become, "the end of the matter; all has been heard. Fear God and keep his commandments, for this is the whole duty of man" (Qoh 12:13). The human experience of vexation only proves our existence in life. However, it does not constitute the be-all and end-all of the God-fearer. As René Descartes, a father of modern philosophy, once stated, "I think, hence I am,"[17] asserting that he existed by the evidence of his ability to think and acquire knowledge, Qohelet asserts that a person exists when they are experiencing the business of life under the sun. Whether those experiences are love or hate (Qoh 9:1), fortune or misfortune, no one has complete control over their fate. However, for the righteous person who lives in the fear of God, Qoh 9:1 states, "The righteous and the wise and their deeds are in the hand of God." To live in the hand of God is to live in honor of God by following his commands. As Deut 33:3 states, "Yes, he loved his people, all his holy ones were in his hand; so they followed in your steps, receiving direction from you." Hence, although life is filled with paradoxical circumstances, the righteous are to rejoice in their existence and praise God, the giver and sustainer of life. Life in the sustaining grace of God is a life that understands it deserves nothing. It is a life that recognizes its very existence is only because of God's grace, and with everything life has to offer, it should be received with gratitude, wisdom, and joy. While there is an affliction in the burden of toiling, God has given the God-fearer the ability to enjoy the rewards of their toil (Qoh 5:19). And to have joy in a world of vanity and affliction is a God-given gift of sustainment, whereby those who fear God find hope for persevering in every day. Hence, Qohelet's projectile theme of sustainment is a guide for living in the stewardship of God's commands until the day of his promised redemption.

LIFE AND THE COMING JUDGMENT

Throughout the Bible, there have been warnings of an immediate and future judgment, a reality that is forced to be reckoned with in the book of Qohelet. Qohelet's theological end goal is an appeal to an event beyond death that will entail a judgment of all of humanity for every deed they have done, whether good or evil (Qoh 12:14). Since the fall, humanity has been in constant rebellion against God, and time and time again God has shown his great mercy by not giving humanity the annihilation that they truly

---

17. Descartes, *Method, Meditations and Philosophy*, 171.

PART III. QOHELET'S THEOLOGICAL AFFINITY

deserve. Nonetheless, there is a time coming that will be a day of reckoning for both the living and the dead (cf. Acts 10:42; 2 Tim 4:1; 1 Pet 4:5), and Qohelet understood this imminent reality. Hence, Alan P. Stanley states, "That God is the rightful 'Judge of all the earth' (Gen. 18:25) has been a stalwart of the biblical story from the beginning (e.g., 16:5; 31:53)."[18] For this reason, Qohelet's frame narrator concludes with an exhortation to fear God and obey his commandments as a duty given to every person living under the sun (Qoh 12:13–14). The Lord's forbearance in judging humanity for their sins is not to be misconstrued. According to the apostle Paul, God's forbearance was to show his righteousness "so that he might be just and the justifier of the one who has faith in Jesus" (Rom 3:26). In other words, God's promise of a seed (i.e., offspring) that would crush the serpent who deceived and corrupted humanity in the garden (Gen 3:15) has been revealed in Jesus, "whom God put forward as a propitiation by his blood, to be received by faith" (Rom 3:25). According to John Walton, "The traditional understanding, at least throughout church history, has been that in Genesis 3:15 we find the promise of victory and the first proclamation of a plan for God's redemption through his Messiah."[19] Hence, it is hopeful that Jesus, who will judge as the justifier, is also just in his judging and will judge righteously. Since there is no distinction in the guilt of humanity, there is no distinction in the approach to God for justification. All of humanity is guilty of offending God, as there is no righteous person who lives (Rom 3:10). And since all of humanity is in the same manner guilty before God, the Lord has provided one way and one way only (i.e., faith in Jesus Christ) for all to receive justification. Romans 3:21 states, "But now apart from the law the righteousness of God has been made known, to which the Law and the Prophets testify" (NIV). Here, the apostle Paul proclaims that the righteousness of God has been revealed apart from the law, implying that a definite and absolute means for justification is now attainable. This revelation is not a new means by which the law of God is replaced. Instead, this revelation is the means by which the law of God is fulfilled. And the Old Testament prophets have all borne witness to the infinite righteousness of God through their proclamation of judgment and redemption that would come through the promised seed, Jesus (cf. Rom 2:4–5; Gal 4:4).

Hence, Qohelet's projectile theme of judgment serves as a guide for life by pointing to a future reality applicable to all humanity. In every instance,

18. Stanley et al., *Four Views on the Role of Works*, 9–10.
19. Walton, *Genesis*, 233–34.

the word "judgment" in Qohelet refers to the final judgment that every person will face. The New Testament testifies to two types of judgments. The first type of judgment takes place at the βῆμα (bēma) seat of Christ. "βῆμα" is the Greek word for a "tribunal," which is defined as "a raised platform mounted by steps and usually furnished with a seat, used by officials in addressing an assembly, often on judicial matters—'judgment seat, judgment place.'"[20] According to Johannes P. Louw and Eugene Albert Nida, in the *Greek-English Lexicon of the New Testament*, "The association of a βῆμα with judicial procedures means that there is almost always an important component of judicial function associated with this term. Therefore in translating βῆμα, it is often best to use a phrase such as 'a place where a judge decides' or 'a place where decisions are made' or 'a judge's seat.'"[21] The apostle Paul tells the church in 2 Cor 5:10 that "we must all appear before the judgment seat [βῆμα] of Christ, so that each one may receive what is due for what he has done in the body, whether good or evil." Unlike the judgment of the wicked, this judgment is not to determine salvation, but rather, it is to determine the gifts the believer has earned based on his earthly deeds (1 Cor 3:11–15).

The second type of judgment occurs at God's great white throne, which is the final judgment that results in the second death of the wicked and those whose names are not found in the Book of Life (Rev 20:1–15). Qohelet gives the implication that the wicked will not survive the final judgment (Qoh 8:12–13), which is attested in Rev 20:14–15, as those judged by the great white throne judgment will be tossed into the lake of fire where the spirit experiences eternal death. Hence, the theme of judgment in Qohelet is essential to recognize as part of the grand terminus of Qohelet's message. Spanning the spectrum of human experience, Qohelet appeals to an endpoint beyond the grave. Although death of the body may be the end of a person's existence under the sun, it is not the ultimate finality. If the death of the body were the ultimate finality, then there would be no purpose in the judgment. Eswine states, "Beyond the grave, the Preacher maintains that there is more than an empty nothing or amnesia that awaits us. We have a future relationship with the One who created us, including his judgment for our treatment of him and others while we lived under the sun, and granting the final vindication of God and the purpose for which he created

---

20. Louw and Nida, *Greek-English Lexicon*, 91.
21. Louw and Nida, *Greek-English Lexicon*, 91.

us (Eccl. 3:17)."[22] In other words, God will have the final word (Qoh 12:14), and Qohelet is exhorting his audience to turn from their wicked ways and to live in the fear of God. For the God-fearer, there is freedom in the hope of surviving the judgment, giving reason to rejoice even amid the vexations of life under the sun (Qoh 9:9; 11:8–9).

Moreover, the judgment cannot be discussed apart from its redeeming factor. As there are two sides to a coin, there is judgment on one side and redemption on the other. As mentioned earlier, the prophets have all borne witness to the infinite righteousness of God through their proclamation of judgment and redemption through a coming Messiah. Hence, Qohelet's horizontal perspective of the "under the sun" motif is a rhetorical strategy intended to capture the minds of his listeners and take them from an explicit view of vanity under the sun to an implicit view of joyful hope in fearing God. Without properly articulating how the "under the sun" motif correlates to the plan of redemption unfolding throughout the entire canon of Scripture, how can we justify a God whom we know to be merciful and graceful in his love?[23] The realism of Qohelet is acknowledging the pessimism of life under the sun as a temporal reality while simultaneously believing in an eschatological hope of a better life for those who abstain from evil and persevere through the vexations of life in the fear of God. While recognizing that all of creation suffers a depreciative value from its fallen state (i.e., all things vanity under the sun), the only glimmer of hope that exists is in the eschatological reward of prolonged life (eternity) in the world to come (cf. Qoh 1:3 Targum Onkelos). Hence, Qohelet's rhetorical strategy consists of three major contextual elements (the context of a fallen world, joy in a world of affliction, and an eschatological appeal) whereby his audience is forced to reckon the value of life under the sun compared to the value of a hopeful reward in a world to come. Hidden in the contours of normalcy under the sun is a curse, often forgotten and unacknowledged. It is a curse of fallen creation veiled by the wicked deceit of secularism,

22. Eswine, *Recovering Eden*, 103.

23. God's love endures through the ages (Deut 7:9; Ps 119:90; Mal 3:6; Heb 13:8). The Christian faith hinges on the preeminence of God's love, which is the motive whereby he sent his Son Jesus Christ into the world to be the savior of those who believe in him (the incarnation; John 3:16). God's love is the foundation whereby every believer receives forgiveness of sins (the atonement; 1 John 2:2). God's love is the council, whereby he directs his followers to the way, truth, and life (the indwelling Holy Spirit; John 14:26). Furthermore, God's love is redeeming, whereby the sinner receives salvation and entry into a life of relationship and a surpassing knowledge of everlasting experience with the intra-trinitarian love of God (consummation; Matt 24).

defined by C. Stephen Evans as "a belief system, attitude or style of life that denies or ignores the reality of God. Derived from a term that means 'worldly,' secularism (and its articulate philosophical expression, secular humanism) focuses on the natural order of things as the only reality."[24] On the contrary, the book of Qohelet positively reflects a biblical worldview of redemption in the appeal to eschatological salvation accompanied by a redeeming judgment. With Qohelet's biblical background, he may have Ps 1 in mind while distinguishing the eschatological outcome of the righteous and the wicked. According to Ps 1:5–6, "The wicked will not stand in the judgment, nor sinners in the congregation of the righteous; for the LORD knows the way of the righteous, but the way of the wicked will perish." This passage parallels Qoh 8:12–13, stating, "Though a sinner does evil a hundred times and prolongs his life, yet I know that it will be well with those who fear God, because they fear before him. But it will not be well with the wicked, neither will he prolong his days like a shadow, because he does not fear before God." The Lord knows his people, those who are obedient, loyal, committed, and refrain from wickedness (2 Tim 2:19). The righteous has an identity in Christ as his children, and Jesus said that his children know him, and he knows his children as the Father knows him (John 10:14–15). Jesus prays to the Father on behalf of those who are his, asking that they may be with him in his kingdom and share in his glory (John 17:24), the redeeming hope of glory that sits on the other side of the judgment.

The judgment theme in Qohelet exhorts its audience to a spiritual formation that transforms a person's attitude toward life and God. Spiritual formation in the Old Testament hinged on the God-fearer's obedience to God and his commands. Qohelet directs his audience's focus back to the law of God and his ordinances for living a righteous and joyful life. In other words, Qohelet is an exhortation of wisdom that serves as a guide for life that purposely emphasizes the dark realities of fallen creation to admonish humanity away from sin and direct humanity back to the Creator. We learn from Qohelet that apart from God, life only succumbs to death, and not just death of the body, but an eternal death that is further revealed in the New Testament vision of eschatological judgment and redemption. However, having favor, unity, and communion with God is the basis for living a genuinely joyful and content life where grace that sustains life under the sun and hope that keeps anticipating eternity persist.

---

24. Evans, *Pocket Dictionary of Apologetics*, 106.

PART III. QOHELET'S THEOLOGICAL AFFINITY

It is difficult to discuss life's vanity without discussing humanity's fallenness and sin. It is difficult to discuss joy without discussing the grace of God that sustains humanity amid the fallenness. Moreover, it is difficult to discuss the judgment without discussing the redemption. That is because each of these factors represents an essential element in God's master plan for the redemption of all creation, as the apostle Paul states, "For the creation was subjected to futility [*mataiotēs*], not willingly, but because of him who subjected it, in hope" (Rom 8:20). Qohelet was preaching from the same perspective, evangelizing a gospel of hope and glory in the one true living God. Hence, Qohelet's function as a guide for life follows the projectile themes of fallenness, sustainment, and judgment, which all give testimony to humanity's sinful rebellion, God's gracious love, and God's preservation of those who fear him. It is a guide for life that follows the premise that humanity enters a fallen world, God sustains humanity amid the fallenness, and God preserves the lives of those who fear him on the day of judgment. This premise aims at a timeless, universal appeal to righteous living and eschatological hope in the fear of God.

Conclusion

*W*HILE MEANINGFUL ADVANCES HAVE *been made in the search for coherence in the literary approach to Qohelet's contradicting motifs, there is still an unsettled incoherency in the overlay of Qohelet's theology. However, in taking a thematic approach, the inconsistencies of Qohelet take on a function of thematic underpinning, whereby coherence in the course followed by the projectile themes of fallenness, sustainment, and judgment forms a framework guiding a theological trajectory aiming at an appeal to righteous living and eschatological hope.* What has been presented in the previous chapters sought to establish a coherent basis for reading and understanding Qohelet's framework and theological worldview. After all that has been discussed, concluding comments on the theological appeal in the trajectory of Qohelet will be offered, along with comments on the overall theological message of Qohelet as a coherent call to righteous living and eschatological hope. Additionally, a final proposal for reading and teaching Qohelet will be given in hopes that the reader, teacher, and student of Qohelet can find a more satisfying coherency in a thematic approach to its literary infrastructure. Hence, a final analysis of the theological trajectory of Qohelet will be presented in this concluding chapter, showing how a thematic approach focused on the theological themes guiding Qohelet's frame of thought allows for a coherence of less conjecture and more contextual affinity to the metanarrative of the Bible. As the book of Qohelet is an essential part of the biblical canon, it should be read and interpreted with fidelity to the testimony and character of God witnessed throughout biblical history. To accomplish these tasks, the appeal in Qohelet's thematic trajectory of fallenness, sustainment, and judgment must be recognized as a coherent call to righteous living and eschatological hope in the framework of Qohelet's theological worldview and systematic.

CONCLUSION

THE THEOLOGICAL APPEAL IN THE TRAJECTORY OF QOHELET

This study has sought to establish a basis for coherency in Qohelet's theological appeal by analyzing a thematic trajectory underpinned by the rhetoric of Qohelet's emphasis on vanity, joy, and judgment. These emphases follow what have been labeled *projectile themes*, which aim at particular points, carrying the audience from one thought to another. These thoughts are deeply correlated and best recognized as the substance forming Qohelet's framework from which Qohelet's teaching flows. In other words, Qohelet's thoughts, revealed by his thematic emphasis and endpoint, function as an evangelistic appeal to a theological worldview, whereby the minds and hearts of his audience are directed to a present and future reality in the fear-God concept. This present and future reality follows the premise that humanity enters a fallen world, God sustains humanity amid the fallenness, and God preserves the lives of those who fear him on the day of judgment.

A systematic approach is taken to establish a basis for coherency in Qohelet's thematic trajectory, whereby each part and chapter contributes to the understanding of Qohelet's projectile themes and overall theological appeal. Before analyzing the projectile themes of Qohelet's thematic and theological trajectory, it was essential to begin by establishing some background context on the world and book of Qohelet. Since the book of Qohelet falls within the wisdom corpus of the Bible, part 1 ("Background Analysis") of this study focused on providing a general and essential background on wisdom as an attribute and genre and a general and essential background on wisdom in the worldview of the ancient Near Eastern and Israelite cultures. The sole purpose of understanding wisdom as an attribute and genre and the perceptions of wisdom in the ancient Near Eastern and Israelite cultures is to establish a fundamental starting point for reading and studying Qohelet. As stated in chapter 1, by classifying literature into genres, rules are set for the author-reader relationship, whereby boundaries are determined by the author for how its audience should respond to and receive its message.[1] Additionally, understanding wisdom as an attribute in the cultural worldviews of the ancient Near East and Israel provides insight into these culture's expressed ethical and moral perceptions, which helps establish the significance of Qohelet's message as it pertains to his theology and view of the world.

---

1. See ch. 1, "Wisdom Tradition in the Ancient Near East and Israelite Culture," 23.

CONCLUSION

Once establishing a starting point for reading and studying Qohelet within the boundaries of its genre, it is essential to evaluate and recognize its canonicity as a book that stands alone, a book within the wisdom corpus of the Bible, and a book as part of the one story of the Bible. The canonicity of Qohelet is an essential factor that has been questioned too often throughout church history, and without a proper understanding of Qohelet and its contribution and placement in the metanarrative of the Bible, its credibility becomes doubted, and interpretations are asserted that contradict Qohelet's theology and worldview with the Bible's redemptive story and future anticipation of glory. However, with the proper understanding of Qohelet's canonicity, it can be asserted that Qohelet is in correlation with the one story of the Bible that testifies to the realities of human experience, the intervention of God, and the anticipated justice for those who fear God. Only then can a student of Qohelet maintain an interpretation that is in affinity and fidelity to the character of God and his divinely inspired word. Hence, the canonicity of Qohelet is a crucial factor in the search for coherency, whereby the theological appeal of Qohelet is shown to be a universal message of hope and redemption for all peoples and nations.

As universally appealing as Qohelet's message is, it would only make sense that Qohelet be the most qualified person in biblical history known to have encountered peoples of all nations and to possess vast, influential wisdom that would capture the attention of his nation's people and those with vastly different worldviews. The only king in the biblical record with such a degree of international reputation, known for his wisdom and influence, is King Solomon, whom the whole earth sought the presence of to hear his wisdom (cf. 1 Kgs 10:24). Qohelet's identity as Solomon is strongly depicted in his claims to be a teacher, the son of King David, and a king himself over Israel in Jerusalem (cf. Qoh 1:1, 12). Furthermore, the testimony of Qohelet's frame narrator depicts his identity as a wise teacher known for arranging proverbs with great care, which is in stark similarity with Solomon, the author of Proverbs. Hence, it is stated that "The Preacher sought to find words of delight, and uprightly he wrote words of truth" (Qoh 12:10). Some may argue from language that Qohelet has to be written centuries later. Still, a man of such vast wisdom, knowledge, and interaction with foreign nationals could very well be a reason for the use of loanwords.[2] Even then, there is no other depiction in the biblical history of a king in Israel with such fame and influence. Hence, the argument for Solomon as

---

2. See ch. 2, "Canonicity of Qohelet in the Wisdom Corpus and the Bible," 43–46.

the person of Qohelet allows for the best coherent approach to reading and studying Qohelet in that it presupposes a teacher of a learned theology and worldview that understands the history of the creation, its current condition, and future promise (Gen 3). With a Solomonic view of Qohelet's identity, coherency is more attainable in the thematic motifs underpinning the broader projectile themes of Qohelet's message (i.e., fallenness, sustainment, and judgment).

After gaining some background context into the book of Qohelet in part 1, part 2 ("Analysis for Coherence") discusses three modern scholarly attempts in the search for coherency in Qohelet and examines what has been labeled in this study as Qohelet's *projectile themes*. The presentation of Qohelet's projectile themes is where the thesis of this study is fleshed out in arguing for a thematic reading that emphasizes coherency in Qohelet's appeals to the themes of fallenness, sustainment, and judgment with his emphasis on the motifs of vanity, joy, fear God, and judgment. Furthermore, the framework of Qohelet depicted in the theological worldview gathered in the background analysis and the thematic trajectory depicted in the emphasized motifs of Qohelet help us understand the frame of thought from which Qohelet was teaching. Hence, after discussing previous attempts to find coherency in Qohelet from modern scholars, such as J. A. Loader, who argues for an "adequate literary explanation" of Qohelet in the tensions he calls "polar structures," Michael V. Fox, who argues that "harmonization is a proper and necessary part of the reading process of Qohelet," and Eunny P. Lee, who argues that the contradictions in Qohelet have "their place in the author's overall rhetorical strategy," the argument for the central thesis is presented. What is determined and asserted is that Qohelet's theological trajectory is a culmination of thematic underpinning inherent to the *projectile themes of fallenness, sustainment, and judgment*, whereby the supposed contradicting motifs, such as vanity and vexation, joy and gift, and judgment, take on a function of thematic grain carried along by the projectile themes guiding Qohelet's frame of thought aimed at an appeal to righteous living and eschatological hope. And it is in this message of Qohelet that the trajectory of fallenness, sustainment, and judgment coheres with the messianic vision of the Old Testament and the eschatological hope of the New Testament, whereby Qohelet's role takes on the function of an evangelist, apologist, and *preacher* whose message has become timeless and universally appealing to all peoples and nations.

CONCLUSION

Part 3 ("Qohelet's Theological Affinity to the Metanarrative of the Bible") is a crucial task in the search for coherency in Qohelet. This part is intended to tie up loose ends with any skepticism about Qohelet's canonicity and coherent contribution to the one story of the Bible. Chapter 6 shows how the projectile themes of fallenness, sustainment, and judgment in Qohelet are rooted in salvation history, aiming at a messianic and eschatological vision revealed in the New Testament. One of the injustices made by modern scholarly attempts is showing how Qohelet maintains affinity and fidelity to the metanarrative of the Bible. In examining what the New Testament reveals about Qohelet's theology in the context of sin (fallenness), grace (sustainment), and redemption (judgment), it becomes apparent that Qohelet has always been a vision of glory and redemption, whereby the applicability of Qohelet's theology to Christian living testifies to the themes of fallenness, sustainment, and judgment alluded in the New Testament's universal appeal to righteous living in faith and faithfulness to God in Christ Jesus.

Hence, the final task in this study's analysis of coherency in Qohelet's thematic trajectory is to show how Qohelet's theological appeal is a timeless, universal appeal applicable to the modern-day church. Throughout the Bible, God's redemptive work has been unfolding in the teachings and warnings against sin, the promise of sustainment in God's grace to persevere in righteousness, and the eschatological hope of withstanding in the final judgment for those who fear God. And now, the righteousness of God has been revealed in Jesus, the Messiah/Christ, who calls all people and nations to faith in him. Qohelet's theological trajectory of fallenness, sustainment, and judgment appeal to these core elements of the biblical message, thus making Qohelet a message of wisdom for guiding its reader to a life of righteousness and hope. Qohelet is, therefore, an essential book of the Christian canon that should be read with an emphasis on the projectile themes of fallenness, sustainment, and judgment, which coincide with the New Testament's appeal to the eschatological hope of redemption. God's call to righteousness, justification, and redemption in Jesus are core doctrines of the faith that affirm Qohelet's theological appeal in the thematic trajectory of fallenness, sustainment, and judgment, which function as a guiding light to life in the fear of God.

CONCLUSION

QOHELET AS A COHERENT CALL TO RIGHTEOUS LIVING AND ESCHATOLOGICAL HOPE

Righteousness and redemption are inherent to Qohelet's message, and his differentiating emphasis on the one who fears God and the wicked hints at the end target of his theological trajectory. Qohelet's end target is summed up in Qoh 12:12–14, stating, "My son, beware of anything beyond these. Of making many books there is no end, and much study is a weariness of the flesh. The end of the matter; all has been heard. Fear God and keep his commandments, for this is the whole duty of man. For God will bring every deed into judgment, with every secret thing, whether good or evil." Two points in this end-of-the-matter summary appeal to a call to righteous living and eschatological hope. First, there is the call to the priority of living in the fear of God. Rather than seeking what can never be fully attainable, the priority is for humanity to live not for their own earthly or material gain but for the glory, honor, and praise of the Creator. Second, there is the call to hope that the judgment of those who do good in the sight of God will be preserved. Hence, Qoh 12:14 brings the audience back to Qoh 8:12–13, stating, "Though a sinner does evil a hundred times and prolongs his life, yet I know that it will be well with those who fear God, because they fear before him. But it will not be well with the wicked, neither will he prolong his days like a shadow, because he does not fear before God." In other words, the end-of-the-matter summary of Qohelet's message redirects the audience from the vexing task of pursuing what lacks in value under the sun to a task that sustains and preserves humanity in the duality (i.e., the *already but not yet*) of the present and future realities. Zack Eswine states,

> Part of our help to pursue our human purpose also comes when recognizing that all the secrets of this vain life, along with everything good and evil, will be brought to light, sorted out, and set right. Every neighbor will stand before God to be judged by his good character (Eccl. 12:14).... For many of us, judgment scares, threatens, and spooks us. But for the Preacher, judgment blesses us. For in it, a distinction will finally be made which lost Eden has refused to own. "The righteous" and "the wicked" and their ways within their seasons and times, will finally hear what was and is true about them.[3]

---

3. Eswine, *Recovering Eden*, 221–22.

CONCLUSION

In chapter 7, it is mentioned that the judgment cannot be discussed apart from its redeeming factor, and furthermore, redemption cannot be discussed apart from its demand for righteousness. Qohelet knows this and, therefore, uses a rhetorical strategy of emphasizing what seems, on the surface, contradictory and negating of the biblical call to righteousness. Qohelet begins his teaching with an immediate appeal to the evil that has consumed the earth and humanity by dramatically stating, "Vanity of vanities, says the Preacher, vanity of vanities! All is vanity" (Qoh 1:2). In other words, the earth and humanity are broken, as Qohelet states, "What is crooked cannot be made straight, and what is lacking cannot be counted" (Qoh 1:15). Qohelet is describing a condition that every human can identify. Even atheists can identify with the vanity and vexation of life, but they cannot explain its reason or figure out its solution. Qohelet, however, has a solution that he hints at with subtlety. Kent Sparks notes, "Qohelet's intentions are frequently misunderstood by scholars who fail to understand his intellectual subtleties."[4] With Qohelet's six repeated references to fear God (Qoh 3:14; 5:7; 8:12–13; 12:13), Qohelet is shifting his appeal to a call to righteousness in the righteous God. Hence, taking a messianic and eschatological view, Daniel L. Akin and Jonathan Akin state, "Solomon lays out his exasperation over leadership failures (perhaps even convicted about his own failures), death, and the lack of justice in the world. The Teacher cries out for solutions to these problems, and Jesus is the answer to each!"[5] Throughout the Old Testament, the call to righteousness in the fear of God has appealed to covenantal response. Anyone who answers the call receives the gift of grace, whereby mercy and forgiveness of sins are given. Such a universal call to righteousness is testified in the pagan nation of Nineveh's repentance recorded in Jonah. Nineveh was a pagan nation, yet, out of his lovingkindness, God had mercy on them in their repentance (Jonah 3:5–10). Like the prophets of the Old Testament, Qohelet appealed to the nations by admonishing the idolatry of a self-indulgent world and admonishing them to turn away from selfish pleasures and live in the righteousness of God.

Qohelet's message hints at righteousness as a requirement for redemption—not a works-based redemption, but a basis of redemption rooted in glory, honor, and praise to the Creator. In other words, Qohelet teaches a way of life that brings glory, honor, and praise in the stewardship of what

---

4. Sparks, "In the Footsteps of the Sages," 81.
5. Akin and Akin, *Exalting Jesus in Ecclesiastes*, 58.

CONCLUSION

God has allotted each person. Hence, Qohelet states, "Behold, what I have seen to be good and fitting is to eat and drink and find enjoyment in all the toil with which one toils under the sun the few days of his life that God has given him, for this is his lot. Everyone also to whom God has given wealth and possessions and power to enjoy them, and to accept his lot and rejoice in his toil—this is the gift of God" (Qoh 5:18–19). In other words, Qohelet says people should be content and rejoice in what God has given them. It is only by God's gracious gift whether that person has much or little, and to steward life well in glory, honor, and praise to the Creator is to show gratitude with a heart of thanksgiving to God and good stewardship over the lot God has given. Essentially, Qohelet is appealing to stewardship rooted in the fear of God and his commands, whereby glory, honor, and praise are lived out in trust and reverence to God. According to Walter C. Kaiser Jr.,

> If we have been following our author's aim carefully, we should have added up all the parts of the preceding argument and concluded that the chief end of man is to "fear God and keep his commandments, for this is the 'manishness' of a man and 'womanliness' of a woman" (12:13). What is the "profit" of living? What does a man get for all his work? He gets the living God! And his whole profit consists of fearing Him and obeying His Word.[6]

Hence, Qohelet's call to righteousness is inherent to his appeal to joyful living in the fear of God. The person who despises God will never experience true joy, and those who do not have true joy will never be pleased and content with what God has given them. Their pursuits will only vex them because they are trying to fill a void the world cannot satisfy. As Qohelet states, "All things are full of weariness; a man cannot utter it; the eye is not satisfied with seeing, nor the ear filled with hearing" (Qoh 1:8). But for the God-fearer righteousness is lived out with satisfaction in God, whereby peace and hope in a redeeming reality become the priority for living. That is living not for what one might gain under the sun but for what one might gain beyond the sun when death of the body comes.

When read carefully, it is not difficult to see that Qohelet hints at the redeeming factor of judgment for the person who fears God and conducts their life in righteous living. Amid the appeal to vanity and strife in the fallenness of humanity and creation, it is the appeal to a time when each person will face a judgment of accountability for how they lived their lives under the sun. And the very element of judgment brings to full circle the coherent

---

6. Kaiser, *Coping with Change*, ch. 4, sect. D.

call to righteous living and the eschatological hope of redemption. Just as the apostle Paul was a Jew trained in the Scriptures (Acts 22:3), Qohelet also, being a king of the Jews, was raised in the religious customs and given vast wisdom by God, whereby he would have had a shared understanding with Paul on the eschatological hope of glory. That is a hope whereby the God-fearing, righteous person looks to the promises of God to restore creation. Hence, Edward M. Curtis states, "Thus Qoheleth points his readers to a path of God-centered living that the fuller revelation of the New Testament will affirm is the way to life as it was meant to be. It leads to a life that brings glory to God and brings blessing to the person who lives by faith; it is also the key to a life that generates a profit that death cannot erase."[7] Perhaps Qohelet has this view in mind when he states, "He has made everything beautiful in its time. Also, he has put eternity into man's heart, yet so that he cannot find out what God has done from the beginning to the end" (Qoh 3:11). Qohelet's appeal to eternity was not random. Just after he appeals to the cyclic times and seasons of human experience under the sun, Qohelet shifts his appeal to the heart's desire for eternity residing in every human. Qohelet's correlation of the seasons, restricted by time and governed under the sun, with eternity, which is not bound to time and exists beyond the sun, speaks to the mystery of God's intervening work from the beginning of creation to the end of time. However, if one must ask what end Qohelet meant if he had no view of something beyond the grave, it was the view of judgment, whereby "the Lord will seek out the one who is weak and poor from the hand of the wicked one that has persecuted him."[8] It is the end of time, when God makes all things new, ushering in the redemption of all creation (Rev 21:5), which is reminiscent of the same hope of redemption exhorted by the apostle Paul when he stated, "For the creation was subjected to futility, not willingly, but because of him who subjected it, in hope that the creation itself will be set free from its bondage to corruption and obtain the freedom of the glory of the children of God" (Rom 8:20–21). This hope is a testimony of God's love for his creation and his plan to bring about justice in his unfolding work of redemption for those who fear him (the righteous). David George Moore and Daniel L. Akin state, "Everything God does is eternally significant. When we are submissive to what he is seeking to accomplish, we find ourselves participating in the eternal as well."[9] Hence,

---

7. Curtis, *Ecclesiastes and Song of Songs*, 7.
8. Clem et al., *Targum Onkelos, Jonathan*, Eccl 3:15.
9. Moore and Akin, *Ecclesiastes, Song of Solomon*, 45.

CONCLUSION

Qohelet aims to instill a perspective of eternity that already exists in the hearts of his audience. A perspective that encourages righteous living and hope for a time when the human experience will be in the fullness of glory, whereby the redeemed (i.e., those who are preserved in the judgment) enter into the reality of eternity. In reading Qohelet, it is essential to recognize the hints that give nuance to the coherent call to righteous living and the eschatological hope in the fear of God, whereby, in the coherency of these appeals, Qohelet testifies to the one story of the Bible, unfolding throughout history and God's redemptive plan.

READING AND TEACHING QOHELET

Reading Qohelet has always been challenging, as demonstrated by the various interpretations and scholarly attempts to find coherence in its message.[10] On the one hand, Qohelet has been misconstrued as an emotional monologue of despair from an old king who is frustrated with life. On the other hand, Qohelet has been misconstrued as a nonsensical, ill-advised compilation of isolated discourses of contradictions. Sidney Greidanus states, "A major reason for this difficulty is that Old Testament scholars are not agreed on key issues: the number of authors involved in writing this book; the identity of the main author; when, where, and why the book was written; the quality of the Hebrew style; which sections are poetry and which are prose; the book's structure, or lack thereof; and whether its message is pessimistic or positive."[11] This study has addressed some of these issues, primarily on authorship, language, style, and hermeneutical approach.[12] While all of these issues will play a role in a person's interpretation, the hermeneutical approach is often the driving factor. However, the most incoherent views on Qohelet have frequently resulted from a strictly literary approach focused on isolating words, phrases, and textual units. While the literary approach has been the traditional approach to biblical commentaries, modern scholarship has now concentrated on theological themes as an interpretive thread tying all other textual elements together. Hence, it is recommended that the approach to reading Qohelet be a thematic approach depicted from its literary infrastructure rather than

---

10. Refer to ch. 2, "Canonicity of Qohelet in the Wisdom Corpus and the Bible," and ch. 4, "Modern Scholarly Attempts to Find Coherency in Qohelet."

11. Greidanus, *Preaching Christ from Ecclesiastes*, 1.

12. Refer to part 1, "Background Analysis," and part 2, "Analysis for Coherence."

a literary approach isolating its words, phrases, and textual units from its theological significance and correlation. In doing so, the overarching themes of Qohelet take precedence and reduce the risk of being negated to the detriment of a proper and meaningful interpretation that maintains an affinity to the canonicity of Qohelet and fidelity to the character and promises of God witnessed throughout the entirety of the Bible. Richard Alan Fuhr Jr. and Andreas J. Köstenberger state, "Interpretive *correlation* involves allowing the Bible to function as its own best commentary through linguistic, grammatical, literary, and topical parallels."[13] Such parallels often function as thematic grain inherent to the book's theological themes. As stated earlier in the introduction, biblically speaking, when themes transcend an individual book, there is an implication that external factors and sources are likely influencing the author's frame of thought.[14] When a motif is repeated in the content of a book, this typically functions as a clue toward the subject matter. Motifs help guide the reader to a coherent reading and keep the reader in tune with the author's flow of thought, whether implicitly or explicitly expressed. In the case of Qohelet, a book undoubtedly challenging to read with any immediate coherency, it requires a crucial level of sensitivity and patience when reading and interpreting.

The concept of projectile themes presented as an approach to Qohelet in this study[15] represents a thematic reading approach that focuses on drawing theological connections between the words, phrases, and literary units of Qohelet and its overarching contextual background. This approach begins by learning as much background about the book, its author, and its audience before making any endeavor to make sense of its content. The background context consists primarily of the historical-cultural, literary, and theological context, allowing for a more accurate and coherent reading. Fuhr and Köstenberger state, "Concerning accurate interpretation, perhaps the most important principle to remember is the contextual principle. The contextual principle simply affirms that the text of any portion of Scripture must always be understood within the confines of its historical-cultural, literary, and theological-canonical context."[16] In reading Qohelet, it is recommended to begin with a historical-cultural and literary analysis, whereby

13. Fuhr and Köstenberger, *Inductive Bible Study*, 40.
14. Refer to introduction, "The Concept of Projectile Themes."
15. Refer to introduction and ch. 5, "Coherency in the Theological Trajectory of Qohelet's Projectile Themes."
16. Fuhr and Köstenberger, *Inductive Bible Study*, 24.

contextual knowledge of the genre, text structure and style, cultural origins, date of composition, the life of the author, and identification of audience are discovered. Although these contextual elements, such as the author or audience, may not always be identifiable, literary clues can often lead to highly plausible assumptions, such as the case for the Solomonic authorship and universal audience of Qohelet. In essence, establishing a contextual basis from a historical-cultural and literary analysis can be thought of as establishing the plot of a story that is essential to reading comprehension. Once the historical-cultural context has been established, the literary context can be evaluated by careful reading, paying close attention to literary structure, catchwords, and phrases, such as literary devices and thematic motifs. One of the challenges to reading Qohelet is its frequent shift in thought, as if Qohelet was attempting to fit all of life's experiences into this one sermon to make his point. Nonetheless, every word of Qohelet's message is vital to his rhetorical strategy and concluding thought, so it is important to avoid drawing immediate conclusions in the literary analysis.

When reading Qohelet thematically, it is essential to recognize thematic units that correlate with the overall message of the Bible in light of its context. In other words, to discover any meaningful theological significance in Qohelet, a correlation must be drawn from each literary unit, catchword, or phrase to the broader themes (e.g., projectile themes) charting Qohelet's frame of thought. Fuhr and Köstenberger make two points regarding establishing a book's theological and canonical context:

> *Theological* context tends to emphasize the covenant relationship that God has with his people and the representation of that relationship in the progression of salvation history. . . . *Canonical* context concerns not just the place in the timetable of revelation in which a biblical writer lived or wrote but also the way in which individual books of the Bible function together to form one comprehensive book.[17]

Theological and canonical contexts should always maintain affinity and fidelity to the overall message of the Bible. Hence, when reading Qohelet, it helps to ask if our interpretation of Qohelet contradicts the message and character of God witnessed throughout the Scriptures. If there is any inkling of contradiction, it may be necessary to take another reading and more time to meditate on the discourse at hand, whereby the sensitivity and patience aspect of reading Qohelet comes into play. As stated earlier, if

---

17. Fuhr and Köstenberger, *Inductive Bible Study*, 27.

the articulations of Qohelet's theological message are narrow, conflict will inevitably arise between the interpretation and application of the text.

Reading and interpretation have an inevitable impact on teaching. Improper reading leads to misinterpretation and incorrect teaching that disservice those learning. It is essential to recognize that different books may require different approaches. Hence, when it comes to teaching Qohelet, the thematic approach should be maintained, emphasizing Qohelet's theological themes that encapsulate the entirety of the text. Only because of the vast rhetorical devices Qohelet uses throughout his teaching can these theological themes be presented as a series, whereby each theme functions as a critical point that can be taught in succession, such as the projectile themes of fallenness, sustainment, and judgment presented in this study. As overwhelming as Qohelet can be for any experienced reader, it can be just as much or more challenging for a less skilled reader. Hence, whether teaching Qohelet in a sermon or a small Bible study, the best approach would be to use a series of successive lessons that follow a systematic and coherent trajectory derived from a careful exposition. According to Andreas J. Köstenberger and Richard D. Patterson, "Once you have done your exegesis, you are ready to begin preparing your sermon or Bible study. While a study or sermon may take many forms—topical, textual, or expository—our primary concern is to prepare an expository message. It is our conviction that the majority of preaching should be expository, that is, explaining a biblical text."[18] Especially in the context of Qohelet, it is hardly a book that would allow for a topical approach. Qohelet contains too many rhetorical shifts, from which the most basic reading does not appear linear in thought. Scholars have been referring to these shifts as the supposed contradictions of Qohelet. Nonetheless, Qohelet's textual shifts from vanity to joy to judgment can be correlated with its broader themes of fallenness, sustainment, and judgment, which in turn correlate with the metanarrative of sin, grace, and redemption of the Bible's one story. Hence, the hermeneutical process requires careful observation, whereby themes are discovered and classified into a coherent system of thought, and the emphasis on Qohelet's theological motifs (e.g., vanity, joy, judgment) establishes the framework for reading and teaching Qohelet in any setting, allowing for a more coherent exposition and fruitful service to those learning.

How often do we hear Qohelet preached from the pulpit? Or how often do we hear of a small group focusing on teaching through the book of

---

18. Köstenberger and Patterson, *Invitation to Biblical Interpretation*, 741.

CONCLUSION

Qohelet? A verse of Qohelet may be used as a cross-reference from time to time but is rarely expounded upon in a sermon. Greidanus quotes D. Brent Sandy and Ronald L. Giese, stating,

> The Book of Ecclesiastes is one of the most important possessions of the Christian church, since it compels us to continually evaluate and correct our understanding of God and our teaching about God in the light of the whole of biblical revelation. . . . The reflections of the sage in Ecclesiastes unmask the myth of human autonomy and self-sufficiency and drive us in all our frailty and inability to find meaning in a crooked world in the Creator-creature relationship—the ultimate polarity.[19]

In essence, Qohelet gives us a glimpse into an evangelistic approach to proclaiming God's sovereignty, goodness, and justice to the world. As stated earlier, Qohelet takes on the role of an evangelist, apologist, and *preacher*, whereby his message functions as a universal appeal for all nations. In his message, Qohelet coheres with the messianic vision of the Old Testament and the eschatological hope of the New Testament gospel.[20] For this reason, Qohelet must be taught as a whole, whereby the totality of Qohelet's trajectory from the fallenness of humanity, the sustaining grace of God, and the redeeming hope of glory for those who fear God is conveyed to a lost and hopeless world and a misunderstood church. Teaching from Qohelet holds one of the most significant values to the church, reminding us of the redemptive-historical progression and the hope of a promised fulfillment of Messiah/Christ.

On the one hand, teaching Qohelet from the view of the redemptive-historical progression follows the trajectory of God's redemptive plan unfolding through the ages of human history, whereby longitudinal themes can be traced from the Old Testament to New Testament progression of salvation history. On the other hand, teaching Qohelet in light of the New Testament revelation of Messiah/Christ and the gospel of Jesus points to a future eschatological hope and judgment, whereby the promise of eternal life to those who have been justified and made righteous by placing their faith in the Son of God maintains affinity to the continuity of the *missio Dei* (mission of God) to bring about the restoration of all creation. As Qohelet's theological worldview expressed in his rhetoric was intended to persuade

19. Greidanus, *Preaching Christ from Ecclesiastes*, 2.
20. Refer to ch. 5, "Coherency in the Theological Trajectory of Qohelet's Projectile Themes."

his audience to hope for a future state of glory, whereby those who fear God will stand in the day of judgment and receive the reward of entry into a world to come, the new heaven and new Earth (Rev 21), our teaching of Qohelet shall remain the same. No matter what approach a person takes to teach Qohelet, they should always seek and strive to maintain affinity with the metanarrative of the Bible and fidelity to the character of God. Hence, the suggestion here is to read and teach Qohelet from a thematic approach that is sensitive to the redemptive-historical progression and longitudinal themes of the Bible that maintain an affinity between Qohelet's theology and the one story of the Bible.

Appendix:
Chart of Correlating Themes and Passages in Qohelet

THE FOLLOWING CHART ILLUSTRATES the correlation between passage units (units of thought) within Qohelet and their correspondence with the projectile themes of fallenness, sustainment, and judgment. Although there may be some thematic overlap within these passages, their correlation is linked to Qohelet's main thought expressed in each unit. While all passage units may not explicitly reference the themes of fallenness, sustainment, and judgment, there is nonetheless an implicit reference to these themes stemming from Qohelet's rhetoric and frame of thought. Therefore, the chart is divided into three columns representing each projectile theme (thematic columns), and a fourth column summarizes each passage unit listed under each thematic column. While the passage summary is not intended to be an interpretive exposition of each unit, it is a summary of what is believed to be Qohelet's main point, giving implications to each passage unit's respective thematic correlation.

APPENDIX: CHART OF CORRELATING THEMES AND PASSAGES

Chart of Correlating Themes and Passages in Qohelet

Fallenness	Sustainment	Judgment	Passage Summary
Qoh 1:2–11			All is vanity! The cycles of life and the spheres of the Earth continue while the dead are forgotten.
Qoh 1:12–18			Seeking wisdom is vanity. Too much wisdom is vexing, and too much knowledge brings sorrow.
Qoh 2:1–11			A person can fill their heart with self-indulging pleasures, earthly treasures, and rewards only to find that all they expended in achieving and acquiring was vanity and striving after wind. In the end, it amounts to nothing of value. Not worth it!
Qoh 2:12–17			Wisdom is compared to light and folly to darkness. Light is better than darkness, with much more to gain. However, although wisdom is better than folly, the wise are no better than the foolish. The wise and the foolish face life's experiences the same way.
Qoh 2:18–23			The toil of life is vexing and vanity in that it leaves no value. In the end, it cannot be taken with you but is passed on to someone who did not work for it and did not give any expense of wisdom and strife for it.
	Qoh 2:24–26		Although there is vexation and vanity in toiling and its rewards, we should find enjoyment and make the soul see good in them. Enjoyment is from God, and all we do is in the hand of God. Meaningful enjoyment in the toil of life and its rewards can only be truly experienced when pursued in honor of God.
	Qoh 3:1–8, 11		There is no rest under the sun. Life under the sun is filled with many matters, and there is a season for every one of them. Still, God has made everything beautiful in its time.

APPENDIX: CHART OF CORRELATING THEMES AND PASSAGES

Fallenness	Sustainment	Judgment	Passage Summary
	Qoh 3:9–15		The business of being busy is both a curse (an effect of the fall) and a blessing (a sustaining grace of God to preserve man). God has placed a desire for eternity in the hearts of humanity. The paradox is that although we have a longing and desire for things eternal (e.g., life, rewards, pleasure, wisdom), we still cannot fathom what God has done from the beginning to the end. It is reiterated that we should find enjoyment and make the soul see good in the toil and its rewards (e.g., eating and drinking). God's sustainment in the vexing and strife of toiling is in the joy that comes from him.
		Qoh 3:16–17	There is a time for every matter and work, including the judgment of both the righteous and the wicked.
Qoh 3:18–21			All men will die, whether righteous or wicked. They will both go back to the dust as man was created.
	Qoh 3:22		Humanity should enjoy the rewards of their toil while they have life. Joy in their toil is a God-given gift of grace and sustainment.
Qoh 4:1–3			There is a vexing evil under the sun that impinges on the value of life.
Qoh 4:4–8			Toiling in envy and covetousness is striving after wind. It is never satisfying and leaves a person deeply unhappy.
	Qoh 4:9–12		Two are better than one. The toil is shared, and the rewards are pleasurable. Two can lift each other up when they become weary.
Qoh 4:13–16			Wisdom can elevate a person to a higher status, and foolishness can lower a person to a lower status. In the end, it does not matter. The poor man who is elevated to a king will not be remembered.
		Qoh 5:1–7	Fear God and give him reverence, lest God be angry and destroy the work of your hands!
Qoh 5:8–17			There is evil in the love of wealth and the love of money.

APPENDIX: CHART OF CORRELATING THEMES AND PASSAGES

Fallenness	Sustainment	Judgment	Passage Summary
	Qoh 5:18–20		A person should take joy in their toil and wealth as the gift of God! For joy itself is a gift that preoccupies the mind amid the evil vexation and strife of the world.
Qoh 6:1–9			Evil and vexation in wealth are caused by greed—never satisfied and never content, but always hungry (appetite) and wanting more.
Qoh 6:10–12			Better are the eyes that see good and reason for content than the appetite that only hungers for more wealth. The appetite never rest but spends life in toil for something lacking value.
		Qoh 7:1–2	Consider what happens after death. People are too fixated on life under the sun and live like they will never die. This could lead to many different evils. However, the judgment will come for all as death comes to all.
	Qoh 7:3–4		Gladness is renewed in the heart in sorrow, and the wise person in a house of mourning remains humble.
	Qoh 7:5–10		The foolish do not rejoice in God's goodness. They celebrate the temporary, worthless goods of the world. But the lowly and wise see God's goodness and look ahead with joy and patient endurance.
		Qoh 7:11–18	God is sovereign. Foolishness can also destroy people and make them wicked, so it is better to grasp wisdom and humility (fear of God) than foolishness and wickedness. The God-fearer will be sustained.
		Qoh 7:19–22	Wisdom is great, but it does not prevent a person from sinning. Have mercy and grace toward the offense of others, as you have also been guilty of offense.
Qoh 7:23–29			The wickedness of folly and the foolishness of madness (sin) lure a person to trap and snare them. God made humanity to be upright, yet they have rebelled against God.
	Qoh 8:1		There is peace in wisdom. There is a countenance that derives from knowledge and understanding (perception/perspective) that changes a man's hardness to joy!

APPENDIX: CHART OF CORRELATING THEMES AND PASSAGES

Fallenness	Sustainment	Judgment	Passage Summary
		Qoh 8:2–5	There seems to be a possible allusion to God's kingship. Although there is wisdom here for human relations to kingship under the sun, Qohelet also had a king to whom he was accountable, and that king was Yahweh. It is possible that these verses were spoken with the kingship of Yahweh in mind, and those who keep his command (fear God) will be preserved in judgment.
		Qoh 8:6–9	Back to the times and seasons for everything under the sun, no one knows what will happen from one day to the next, and there is no way of escaping the death of the body. Here, there is a reference to the detriment of wickedness, which may be an implication of the second death of the wicked (the spiritual death/to his hurt).
		Qoh 8:10–13	The deeds of the wicked will not go without judgment. The wicked do not see the penalties and consequences of their deeds when they continuously get away with them. Hence, their wickedness increases. Although the wicked get away with their evil deeds in this life, they will still be held accountable to God on the day of judgment. But Qohelet says *he knows* it will go well for the God-fearer (on the day of judgment). The God-fearer will have prolonged days in the next life. Qohelet is contrasting the prolonged days of the wicked under the sun with the prolonged days of the God-fearer in the next life.
Qoh 8:14			The paradox is that good things happen to bad people and bad things to good people. There is nothing anyone can do about that.
	Qoh 8:15–17		Although no one can ever fully understand God's ways, the best thing to do is rejoice in the life that God has given. Though toil and uncertainties are an affliction, joy is still possible when realizing that God, who gives and sustains life, is in control.

APPENDIX: CHART OF CORRELATING THEMES AND PASSAGES

Fallenness	Sustainment	Judgment	Passage Summary
		Qoh 9:1–2	The deeds and the lives of the righteous and the wicked are in God's hands. Love (life) or hate (death) awaits them in the judgment! Death and judgment are the same for all, just as it is the same for all under the sun.
Qoh 9:3			It is an evil affliction that the same events happen to everyone. This is due to the fallenness of humanity and creation. The cause of evil is humanity who live their lives full of evil.
	Qoh 9:4		There is hope for those who have not died in their evilness. Even the one who is alive in the lowest state (humility) is better than the one who lived in the highest state (arrogance) and is now dead. For the living, there is hope for repentance.
Qoh 9:5–6			The living are conscious and known. The dead have no consciousness and are not remembered. Their love (for wealth and power), their hate (toward others), and their envy (covetousness) die with them.
	Qoh 9:7–10		Qohelet exhorts the value of being joyful in the gifts of God as he approved of the rewards of our toil. Take pleasure in them. We are reminded that two are better than one. The two are even better when there is love and youth. There is an advantage to bearing the weight of the toil for the husband and wife. They can share in the burdens and the rewards. They can share joy and celebration. Find enjoyment and make the soul see good in life under the sun. Everyone gets one life under the sun, a gift from God, regardless of the strife. So make the best of it.
Qoh 9:11–12			Life is filled with uncertainty. No one knows the time or day they will die. Death has its origin in evil, and it is an affliction to the fallen world, and it could befall humanity at any time.
	Qoh 9:13–18		Wisdom is mighty, with the power to keep people safe and sustain humanity. However, wisdom among fools is despised and not remembered.
		Qoh 10:1–3	Even a little foolishness can ruin the reputation of the wise.

APPENDIX: CHART OF CORRELATING THEMES AND PASSAGES

Fallenness	Sustainment	Judgment	Passage Summary
Qoh:10:4–11			The lack of wisdom leads to foolish decisions and danger.
Qoh 10:12–15			The words of a fool are vain and lead to evil madness.
	Qoh 10:16–20		A nation is strong and prosperous with a wise king, and people are beyond reproach when they maintain reverence for their king.
	Qoh 11:1–6		This is a reminder that no one knows what will happen from one day to the next. The mystery of what is to be is best left in God's hands.
		Qoh 11:7–10	Life is good despite its vexations. If a person lives long under the sun, he should rejoice, especially in his youth, but remember that life will inevitably have its evils. It is good to enjoy life but know that God will bring every deed into judgment.
	Qoh 12:1–8		Hold fast to the trust you had in God in your youth, in the days of innocent youth, before the vexations and vanities of life became your experience. Remember God and hold fast to the reverential fear you had for him as a youth, and never let that depart all the days of your life under the sun.
		Qoh 12:9–14	The whole duty of humanity is to fear God and keep his commandments, knowing that God will bring every deed into judgment, whether good or evil.

Bibliography

Akin, Daniel L., and Jonathan Akin. *Exalting Jesus in Ecclesiastes*. Christ-Centered Exposition Commentary. Nashville: B&H, 2016.

Baker, Warren, and Eugene Carpenter. *The Complete Word Study Dictionary: Old Testament*. Chattanooga, TN: AMG, 2003.

Barnes, William H. *1–2 Kings*. Cornerstone Biblical Commentary 4B. Carol Stream, IL: Tyndale House, 2012.

Bartholomew, Craig G. *Ecclesiastes*. Baker Commentary on the Old Testament Wisdom and Psalms. Grand Rapids, MI: Baker, 2009.

Barton, John, and John Muddiman, eds. *The Oxford Bible Commentary*. Oxford: Oxford University Press, 2001.

Beale, G. K. *The Book of Revelation: A Commentary on the Greek Text*. New International Greek Testament Commentary. Grand Rapids, MI: Eerdmans, 1999.

———. *We Become What We Worship: A Biblical Theology of Idolatry*. Downers Grove, IL: IVP, 2018.

Blocher, Henri. "Yesterday, Today, Forever Time, Times, Eternity in Biblical Perspective." *Tyndale Bulletin* 52.2 (2001) 182–201.

Blomberg, Craig L. *Matthew*. The New American Commentary 22. Nashville: Broadman & Holman, 1992.

Boda, Mark J. *1–2 Chronicles*. Cornerstone Biblical Commentary 5A. Carol Stream, IL: Tyndale House, 2010.

Brand, Chad, et al., eds. *Holman Illustrated Bible Dictionary*. Nashville: Holman Bible, 2003.

Bray, Gerald L., and Thomas C. Oden, eds. *We Believe in One God*. Ancient Christian Doctrine 1. Downers Grove, IL: IVP, 2009.

Brueggemann, Walter. *Solomon: Israel's Ironic Icon of Human Achievement*. Studies on Personalities of the Old Testament. Columbia, SC: University of South Carolina, 2005.

Carpenter, Eugene. "קֹהֶלֶת." In *NIDOTTE* 3:887.

Chang, Frances Tsai-Fen. "Suffering and Enjoyment/Hope in the Progress of Revelation: Qohelet and Romans 8:18–39." PhD diss., Dallas Theological Seminary, 2011. https://www.proquest.com/pqdtglobal/docview/885129002/abstract/6FDF4543BF914F7BPQ/1.

Clem, Eldon, et al., eds. *Targum Onkelos, Jonathan, and the Writings (English)*. Accordance electronic ed. Altamonte Springs, FL: OakTree Software, 2014.

Coleson, Joseph. "Joshua." In *Joshua, Judges, Ruth*. Cornerstone Biblical Commentary 3. Carol Stream, IL: Tyndale House, 2012.

BIBLIOGRAPHY

Crenshaw, James L. *Qoheleth: The Ironic Wink.* Columbia, SC: University of South Carolina Press, 2013.

Currid, John D. *Ecclesiastes: A Quest for Meaning: Ecclesiastes Simply Explained.* Welwyn Commentary Series. Welwyn Garden City, UK: EP, 2016.

Curtis, Edward M. *Ecclesiastes and Song of Songs.* Teach the Text Commentary. Grand Rapids, MI: Baker, 2013.

———. *Interpreting the Wisdom Books: An Exegetical Handbook.* Handbooks for Old Testament Exegesis. Grand Rapids, MI: Kregel, 2017.

Descartes, Renè. *The Method, Meditations and Philosophy of Descartes.* Translated by John Vietch. Universal Classics Library. London: M. Walter Dunne, 1901.

Dodson, Derek S., and Katherine E. Smith, eds. *Exploring Biblical Backgrounds: A Reader in Historical and Literary Contexts.* Waco, TX: Baylor University Press, 2018.

Easton, M. G. *Illustrated Bible Dictionary and Treasury of Biblical History, Biography, Geography, Doctrine, and Literature.* New York: Harper & Brothers, 1893.

Eaton, Michael A. *Ecclesiastes: An Introduction and Commentary.* Tyndale Old Testament Commentaries 18. Downers Grove, IL: IVP, 1983.

Elwell, Walter A., and Robert W. Yarbrough. *Encountering the New Testament: A Historical and Theological Survey.* 3rd ed. Encountering Biblical Studies. Grand Rapids, MI: Baker, 2013.

Enns, Peter. *Ecclesiastes.* The Two Horizons Old Testament Commentary. Grand Rapids, MI: Eerdmans, 2011.

Erickson, Millard J. *Introducing Christian Doctrine.* Edited by L. Arnold Hustad. 2nd ed. Grand Rapids, MI: Baker, 2001.

Estes, Daniel J. *Handbook on the Wisdom Books and Psalms.* Grand Rapids, MI: Baker, 2005.

Eswine, Zack. *Recovering Eden: The Gospel According to Ecclesiastes.* The Gospel According to the Old Testament. Phillipsburg, NJ: P&R, 2014.

Evans, C. Stephen, ed. *Pocket Dictionary of Apologetics and Philosophy of Religion.* Downers Grove, IL: IVP, 2002.

Farmer, Kathleen A. *Who Knows What Is Good? A Commentary on the Books of Proverbs and Ecclesiastes.* International Theological Commentary. Grand Rapids, MI: Eerdmans, 1991.

Ferguson, Everett. *Backgrounds of Early Christianity.* Grand Rapids, MI: Eerdmans, 2003.

Firth, David G., and Lindsay Wilson, eds. *Exploring Old Testament Wisdom: Literature and Themes.* London: Apollos, 2016.

Fox, Michael V. *Ecclesiastes.* The JPS Bible Commentary. Accordance electronic ed. Philadelphia: JPS, 2004.

———. *Qohelet and His Contradictions.* Decatur, GA: The Almond, 1989.

———. *A Time to Tear Down and a Time to Build Up: A Rereading of Ecclesiastes.* Eugene, OR: Wipf & Stock, 2010.

Fredericks, Daniel C., and Daniel J. Estes. *Ecclesiastes and The Song of Songs.* Apollos Old Testament Commentary. Downers Grove, IL: IVP, 2010.

Fretheim, Terence. "Yahweh." In *NIDOTTE* 4:1, 293.

Fuhr, Richard Alan, Jr. "An Analysis of the Interdependency of the Prominent Motifs Within the Book of Qohelet." PhD diss., Southeastern Baptist Theological Seminary, 2008. https://www.proquest.com/pqdtglobal/docview/304813496/3E3C8E2EE48846B8PQ/1.

BIBLIOGRAPHY

Fuhr, Richard Alan, Jr., and Andreas J. Köstenberger. *Inductive Bible Study: Observation, Interpretation, and Application Through the Lenses of History, Literature, and Theology*. Nashville: B&H, 2016.

Garrett, Duane A. *Proverbs, Ecclesiastes, Song of Songs*. The New American Commentary 14. Nashville: Broadman & Holman, 1993.

Gentry, Peter J., and Stephen J. Wellum. *Kingdom Through Covenant: A Biblical-Theological Understanding of the Covenants*. 2nd ed. Wheaton, IL: Crossway, 2018.

German Very Easy. "The Zwar-Aber Conjunction in German." n.d. https://www.germanveryeasy.com/zwar-aber.

Gilbrant, Thoraf, and Gregory A. Lint, eds. *The Old Testament Hebrew-English Dictionary*. CBL. Tulsa, OK: Empowered Life, 1998.

Gordis, Robert. *Koheleth, the Man and His World: A Study of Ecclesiastes*. 3rd ed. New York: Schocken, 1968.

Goswell, Gregory. "The Order of the Books in the Greek Old Testament." *Journal of the Evangelical Theological Society* 52.3 (Sept. 2009) 429–65.

Grant, Jamie A. "Wisdom and Covenant." In *DOT* 891–94.

———. "Wisdom Poem." In *DOT* 858–63.

Greidanus, Sidney. *Preaching Christ from Ecclesiastes*. Grand Rapids, MI: Eerdmans, 2010.

Günthner, Susanne. "Concessive Patterns in Interaction: Uses of Zwar . . . aber ('True . . . but') Constructions in Everyday Spoken German." Special issue, *Language Sciences: Adverbial Patterns in Interaction* 58 (Nov. 1, 2016) 144–62.

Guthrie, Donald. *Hebrews: An Introduction and Commentary*. Tyndale New Testament Commentaries 6. Downers Grove, IL: IVP, 1983.

Hallo, William W., and K. Lawson Younger Jr., eds. *Canonical Compositions from the Biblical World*. The Context of Scripture 1. Leiden, Netherlands: Brill, 2003.

Hamilton, Victor P. *The Book of Genesis, Chapters 1–17*. New International Commentary on the Old Testament. Grand Rapids, MI: Eerdmans, 1990.

Hess, Richard S. "Wisdom Sources." In *DOT* 894–901.

Horton, Michael S. "Covenant Theology." In *Covenantal and Dispensational Theologies: Four Views on the Continuity of Scripture*, edited by Brent E. Parker and Richard J. Lucas. Spectrum Multiview Books. Downers Grove, IL: IVP Academic, 2022.

———. *Introducing Covenant Theology*. Grand Rapids, MI: Baker, 2006.

House, Paul R. *1, 2 Kings*. The New American Commentary 8. Nashville: Broadman & Holman, 1995.

Inrig, Gary. *I and II Kings*. Holman Old Testament Commentary 7. Nashville: B&H, 2003.

Jackson, David R. "Solomon." In *DOT* 733–37.

Johnston, Gordon H. "הֶבֶל, הָבַל." In *NIDOTTE* 1:981.

Kaiser, Walter C., Jr. *Coping with Change—Ecclesiastes*. Scotland: Christian Focus, 2013.

Kaiser, Walter C., Jr., and Moisès Silva, eds. *Introduction to Biblical Hermeneutics: The Search for Meaning*. Grand Rapids, MI: Zondervan, 2007.

Kapic, Kelly M. *A Little Book for New Theologians*. Downers Grove, IL: IVP, 2012.

Keil, C. F., and F. Delitzsch. *Commentary on the Old Testament*. 10 vols. Accordance electronic ed. Peabody, MA: Hendrickson, 1996.

Kim, Jimyung. "Reanimating Qohelet's Contradictory Voices: Studies of Open-Ended Discourse on Wisdom in Ecclesiastes." PhD diss., Texas Christian University, 2016. https://www.proquest.com/pqdtglobal/docview/1823621551/abstract/B6695D9EAA141E5PQ/1.

Kitchen, K. A. *The Bible in Its World: The Bible and Archaeology Today*. Eugene, OR: Wipf & Stock, 2004.

———. *On the Reliability of the Old Testament*. Grand Rapids, MI: Eerdmans, 2006.

Köstenberger, Andreas J., and Richard D. Patterson. *Invitation to Biblical Interpretation: Exploring the Hermeneutical Triad of History, Literature, and Theology*. Invitation to Theological Studies. Grand Rapids, MI: Kregel, 2011.

Kynes, Will. *The Oxford Handbook of Wisdom and the Bible*. Oxford: Oxford University Press, 2021.

———. "The 'Wisdom Literature' Category: An Obituary." *The Journal of Theological Studies* 69.1 (April 2018) 1–24.

Lambert, W. G. *Babylonian Wisdom Literature*. Oxford: Clarendon, 1960.

Lee, Eunny P. "The Vitality of Enjoyment in Qohelet's Theological Rhetoric." PhD diss., Princeton Theological Seminary, 2004. https://www.proquest.com/pqdtglobal/docview/305149809/abstract/DA5B8B6C921E4E17PQ/1.

Levine, E. "The Humor in Qoheleth." *ZAW* 109 (1977) 71–83.

Loader, J. A. *Ecclesiastes: A Practical Commentary*. Translated by John Vriend. Text and Interpretation. Grand Rapids, MI: Eerdmans, 1986.

———. *Polar Structures in the Book of Qohelet*. Berlin: de Gruyter, 1979.

Lohfink, Norbert. "כַּעַס כָּעַס." In *TDOT* 7:284.

Longman, Tremper III. *The Book of Ecclesiastes*. New International Commentary on the Old Testament. Accordance electronic ed. Grand Rapids, MI: Eerdmans, 1998.

———. *Ecclesiastes*. Cornerstone Biblical Commentary 6. Carol Stream, IL: Tyndale House, 2006.

Louw, Johannes P., and Eugene Albert Nida. *Greek-English Lexicon of the New Testament: Based on Semantic Domains*. New York: United Bible Societies, 1996.

Lubeck, R. J. Review of *Theological Diversity and the Authority of the Old Testament*, by John Goldingay. *Journal of the Evangelical Theological Society—Book Reviews* 31.4 (Dec. 1988) 486–87.

Lyon, Ashley E. *Reassessing Selah*. Athens, GA: College & Clayton, 2021.

Matthews, Victor H., and Don C. Benjamin. *Old Testament Parallels: Laws and Stories from the Ancient Near East*. 4th ed. New York: Paulist, 2016.

Matthews, Victor Harold, et al. *The IVP Bible Background Commentary: Old Testament*. Electronic ed. Downers Grove, IL: IVP, 2000.

McKenzie, Steven L. *Introduction to the Historical Books: Strategies for Reading*. Grand Rapids, MI: Eerdmans, 2010.

Meade, John D. "Circumcision of Flesh to Circumcision of Heart: The Typology of the Sign of the Abrahamic Covenant." In *Progressive Covenantalism: Charting a Course Between Dispensational and Covenantal Theologies*, edited by Stephen J. Wellum and Brent E. Parker. Nashville: B&H Academic, 2016.

Merkle, Benjamin L. *Discontinuity to Continuity: A Survey of Dispensational and Covenantal Theologies*. Bellingham, WA: Lexham, 2020.

Merriam-Webster's Collegiate Dictionary. Springfield, MA: Merriam-Webster, Inc., 2003.

Moore, David George, and Daniel L. Akin. *Ecclesiastes, Song of Solomon*. Holman Old Testament Commentary 14. Nashville: B&H, 2003.

Mung, Yat-Shing Edwin. "Qoheleth and Social Justice: A Rhetorical and Social Reading." PhD diss., Trinity International University, 2015. https://www.proquest.com/pqdtglobal/docview/1832951571/abstract/F3CD463D51994437PQ/3.

Murphy, Roland E. *Ecclesiastes*. Word Biblical Commentary 23A. Nashville: Thomas Nelson, 1992.

———. "Wisdom in the OT." In *ABD* 6:920–31.

———. *Wisdom Literature*. The Forms of the Old Testament Literature 13. Grand Rapids, MI: Eerdmans, 1981.

Neusner, Jacob, trans. *The Mishnah: A New Translation*. New Haven, CT: Yale University Press, 1988.

O'Donnell, Douglas Sean. *Ecclesiastes*. Reformed Expository Commentary. Phillipsburg, NJ: P&R, 2014.

Osborne, Grant R. *The Hermeneutical Spiral: A Comprehensive Introduction to Biblical Interpretation*. Rev. and exp. 2nd ed. Downers Grove, IL: IVP, 2006.

Oswalt, John N. *The Bible Among the Myths: Unique Revelation or Just Ancient Literature?* Grand Rapids, MI: Zondervan, 2009.

Parsons, Greg W. "Guidelines for Understanding and Proclaiming the Book of Ecclesiastes, Part 1." *Bibliotheca Sacra* 160.638 (2003) 159–73.

Pate, C. Marvin. *Romans*. Teach the Text Commentary. Grand Rapids, MI: Baker, 2013.

Perdue, Leo G. "Cult, Worship: Wisdom." In *DOT* 78–85.

———. *Wisdom and Cult: A Critical Analysis of the Views of Cult in the Wisdom Literatures of Israel and the Ancient Near East*. Atlanta: Scholars Press, 1977.

Pitkänen, Pekka. "Historical Criticism." In *DOT* 280–87.

Pratt, Richard L., Jr. *I and II Corinthians*. Holman New Testament Commentary 7. Nashville: B&H, 2000.

Pritchard, James Bennett, ed. *The Ancient Near Eastern Texts Relating to the Old Testament*. 3rd ed. with supplement. Princeton, NJ: Princeton University Press, 1969.

Provan, Iain. *Ecclesiastes, Song of Songs*. The NIV Application Commentary. Grand Rapids, MI: Zondervan, 2001.

Ryken, Leland, et al., eds. *Dictionary of Biblical Imagery*. Downers Grove, IL: IVP, 1998.

Sáenz-Badillos, Angel. *A History of the Hebrew Language*. Translated by John Elwolde. Cambridge: Cambridge University Press, 1993. https://doi.org/10.1017/CBO9781139166553.

Samra, Jim. *James, 1 and 2 Peter, and Jude*. Teach the Text Commentary. Grand Rapids, MI: Baker, 2016.

Sandmel, Samuel. "Parallelomania." *Journal of Biblical Literature* 81.1 (1962) 1–13. https://doi.org/10.2307/3264821.

Saucy, Robert L. *The Case for Progressive Dispensationalism: The Interface Between Dispensational and Non-Dispensational Theology*. Grand Rapids, MI: Zondervan, 1993.

Schreiner, Thomas R. *1, 2 Peter, Jude*. The New American Commentary 37. Nashville: Broadman & Holman, 2003.

Sheppard, G. T. "Wisdom." In *ISBE* 4:1074–76.

Silva, Moisés. "Worthless." In *NIDNTTE* 1:83.

Smith, Justin Marc. *Why Βίος? On the Relationship Between Gospel Genre and Implied Audience*. Library of New Testament Studies 518. London: Bloomsbury, 2015.

Sneed, Mark R. "Is the 'Wisdom Tradition' a Tradition?" *Catholic Biblical Quarterly* 73.1 (2011) 50–71.

———, ed. *Was There a Wisdom Tradition? New Prospects in Israelite Wisdom Studies*. Williston, VT: Society of Biblical Literature, 2015.

Sparks, Kent. "In the Footsteps of the Sages: Interpreting Wisdom for Preaching." *Faith and Mission* 13.1 (1995) 70–81.

BIBLIOGRAPHY

Stanley, Alan P., et al. *Four Views on the Role of Works at the Final Judgment.* Edited by Stanley N. Gundry. Counterpoints. Grand Rapids, MI: Zondervan, 2013.

Strong, James. *Strong's Hebrew and Chaldee Dictionary of the Old Testament.* Hawthorne, CA: BN, 2012.

Sweeney, Marvin A. "Form Criticism." In *DOT* 227–41.

Thompson, J. Arthur. "Queen of Sheba." In *ZEB* 5:7.

"Vayikra Rabbah 28:1." Sefaria. https://www.sefaria.org/Vayikra_Rabbah.28.1

Von Rad, Gerhard. *Wisdom in Israel.* Translated by James D. Martin. London: SCM, 1972.

Walsh, J. T. "Despair as a Theological Virtue in the Spirituality of Ecclesiastes." *BTB* 12 (1982) 46–49.

Waltke, Bruce K., and Charles Yu. *An Old Testament Theology: An Exegetical, Canonical, and Thematic Approach.* Grand Rapids, MI: Zondervan, 2007.

Walton, John. *Genesis.* The NIV Application Commentary. Grand Rapids, MI: Zondervan, 2001.

Webb, Barry G. *Five Festal Garments: Christian Reflections on the Song of Songs, Ruth, Lamentations, Ecclesiastes, Esther.* New Studies in Biblical Theology 10. London: Apollos, 2000.

Wells, Calvin Richard. "Hebrew Wisdom as the Sitz Im Leben for Higher Education in Ancient Israel." PhD diss., University of North Texas, 1997. https://www.proquest.com/pqdtglobal/docview/304368226/abstract/E84545F6C6074CEEPQ/2.

Wilkins, Michael J. "Matthew." In *Matthew, Mark, Luke.* Zondervan Illustrated Bible Backgrounds Commentary: New Testament 1. Grand Rapids, MI: Zondervan, 2002.

Williamson, Paul R. "Canon." In *DOT* 35–41.

———. *Sealed with an Oath: Covenant in God's Unfolding Purpose.* New Studies in Biblical Theology 23. London: Apollos, 2007.

Wilson, Gerald H. "חָכַם." In *NIDOTTE* 2:128.

Wright, Archie T. *The World of the New Testament: Cultural, Social, and Historical Contexts.* Grand Rapids, MI: Baker Academic, 2013.

Wright, Christopher J. H. *Hearing the Message of Ecclesiastes: Questioning Faith in a Baffling World.* Grand Rapids, MI: Zondervan, 2023.

Wright, J. Robert, ed. *Proverbs, Ecclesiastes, Song of Solomon.* Ancient Christian Commentary on Scripture 9. Downers Grove, IL: IVP, 2005.

Würthwein, Ernst. *The Text of the Old Testament: An Introduction to the Biblia Hebraica.* 3rd ed. Grand Rapids, MI: Eerdmans, 2014.

Index

Abraham, 52
Adam, 52, 103–4, 116–17, 129, 135
Akin, Daniel L., 16, 16n46, 49, 49n27, 50n30, 133, 133n2, 153, 153n5, 155, 155n9
Akin, Jonathan, 133, 133n2, 153, 153n5

Baker, Warren, 134n5
Barnes, William H., 70, 70n21
Barré, 38
Bartholomew, Craig G., 107, 107n26
Barton, John, 64n9
Beale, G. K., 118, 118n6, 120, 120n9
Benjamin, Don C., 30, 30nn18–22, 31n23
Blocher, Henri, 6–7, 7n19
Blomberg, Craig L., 119, 119n8
Boda, Michael J., 36, 36n36
Bray, Gerald L., 51n34
Brueggemann, Walter, 60, 60n4, 64, 64n10, 67n14, 68, 68n16, 72, 72n23

Camus, Albert, 84
Carpenter, Eugene, 41n3, 134n5
Chang, Frances Tsai-Fen, 17, 17n50
Chavalas, 29, 33
Clem, Eldon, 59n1, 155n8
Coleson, Joseph, 36, 37n37
Crenshaw, James L., 41n4, 87, 87n33, 88, 97, 97n7, 97n10
Currid, John D., 100, 100n16, 139, 140n15

Curtis, Edward M., 3, 3n10, 6, 6n17, 13, 13n38, 28, 28n15, 47–48, 48n23, 155, 155n7

David, 5, 16, 43, 45, 50, 59, 62, 69, 72–73, 81, 130, 149
Delitzsch, F., 43, 43n9, 44n12, 69, 69n18, 82
Dell, Katharine J., 3, 3n11, 5, 5n15, 25, 42, 42n6
Descartes, René, 141, 141n17
Didymus, 46
Dietrich, Walter, 64, 64n9
Dodson, Derek S., 55, 55nn43–44

Easton, M. G., 36, 36n35
Eaton, Michael A., 49–50, 50n31, 54, 54n41, 61, 61n5, 109, 109n29
Elwell, Walter A., 127, 127n16, 128, 128nn17–18, 129, 129n19
Enns, Peter, 19, 19n55, 42n5, 43, 43n7, 50, 51n32
Erickson, Millard J., 12, 12n35, 134, 134n4
Estes, Daniel J., 4, 4n14, 45, 45n16, 46nn17–18, 64, 65nn11–12, 73, 73n25, 123, 123n14
Eswine, Zack, 102, 103n20, 104, 104n22, 105, 105n23, 135, 135n6, 139, 139n14, 143, 144n22, 152, 152n3
Evagrius of Pontus, 51
Evans, C. Stephen, 145, 145n24
Eve, 103–4, 116, 135

Farmer, Kathleen A., 14, 15n43, 99, 99n13, 103, 103n21, 108, 108n28, 111, 111n33
Ferguson, Everett, 118n7
Firth, David G., 3n11, 5n15, 42n6
Fox, Michael V., 2, 2n5, 3, 3n7, 4, 4n12, 5, 5n16, 7n20, 15n44, 16, 16n48, 24, 26n11, 44, 44n10, 49, 49n26, 80, 80nn7-8, 83, 83nn16-19, 84, 84nn20-22, 85, 85nn23-27, 86, 86nn29-31, 87, 87n34, 88, 88nn35-37, 89, 89nn38-39, 94, 150
Fredericks, Daniel C., 44-45, 64, 65nn11-12, 73, 73n25, 123, 123n14
Fretheim, Terence, 36n34
Fuhr, Richard Alan, Jr., 10, 10n30, 12, 12n36, 17, 17n51, 157, 157n13, 157n16, 158, 158n17

Garrett, Duane A., 44-45, 45n15, 82n13
Gentry, Peter J., 1n1, 130, 130n20, 135, 135n7
Giese, Ronald L., 160
Gilbrant, Thoraf, 27n12
Gordis, Robert, 45, 59, 59n2, 60n3, 66n13, 67, 67n15, 73, 74n26, 88
Goswell, Greg, 49, 49n29
Grant, J. A., 37-38, 38n39, 38n42, 39n43
Gregory of Nyssa, 46, 49
Greidanus, Sidney, 156, 156n11, 160, 160n19
Gunkel, Hermann, 25, 25n6
Guthrie, Donald, 121, 121n10

Hallo, William W., 31-32, 32n25, 32n27
Hamilton, Victor P., 117, 117n3
Hammurapi of Babylon, 33
Herod the Great, 48n24
Hess, R. S., 13, 13n39, 39, 39n44
Hezekiah, 59-60
Horton, Michael S., 1n1
House, Paul R., 71, 71n22

Inrig, Gary, 69, 69n19
Iser, 11
Israel (Jacob), 52

Jackson, D. R., 68, 68n17
Jackson, Paul, 140, 140n16
James, 121, 128, 139
Jesus Christ, 18, 70, 72-73, 115, 117-32, 142-43, 144n23, 145, 151, 160
Job, 30-31, 38
Johnston, D., 65n12
Johnston, Gordon H., 96n2
Jude, 128

Kaiser, Walter C., Jr., 11, 11n32, 16, 154, 154n6
Kapic, Kelly M., 35, 35n33
Keil, C. F., 43, 43n9, 44n12, 69, 69n18
Kim, Jimyung, 3, 3n9, 9, 9n27
Kitchen, K. A., 34n31
Köstenberger, Andreas J., 10, 10n30, 12, 12n36, 157, 157n13, 157n16, 158, 158n17, 159, 159n18
Kynes, Will, 24, 24n2, 26, 26n10

Lambert, W. G., 24n2
Lee, Eunny P., 3, 3n8, 7n20, 9, 9n26, 16, 16n49, 53, 53n38, 82, 82n12, 89-90, 90nn40-41, 91, 91nn42-44, 92, 92nn45-46, 93, 93nn47-49, 94, 94nn50-51, 150
Leupold, H. C., 54, 109
Levine, E., 2n3
Lint, Gregory A., 27n12
Loader, J. A., 2, 3n6, 7n20, 16, 16n47, 78-79, 79nn2-4, 80, 80nn5-6, 81, 81nn9-11, 82, 82nn14-15, 83-86, 89, 94, 150
Lohfink, Norbert, 99, 99n15
Longman, Tremper, III, 14, 14n42, 40, 40n1, 44, 44nn12n12-13, 45n14, 48, 48nn24-25, 52, 53n37, 54, 54n39, 61, 61nn6-7, 137, 137n11, 138, 138n13
Louw, Johannes P., 136n8, 143, 143nn20-21
Lubeck, R. J., 12, 13n37
Lyon, Ashley E., 25n6

Matthews, Victor H., 29-30, 30n17, 30nn18-22, 31n23, 33, 33n29

McKenzie, Steven L., 78, 78n1
Meade, John D., 1n1
Menelik (child of Solomon), 70
Merkle, Benjamin L., 1n1
Messiah/Christ. *See* Jesus Christ
Moore, David George, 16, 16n46, 49, 49n27, 50n30, 155, 155n9
Moses, 120
Muddiman, John, 64n9
Mung, Yat-Shing Edwin, 15–16, 16n45
Murphy, Roland E., 24, 24n3, 37, 37n38, 38, 38nn40–41, 41n4, 56, 56n46

Neusner, Jacob, 2n3
Nida, Eugene Albert, 136n8, 143, 143nn20–21
Noah, 52

Oden, Thomas C., 51n34
O'Donnell, Douglas Sean, 122, 122n13, 132, 132n1, 136, 136n9, 137, 137n10
Origen, 46
Osborne, Grant R., 7–8, 8n21, 8n24, 9, 9n25, 11, 11nn33–34
Oswalt, John N., 33, 34n30

Parsons, Greg W., 97, 97n8
Pate, C. Marvin, 122, 122n12
Patterson, Richard D., 159, 159n18
Paul, 55–56, 116–18, 122, 124–25, 128, 136, 140, 142–43, 155
Perdue, Leo G., 24n2, 28n14
Peter, 117, 121
Pitkänen, P., 28, 28n16
Pratt, Richard L., Jr., 124, 124n15
Pritchard, James Bennett, 32, 32nn26–27
Provan, Iain, 18, 18n54, 115, 115n1, 138, 138n12

Queen of Sheba, 61, 68–72

Ryken, Leland, 98n11, 133n3

Sáenz-Badillos, Angel, 44, 44n11
Samra, Jim, 121, 121n11
Sandmel, Samuel, 32, 33n28

Sandy, D. Brent, 160
Saucy, Robert L., 1n1
Saul, 50
Schifferdecker, K., 41n4
Schreiner, Thomas R., 117, 117n4
Sheppard, G. T., 13–14, 14nn40–41
Silva, Moisés, 11n32, 96n5
Smith, Justin Marc, 23, 23n1
Smith, Katherine E., 55, 55nn43–44
Sneed, Mark, 24, 24n2, 24nn4–5, 25, 25nn7–9, 26
Solomon, 5–6, 15–16, 26, 43, 46, 51, 58–74, 81, 100, 105, 149, 153
Sparks, Kent, 153, 153n4
Stanley, Alan P., 142, 142n18
Strong, James, 98n12
Sweeney, M. A., 62, 63n8

Thompson, J. Arthur, 70, 70n20

von Rad, Gerhard, 57, 57n47

Walsh, J. T., 2n3, 41n4
Waltke, Bruce, 110n32
Walton, John, 142, 142n19
Webb, Barry G., 2, 2n4, 54, 54n42, 55, 56n45, 97, 97n9
Webb, William J., 10–11
Wells, Calvin Richard, 31n24
Wellum, Stephen J., 1n1, 130, 130n20, 135, 135n7
Wilkins, Michael J., 72, 72n24
Williamson, Paul R., 1n1, 4, 4n13, 6, 6n18, 18, 18n53, 46, 47n20
Wilson, Gerald H., 27, 27n13
Wilson, Lindsay, 3n11, 5n15, 42n6
Wright, Archie, 118n7
Wright, Christopher J. H., 108, 108n27, 110, 110n30
Wright, J. Robert, 46n19, 49n28, 51n35
Würthwein, Ernst, 51, 51n33, 54n40

Yarbrough, Robert W., 127, 127n16, 128, 128nn17–18, 129, 129n19
Younger, K. Lawson, Jr., 31–32, 32n25, 32n27
Yu, Charles, 110n32

www.ingramcontent.com/pod-product-compliance
Lightning Source LLC
Chambersburg PA
CBHW062045220426
43662CB00010B/1660